Weaponizing
WATER

Weaponizing WATER

Water Stress and Islamic Extremist Violence in Africa and the Middle East

Marcus D. King

LYNNE
RIENNER
PUBLISHERS

BOULDER
LONDON

Published in the United States of America in 2023 by
Lynne Rienner Publishers, Inc.
1800 30th Street, Suite 314, Boulder, Colorado 80301
www.rienner.com

and in the United Kingdom by
Lynne Rienner Publishers, Inc.
Gray's Inn House, 127 Clerkenwell Road, London EC1 5DB
www.eurospanbookstore.com/rienner

© 2023 by Lynne Rienner Publishers, Inc. All rights reserved

Library of Congress Cataloging-in-Publication Data
Names: King, Marcus DuBois, author.
Title: Weaponizing water : water stress and Islamic extremist violence in
    Africa and the Middle East / Marcus D. King.
Description: Boulder, Colorado : Lynne Rienner Publishers, Inc., 2023. |
    Includes bibliographical references and index. | Summary: "Explores the
    linkages between water stress and conflict in the activities of Islamic
    extremist groups across Iraq, Nigeria, Somalia, and Syria"— Provided by
    publisher.
Identifiers: LCCN 2022033694 (print) | LCCN 2022033695 (ebook) | ISBN
    9781955055833 (hardcover) | ISBN 9781955055949 (ebook)
Subjects: LCSH: Water-supply—Political aspects—Middle East. |
    Water-supply—Political aspects—Africa. | Islamic
    fundamentalism—Middle East. | Islamic fundamentaism—Africa. |
    Violence—Middle East. | Violence—Africa. | IS (Organization) | Shabaab
    (Organization).
Classification: LCC HD1698.K3 K54 2023 (print) | LCC HD1698.K3 (ebook) |
    DDC 333.9100956—dc23/eng/20221125
LC record available at https://lccn.loc.gov/2022033694
LC ebook record available at https://lccn.loc.gov/2022033695

British Cataloguing in Publication Data
A Cataloguing in Publication record for this book
is available from the British Library.

Printed and bound in the United States of America

∞   The paper used in this publication meets the requirements
       of the American National Standard for Permanence of
       Paper for Printed Library Materials Z39.48-1992.

5 4 3 2 1

Contents

List of Tables and Figures	vii
Acknowledgments	ix
1 Water Stress and Violent Extremism	1
2 The Islamic State of Syria and Iraq	35
3 Extremist Violence in Nigeria	109
4 Al-Shabaab in Somalia	149
5 Stemming the Tide of Water Weaponization	195
Bibliography	215
Index	235
About the Book	245

Tables and Figures

Tables

1.1	The Categories of Water Weaponization	16
2.1	Chronology of IS Names	62
2.2	Origin of IS Foreign Fighters	69
2.3	Dams Occupied by Islamic State	77
2.4	Summary of Water Weaponization Incidents in Syria and Iraq	81
3.1	Summary of Water Weaponization Incidents in Nigeria	136
4.1	Selected Mass Casualty Attacks by al-Shabaab	154
4.2	Summary of Water Weaponization Incidents in Somalia	180

Figures

1.1	A Representative Water Stress and Conflict Cycle	13
2.1	Map of Syria	37
2.2	Map of Iraq	45
2.3	Water Stress and Conflict Cycle in Syria and Iraq	59
3.1	Political Map of Nigeria	110
3.2	Water Stress and Conflict Cycle in Northern Nigeria	137
3.3	Water Stress and Conflict Cycle in Nigeria's Middle Belt	141
4.1	Political Map of Greater Somalia	150
4.2	Water Stress and Conflict Cycle in Somalia	182

Acknowledgments

FOREMOST, I MUST EXPRESS MY GRATITUDE TO THE TEAM OF graduate student research assistants at George Washington University's Elliott School of International Affairs: Nandini Ajmera, Siree Allers, Julia Burnell, Luke Farrell, Keida Gaba, Rianna LeHane, Duncan Matthewson, Sabreen Rash, and Anuka Upadhye. I am also grateful to Katherine A. Weingartner for her research contributions.

I benefited greatly from Peter Schwartzstein's vast knowledge of Syria and Iraq, which I gleaned from conversations during his visits to Washington, DC. I would also like to acknowledge the constant encouragement of John Oldfield, CEO of Accelerate Global, throughout the various phases of my research and related workshops. Ana Mulio Alvarez provided insightful comments on early drafts. Megan, Marcelle, and Eva were supportive and patient during long stretches of family vacations spent writing.

Above all, the research for the book and the many opportunities I have had to present it at conferences would not have been possible without the support of an anonymous donor through the Special Opportunities for Advanced Research (SOAR) Initiative at George Washington University's Elliott School.

Despite all of the contributions from this group of talented individuals, I bear sole responsibility for the views expressed throughout this book.

1

Water Stress and Violent Extremism

WATER CONDITIONS HAVE REACHED THE POINT OF CRISIS IN many parts of the world. The United Nations estimates that by 2025, 1.8 billion people will be living in areas of absolute water scarcity. Absolute scarcity occurs when there is an insufficient volumetric supply of water to sustain human life and the natural ecosystem simultaneously. It is calculated as a ratio of human water consumption to available water supply. *Volumetric availability* generally refers to the physical abundance of fresh or potable water rather than the availability of water used for other human needs such as sanitation.

Aside from scarcity, the UN projects that two-thirds of the world's population could be subject to *water stress*, which in this volume refers to volumetric supply scarcity and encompasses the equally important factors of inadequate water quality and accessibility,[1] that is, the ability of people to use physically available water supplies. Another way of looking at this is to ask whether water is economically exploitable by people living in areas adjacent to the resource. Economic water scarcity exists when there is lack of investment in water infrastructure, policies, and systems or when the population cannot afford to use such water resources. Lack of access to clean drinking water and lack of sanitation are two of the leading causes of human mortality. In 2018, the combination of these factors alone contributed to nearly 800,000 deaths. This number exceeds annual mortality associated with floods, droughts, or violent conflict.[2]

The overall health of the freshwater ecosystem must also be taken into account. Changes in conditions can affect environmental flows,

2   Weaponizing Water

such as the natural filtration provided by wetlands and the movement of bodies of water that carry human waste.

A full understanding of all dimensions of water availability makes it clear that water stress is especially acute in the Middle East and parts of Africa. In Africa, stressed areas include the eastern "horn" of the continent and the Sahel, a band of territory that forms the climate zone between the arid areas of the northern continent and the more fertile southern regions. One factor that these regions have in common is that they experience chronically arid climate conditions and unpredictable, yet prevalent, periods of drought. The Eastern Mediterranean climate zone that encompasses Syria and Iraq shares similar characteristics.

Several parts of the Middle East and Africa additionally suffer from instability resulting from internal conflict, social inequities, and other factors. Compounding these underlying problems, the effects of climate change will further diminish regional food security and social stability. It is difficult to predict exactly how these natural events will unfold. Climate forecasts are hampered because their greenhouse gas (GHG) emissions scenarios rely on national regulatory and energy policies, which change with politics, rather than on natural changes alone. However, various regional models based on a range of scenarios agree that climate impacts on the arid parts of the Middle East and Africa will be negative on balance. Higher temperatures, more frequent droughts, and unpredictable variability in precipitation are outcomes anathema to the farming and animal husbandry that support food systems in these countries.

In terms of precipitation, the net result of changing temperatures, precipitation patterns, and evaporation is that most dry areas will become dryer and wet areas wetter. These effects are already apparent in the arid regions of the Sahel and the Horn of Africa. In the last thirty years, for example, the Horn of Africa, including Somalia, has experienced a persistent decline in rainfall during the primary rainy season, which occurs from March to May. In a region where the maize and sorghum food staples rely on dependable rainfall, lower rainfall has major negative consequences for food security. Crop production is now unable to meet demand on a perennial basis.[3]

Most of the African continent is projected to warm under all scenarios predicted by global climate models. Climate models predict that arid regions of the Horn of Africa, including Somalia, will have higher temperatures and extreme decreases in precipitation compared to both the global average and the rest of Africa.[4]

Climate change is also behind a steady decline in rainfall in many parts of the Middle East. An overall decline in precipitation in the

Mediterranean region from 1971 to 2010 has also been partially attributed to climate change.[5] Extreme temperatures have rendered some areas nearly uninhabitable. In June 2017, the Iranian city of Ahvaz recorded a temperature of 127 degrees Fahrenheit. The heat index, which takes temperature and humidity into account, hit an incredible 142 degrees Fahrenheit, a level that can sustain human life for only a short period of time.[6]

Global climate projections suggest a significant intensification of summer heat extremes in the Middle East and North Africa (MENA), including Iraq, Somalia, and Syria. A study conducted in 2021 used a comprehensive ensemble of regional climate projections to examine temperature projections under what is known as a business as usual scenario. Business as usual is the assumption that global greenhouse gas emissions will continue to increase on essentially the same trajectory as they do today. The findings indicate that in the second half of this century unprecedented super- and ultra-extreme heat wave conditions, with temperatures as high as 132.8 degrees Fahrenheit, will emerge and about half of the MENA population, or approximately 600 million people, could be exposed to annual recurring heat waves for a number of weeks.[7]

Droughts in the Middle East are occurring more frequently, and they are also related to climate change. Writing in the *Proceedings of the National Academy of Sciences*, Colin Kelley and colleagues found that observed trends in precipitation and temperature in climate models strongly suggest that GHG emissions resulting in climate change have increased the probability of severe and persistent droughts in the Eastern Mediterranean region.[8] This study concluded that a reoccurrence of a three-year drought in Syria as severe as that of 2007–2010, which triggered the events described in this volume, is two to three times more likely as a consequence of climate change.[9]

Taken together, the impacts of climate change on temperatures and precipitation will increase water stress in the Middle East and Africa. Water stress compounds food insecurity and reduces populations' resilience to other stressors, such as economic and social cleavages. These factors conflate in war-torn countries, and this volume investigates the correlation between water stress and conflict in the MENA and Africa.

Water Stress and Violent Extremist Organizations

An underlying purpose of this volume is to better understand how natural conditions, including climate trends, pose increasing risks to water

4   *Weaponizing Water*

sources in the Middle East and Africa. The next question we will consider is how water stress has become associated with another growing trend that has recently swept across the region: the rise of violent Islamic extremism.

In 2016, as I first set out to answer how these two trends might be related, I pored over remote-sensing maps of the Middle East and Africa drawn from commercial satellite imagery. I was struck by the correlation between the spheres of influence of violent extremist organizations (VEOs) and the driest lands or areas of sparse vegetation in some of the most arid regions on earth. A quick check of reference sources showed that many of these areas where vegetation had been depleted were also under acute water stress measured by a host of other indicators, including lack of groundwater resources, and represented by the increasing impacts of global climate change.

Glancing at Syria and Iraq, I noted that the Islamic State (IS), which was at the height of its power at that time, had postured forces to maintain control of territory along the banks of the Tigris and Euphrates Rivers. Forces were also seemingly positioned to control key water infrastructure, mostly dams. Turning to Nigeria, I also noticed that the VEO Boko Haram was most active in the dry northeast of the country, including the troubled Lake Chad region. In the last few decades, Lake Chad has shrunk to a fraction of its original size primarily as a result of droughts brought on by a changing climate. I suspected that the proximity of VEOs and key water geographies and features in each country warranted further attention, which led me to one of the main questions addressed by this volume: Can connections between water geography, water stress, and violent extremism lead to a better understanding of the nature of modern warfare of the type increasingly perpetrated by VEOs?

Water Stress and the Spectrum of Conflict

Taking a step back, it is important to note that a growing number of scholars are exploring linkages between water stress and conflict. Many researchers attribute the outbreak of wars in MENA, such as the Syrian Civil War, at least in part to environmental causes. On the other end of the spectrum, copious literature also examines water's role in postconflict situations.

What sets this volume apart is that I concentrate on what occurs at the middle of the conflict spectrum—the stage of ongoing warfare. The coming chapters are concerned with VEOs' use of water as a tool of warfare during ongoing conflict. This phase of conflict is known as *jus in bello*. My intentions are to expand the water and conflict literature and to completely explore the role of water stress across the full spectrum of conflict: preconflict, ongoing conflict, and postconflict situations.

The question of whether water stress leads to conflict is asked often and usually not in a way that allows for nuance. It is valid to ask whether water stress fits anywhere along a conflict spectrum. The historical record tells us that the allocation of water among parties, especially nations, has actually most often been a vehicle for cooperation. In fact, there is near consensus among water analysts and scholars that water stress is unlikely to spark large-scale international violent conflict. So-called water wars have been long predicted by people ranging from Secretaries-General of the United Nations to the mainstream media; both proclaim on a regular basis that the next international war will be fought over water, and that the possibility lies just around the corner. Nevertheless, history tells us that these predictions have seldom, if ever, been realized.

Reflecting the concern with the possibility of a coming water war, the theme of water as an "urgent security issue" topped the agenda at the InterAction Council 29th Annual Plenary Meeting in Canada in 2011. This body, composed of thirty-seven former heads of state and governmental officials and convened in cooperation with the United Nations University, was designed to offer recommendations on long-term issues facing humankind. By the time of the 2011 conference, at least three Secretaries-General had weighed in on the issue. The first was Boutros Boutros-Ghali, who had famously said in 1985 that the next major war in the Middle East would be fought over water, not politics. This assertion was then echoed by UN Secretary-General Kofi Annan in 2001, who observed that water could be a source of conflict in the future. The next UN Secretary-General Ban Ki-moon added in 2007 that the consequences of a coming water war for humanity would be grave because water scarcity threatens economic and social gains.[10]

Although these predictions have not come to fruition, Dr. Fabrice Renaud, head of the Environmental Vulnerability and Energy Security Section of the United Nations University's Bonn-based Institute for Environment and Human Security, and other experts at the high-level InterAction Council meeting concurred that the tradition of water cooperation could be tested. Aggravating factors would be the increasing tensions resulting from growing populations; urbanization; rising industrial, agricultural, and household demands; and the threat multiplier of

6 Weaponizing Water

climate change as supplies of fossil water in underground aquifers, on which many countries rely, are exhausted.[11]

Despite prognostications, an all-out water war between two nations seemingly remains a relatively distant prospect; as of yet, water has been a significant factor in conflicts between nations on discrete occasions. One was a series of confrontations between Israel and its Arab neighbors from November 1964 to May 1967. The flashpoint was control of scarce water resources in the Jordan River drainage basin. The trouble arose when the Arab states deprived Israel of water capacity by diverting the River Jordan's headwaters while Israel was diverting the water of Lake Tiberias and transferring it to its arid south. These actions led to border clashes between Syria and Israel.[12]

The Israeli military attacks against the river diversion effort are considered a factor that led to the Six-Day War in June 1967. Disputes over water allocation were important but certainly not the only factors that contributed to this conflict. Despite this counterexample, prominent water and conflict experts tend to agree that water stress in the context of shared waterways engenders cooperation, not violence, between nations.

The MENA have a limited number of shared watercourses, but there is still substantial historical empirical evidence to support water cooperation, sometimes on a subnational basis.[13] On balance, positive interactions between nation-states around water sharing have taken place formally and informally since at least the time of the ancient Mesopotamian civilization 2,500 years ago. Biblical narratives in the Christian tradition also support water cooperation involving state actors. One of the earliest stories in the Bible describes a peaceful resolution between Abraham and the Philistines over the rights to a well.

But what has become apparent recently is that the dynamic may have changed. As water scarcity increases, cooperation has decreased and the volume of localized violence around water resources has increased but remains diffuse, less publicized, and harder to quantify. It is probable, then, that experts are chronically underestimating the extent to which water stress is already contributing to local conflict in the Middle East and Africa.

Since the late 1990s, both intrastate and interstate clashes that feature water as a potential cause of conflict have soared, according to the authoritative World Water Conflict Chronology maintained by the Pacific Institute.[14] This database reveals that the number of intrastate conflictual events has been about four to five times greater than the number of interstate conflictual events, numbering an average of thirty to forty incidents per year over the past decade.[15]

Peter Schwartzstein, a noted environmental journalist and expert on MENA, explains that in this region, there can be more incentive to violence around water issues among individual communities. It is easier for smaller communities, especially agricultural communities dependent on water, to come to blows than it is for nation-states to mobilize and execute a war. Only the most well-prepared and well-armed nations have the military power to deal with the presumed massive retaliatory repercussions of pilfering large quantities of water from their neighbors. Therefore, a type of conflict deterrence prevails and the options for waging and winning international conflicts over water are limited to Pyrrhic victories.

Deterrence is not a factor, as Schwartzstein observes, at a local level, where resources can be more easily secured or stolen and where the balance of power can be much more fluid than it is among nation-states.[16] Tensions are rising among water users as non-state actors and civil societies oppose one another and the central government over inequitable water allocation. Ethnic and communal groups, such as opposing tribes, compete violently for dwindling water supplies in pastoral settings such as the Nigerian Sahel. However, it is important to note that many forms of action short of war are possible. Instead of physical violence, the panoply of conflict avoidance strategies includes debate, linguistic aggression, demonstrations, migration, and elimination of the sources of environmental degradation of water supplies through such means as investment in climate adaptation programs.

A large body of academic environmental peacebuilding literature casts water as a positive vehicle of cooperation. This situates a role for water squarely on the tail end of the conflict spectrum. Indeed, in ideal situations, discussions over environmental scarcity issues have been proven to facilitate peace by strengthening social cohesion around the realization of common needs. In these cases, skilled mediators have an opportunity to convene stakeholders who have been or would otherwise be belligerents to discuss the common cause of mutually beneficial access to water.

Cooperation thus becomes an iterative process that gains momentum. This dynamic also presents opportunities for the parties to discuss issues that are adjacent to environmental degradation such as those that pertain to the roots of the larger conflict. The idea of environmental cooperation then takes on more expansive significance. It does not signal that there is an absolute absence of conflict, but it demonstrates that there is at least a mutual will to address water challenges through communicative means.[17]

8   Weaponizing Water

It is well documented that conversations about the equitable sharing of water have taken place even among countries that are otherwise at war with each other. In the Middle East, many water conflicts have erupted between Israel and one or more of its neighbors. The Jordan River flows between five particularly contentious riparian states, two of which rely on the river as their primary water supply. This situation led to the so-called picnic table talks that started in 1953 between the Jordanians and Israelis about water flow rates and allocations at the confluence of the Jordan and Yarmuk Rivers. The two countries had deep disagreements over coordinating allocation of the Jordan River basin's waters. The picnic table talks, held in secret, were known as track-two negotiations because they were conducted by hydrological experts, not professional diplomats.[18] The parties met sometimes as often as every two weeks during the summer months and the talks carried on despite the fact that the two nations were officially at war from 1948 until 1994, when a formal peace treaty was signed.

Similarly, the Mekong Committee, established by Cambodia, Laos, Thailand, and Vietnam in 1957, exchanged data and information on the Mekong River basin throughout the major disruption of the Vietnam War.[19] Although the political conditions in the region have changed dramatically, with China acting in a hegemonic role controlling the flow of the river system, cooperation established by this organization continues to this day in the form of the Mekong River Commission.

Overall, mutual development of water technologies and solutions are increasingly viewed as strategic opportunities to facilitate discussion among adversaries. This provides rationale for including water development as part of a liberal internationalist peacebuilding agenda, which has as its goal strengthening global institutions and state-building capacity.[20] Such actions are referred to as hydro-diplomacy.

Again we find that environmental peacebuilding around water issues prevails predominately at an interstate level. Sadly, none of the conflicts involving violent extremism chronicled in this volume has reached a stable peace or a situation that negotiators refer to as ripe for negotiation to test the capacity of environmental peacebuilding. There is little evidence that the VEOs in these cases are willing to negotiate on any issue with national governments.

It is also important to understand that water cooperation may exist in situations where violence is still pervasive. Marwa Daoudy provides examples in Syria and Iraq, two parties that are weaponizing water but that can cooperate as a strategy of domination. She documents how IS and the Syrian government colluded to weaponize water against other parties, including the Kurds, in the complex civil war in that area. In this way, both cooperation and domination become integral to weaponization.[21] The tension between the definitions of cooperation and conflict in the setting of Iraq and Syria is very nuanced and this topic certainly warrants further scholarly attention to test its validity in other settings.

As of 2021, among the cases in this volume, Iraq has been the most free of extremist violence given that the Islamic State has been suppressed if not defeated outright, whereas al-Shabaab and Boko Haram are still launching offensives regularly. However, it is notable that in Iraq water stress still factors into political instability because of shortages in both quality and quantity of the water in the Tigris and Euphrates system.

In the context of cooperation events outnumbering conflict events on the interstate level and of the idea of cooperation itself being nuanced, the following chapters explore ongoing large-scale violence, not between national governments, where little evidence of confrontation exists, but between national governments' substate actors, primarily VEOs. Therefore, I give some attention to the proto-state of Iraqi Kurdistan in the case study of Syria and Iraq. Subnational conflict is the most prevalent form of conflict today; it can be equally disruptive to society as are larger wars and can also result in significant numbers of deaths on the battlefield.

Although there is no clear precedent of an all-out water war in geographies where water resources must be shared across borders, international tensions over access to water have always existed. In fact, the word *rivalry* is derived from the Latin word *rivalus*, meaning "he who shares a river with another." Water conflict analysis in the literature tends to focus on allocation of shared water courses, such as river basins. But the MENA countries examined in this volume only sometimes rely on water from river basins. Some large cities in Iraq, for example, depend on the waters of the Tigris and Euphrates Rivers, but inhabitants of Nigeria, Somalia, and many areas of Syria and Iraq instead rely on rainfall harvesting and groundwater aquifers as primary sources of potable water. Therefore, rather than focusing on shared river basins, this volume takes a different analytic approach by focusing on water balances and ecosystems within states. Although the nations under study do not share disputed water with their neighbors, transboundary droughts are a common experience.

Water Stress and the Environment–Conflict Thesis

Starting in the early 1990s, scholars developed a copious literature interrogating the connections between the environment, including degradation

10 *Weaponizing Water*

and climate change, and conflict through various lenses. It has become an important, if not essential, topic in the emerging field of environmental security. This work was initially based on a series of country case studies by Professor Thomas Homer-Dixon, then at the University of Toronto, in his groundbreaking 1994 book entitled *Environmental Scarcity and Violence*. Homer-Dixon put forward what has now become widely known as the environment–conflict thesis. Scholars of this early environmental security literature were preoccupied with theoretical proof of the connections between scarcity and conflict that are the lived reality of people who are both victims and perpetrators of violence. Attempts by academics to clearly identify and isolate causative factors of violence resulting from climate change, including the increasing prevalence and frequency of drought, have led to a cacophony of results.

Historical evidence suggests that the environment is just one component of a larger, complex web of causality that interacts with a number of alternative cultural, political, and social variables. As a consequence of this complexity, it is credibly theorized that no conflict can be exclusively environmentally *driven*; rather, violence is environmentally induced when ecological factors combine with a number of other factors to create a structure that allows for an escalation into conflict.[22]

Factors that must be considered are the existence of underlying social and ethnic cleavages within a society and sudden onset shocks. In 2016, researchers conducted a global study of the intersection of climate change and conflict and concluded that the "risk of armed-conflict outbreak is enhanced by climate related disaster occurrence in ethnically fractionalized countries."[23]

In recent years, political scientists and others have taken increasingly quantitative approaches to understanding the environment–conflict nexus. In a groundbreaking study, one research team drew from several disciplines to perform a global meta-analysis of sixty quantitative studies on human conflict and to situate them in the context of climate-related events. The researchers assessed a wide scope of conflict, ranging from individual-level and household domestic violence to wars in which countries were the primary belligerents. They found a strong correlation between climate-related events and internal wars, such as those treated in this volume. With each standard deviation of change in the climate toward warmer average temperatures and more extreme rainfall, the median frequency of intergroup internal conflict—that is, civil war—rises by 14 percent.[24] The droughts that occurred between 2011 and 2017 are the geophysical focus of this volume, but they are not the only aspect of the climate that carries strong implications for water stress. Interestingly, water stress can also be caused by too much water, when crops are drowned, sewers overrun, and flooding pollutes potable supplies of surface waters. Through the spread of disease, flooding has consequences for human health and food security.

Critics point to the ambition and scope of the meta-analysis, saying the study covers a too wide range of conflict and climatic events and spatial scales, from single municipalities to countries to the entire world.[25] This line of criticism provided the inspiration for this author to examine individual case studies using less variability in climate change impacts—drought is a constant factor. The case studies herein are limited to nations where VEOs engaged in civil wars primarily within a closed national political system.

Social science in general and the environmental security field specifically have moved beyond the narrow argument of the environment–conflict thesis. Scholars have long observed a correlation between natural resource scarcity coupled with abundance of certain types of resources, such as mineral or alluvial (e.g., surface diamonds), and the initiation of internal conflict by insurgents.[26] Most prominent is the greed and grievance theory based on a study by Paul Collier and Anke Hoeffler that identified a set of recurring variables related to natural resources in large-scale conflict.[27] The theory centers on the predation of natural resources by national governments and rebels. In these situations, natural resources can clearly influence the incidence, duration, and intensity of conflicts, according to their research. Greed and grievance theory is primarily concerned with nonrenewable resources, such as oil and diamonds, which are characterized as easily looted, so it is unclear whether Collier and Hoeffler's theory can be applied to water.

In most situations, water is not lootable or concealable. The greed and grievance theory is especially inapplicable to surface waters, although an argument could be made for single-point water sources, such as individual wells. Also, oil and diamonds provide more reliable support to war economies because of their substitutability for cash payments, a characteristic Collier describes as "fungibility." Although water is not its focus, the study finds that 40 percent of all intrastate conflicts in the past six decades involved disputes over limited natural resources.[28]

The theory of eco-violence argues that environmental scarcity is linked to violent conflict and that this linkage will become more prominent over time. This theory can be traced to Thomas Homer-Dixon, who also examined the role of diminished quality and quantity of natural resources in conflict using case studies from over twenty ongoing conflicts.

12   *Weaponizing Water*

As mentioned, Homer-Dixon's focus was on nonrenewable resources. My argument here is that natural resource scarcity or abundance coupled with poor resource management and societal cleavages like ethnic or communal differences can ignite a competitive quest for resources in the form of insurgency against the government or civil war.[29] Water is often considered a renewable resource, although scarcity is challenging this definition in many parts of the world. Though it might not fit neatly into the eco-violence paradigm as established by Homer-Dixon and Collier, less attention has been paid to the fact that water used in manufacturing processes is necessary to sustain an industrial war economy. Factories that supply war materials often run on hydroelectric power and water is necessary for cooling in all types of utility-scale electricity production.

Homer-Dixon, like many other scholars in the field of environmental security, was not convinced that water would be a cause of interstate wars. His framework allows for only a narrow range of situations that would facilitate a water war between nations, such as when a nation that is upriver in a shared river basin is perceived to be hoarding water or unilaterally constructs a dam, but the downstream or lower-riparian nation has a stronger military. This is currently the case with the impending completion of the Grand Ethiopian Renaissance Dam on the upper Blue Nile. The Nile River supplies over 95 percent of Egypt's water, and Egypt, with its superior military, has on more than one occasion threatened to strike the dam. There is also evidence that Egypt has supported insurgents in destabilizing the government of Sudan, which is the intermediary nation on the Nile River system and could conspire with Ethiopia to restrict water flow. More research is necessary to fully understand how this theory of conflict between riparian parties operates at the subnational level.

The Water Stress and Conflict Cycle

The cases in this volume argue that water stress is indeed one driver of conflict, although other variables certainly exist. Furthermore, within Iraq and Syria, Nigeria, and Somalia, the relationship between water stress and conflict can best be understood as a cycle. The cycle in each case is distinct and sometimes it is more easily discerned than in other countries, but there are striking similarities among the variables in the conflict cycles so that a generic pattern can be recognized. For example, in each case migration is a catalyst for instability. Any attempt to fully capture the water stress and conflict dynamics in a simplistic manner, such as in Figure 1.1, is difficult. However, this cyclic approach can be useful for providing a basic illustration of a complex reality and a basis for further analysis in the case studies.

As illustrated in Figure 1.1, the cycle begins with ecological changes, including climate change and droughts that may lead to increased water stress. Precipitation changes, elevated temperatures, and floods are typical indicators. Delineating the underlying conditions of water stress in a country illuminates the systemic and conflict outcomes visible in the next stages of the cycle because the reasons for water stress elucidate a country's political economy of water access and distribution. The next stage illustrates how water stressors influence these systems that affect human existence. These systems may regulate agriculture, health, or energy production. For example, depleted wheat harvests due to drought led to a breakdown in farming, producing lower agricultural yields and

Figure 1.1 A Representative Water Stress and Conflict Cycle

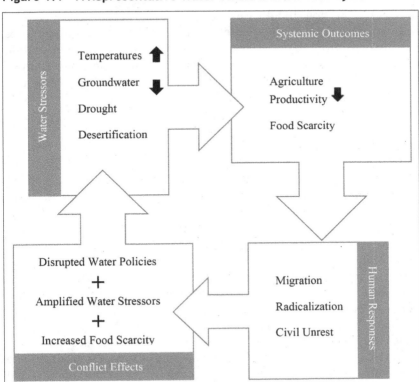

14   *Weaponizing Water*

diminished food security in Syria prior to the outbreak of civil war. The next step shows how humans ultimately respond to the systemic outcomes of water stress. In every case, these responses include internal or out-migration. Radicalization, including adherence to Islamic extremism, and civil unrest are also possible outcomes. In some cases, governments have the opportunity to understand the predicament and make genuine albeit last-minute adjustments to water policies in a desperate attempt to control the negative consequences of water-induced problems before they reach crisis proportions.

However, even if there is a political appetite and a legitimate will to improve living conditions for all people, a national government's options may be curtailed by limited finances. As the following chapters demonstrate, successful policy interventions often require functional, transparent, and well-informed governments. None of the national governments detailed in this volume consistently reach that standard. Migration and the absence of effective governance facilitate a resort to violence perpetrated by citizens who are aggrieved by the situation. Grievance can manifest in various ways, including internal or cross-boundary migration. In all cases, as its water crisis worsens, a country becomes more unstable and violent and the national government loses effective control so that improved water policy implementation becomes impossible. Conflict itself interrupts the implementation of water policies, amplifies water stressors, and erodes the systems that support human security.

Water Weaponization

The concept of environmental terrorism, from which the concept of water weaponization is largely derived, is not new by any standard. In 2001, Elizabeth Chalecki broke ground by defining environmental terrorism as the unlawful use of force against in situ environmental resources so as to deprive populations of their benefit(s) and/or to destroy other property. She made the useful distinction between two types of environmental terrorism: resource-as-tool terrorism and resource-as-target terrorism. Chalecki notes that, under this framework, water can fit into both categories.[30]

Some hint of how water weaponization, an understudied concept, would play in international power dynamics was also foreseen in a 2012 US Intelligence Community Assessment on global water security. The assessment presciently judged that the use of water as a weapon would become more common during the next ten years—taking us just about up to the present—not only on the subnational level but also between states as powerful upstream nations impede or cut off downstream flow. More to the point of this volume, the intelligence report also predicted that water will be used within states to "pressure populations and suppress separatist elements."[31]

Today, it is clear—as it has probably always been—that states with relatively greater water resources exercise strategic advantage, or what has been called hydrohegemony, over their neighbors that occupy inferior downstream positions in riparian river systems.[32] These so-called hegemons have not yet fully weaponized water in a lethal sense, according to the criteria established in this volume and elsewhere, but they have employed water resources as very distinct and sometimes painful leverage over neighboring states.

For example, the Tigris and Euphrates Rivers originate in Turkey and then flow through Syria and Iraq. Turkey is a nation that has long used its position as the upper riparian to its political advantage, especially when dealing with issues relating to either neighboring nation's support of Kurdish separatism. In this volume, I argue that instead of deployment for the somewhat blunt goal of geopolitical leverage, the water weapon is already being used in a more tangible and deadly manner by VEOs in the Middle East and Africa.

It is useful to reflect on the commonly understood meaning of *weapon*. At its most basic, a weapon is a means of gaining advantage over or defending against an adversary in a conflict or contest. Wielded by a nation or a group, a weapon can take the form of an item, action, or offensive capability used or intended to kill, injure, or coerce.[33] In this volume, I classify water weaponization into six categories related to this basic definition: strategic weaponization, tactical weaponization, coercive weaponization, and water used as an instrument of psychological terror, extortion, or incentivization. A seventh category is unintentional weaponization (see Table 1.1). The intent of the perpetrator, including whether for political or military advantage, is also an important consideration. These categories are not necessarily mutually exclusive. For example, a water weapon may be deployed tactically but with the intent of coercion. The case studies will demonstrate this clearly.

Strategic Weaponization

A strategic weapons system is designed to strike an enemy at the source of military, economic, or political power.[34] Strategy is widely considered

Table 1.1   The Categories of Water Weaponization

Strategic	Tactical	Coercive	Unintentional	Instrument of Psychological Terror	Instrument of Extortion or Incentivization
The use of water to destroy large or important areas, targets, populations, or infrastructure	The use of water against targets of strictly military value within the battlespace	The use of water provision to fund territorial administration or weapons acquisition with aspirations of achieving legitimacy	Attempted water weaponization causes collateral damage to the environment or its human component	The use of the threat of denial of access or purposeful contamination of the water supply to create fear among noncombatants	The use of water provision to reward the behavior of subject populations and support legitimacy of the perpetrator

Water Stress and Violent Extremism   17

to be the highest level of battle. This classification system envisions two dimensions of strategic water weaponization. First is the use of water for a spectacular purpose, which might include control of large or important land areas, cities, or facilities on an actual or virtual level. The threat of inundation alone can be sufficient to gain virtual control of an area, including by denying access to the enemy. Second is the use of rent collected from a subjugated population for water provision as an asset to fund VEO activities, including payment of officials' salaries or purchase of weapons. Water can become a conflict commodity, according to Collier, or, literally, a liquid asset. In these cases, water weaponization can be seen as a coercive act. Actions that target or destroy large population centers or strike at the opponent's industrial base or critical infrastructure certainly qualify as strategic weaponization.

Tactical Weaponization

The most clear-cut example of tactical weaponization is when water is employed against targets of strictly military value within a confined battlespace. In these situations, water is the medium of violence itself generally but not exclusively on the battlefield. Targeting enemy positions or military formations by destroying dikes or levees with the aim of deluging them with water is an example of tactical weaponization. In some cases, combatants seek to deny water supply to enemy forces by destroying wells or other water infrastructure. Finally, the use of water cannons to control violent crowds is an example of tactical weaponization in a noncombat situation, but this use is not relevant to the cases in this book.

Coercive Weaponization and Instrument of Terror, Extortion

Water used entirely for terrorism is another possibility. Any category of water weaponization can be classified as terrorism depending on the perpetrator's intent. Water, especially water in small wells rather than lakes and rivers, is universally accessible, somewhat fungible, and a weapon that is easily exploitable by terrorists. The mere threat of denial of access or purposeful contamination of the water supply can have a larger demonstration effect consistent with the ends of terrorism. In an effect closely tied to strategic weaponization, water use for terrorist purposes can reverberate and create fear among noncombatants disproportionate to the terrorist organization's actual area of operations or control.

18   *Weaponizing Water*

On the other side on the coin, water can be used as an instrument of extortion or coercion. In what can popularly be described as a good cop, bad cop routine, terrorist organizations pose as modern-day Robin Hoods, stealing from the rich and giving to the poor. VEOs might offer to meet poor people's basic needs where the federal government is ineffective in doing so, possibly as a result of the instability that the insurgency itself has caused. When VEOs act as gangsters, also known as water mafias, steady water provision to the subjugated population becomes a reward for loyalty. Water might be provided to populations under terrorists' direct control to create legitimacy for VEOs that are seeking to build Islamic caliphates.

Unintentional Weaponization

This research also reveals that attempts to deploy the water weapon in a strategic or tactical way can sometimes backfire because water can be a very blunt weapon. This falls into the category of unintentional weaponization, where the perpetrator's initiation of the act is intentional, but the outcome is not. This situation might be akin to manslaughter rather than murder under a Western legal system. Once waters are released with aggressive intentions, the resulting floods can be difficult if not impossible to control. It is also easy to imagine situations in which it would be impossible for a militant group to deny water to some percentage of the population that opposes them, but not to support others after the deliberate destruction of water infrastructure and systems. When the water weapon backfires, food insecurity and famine may follow in its wake. The cases of Somalia and Nigeria illustrate this point.

Using the Water Weapon

All of the VEOs addressed in this volume have used the water weapon. Some of the national governments that combat these organizations have resorted to its use to a small extent during the time period described in the case studies. This discrepancy is interesting, and I posit that states are bound by norms of modern warfare that are ignored by VEOs.

However, this volume argues that the systematic and comprehensive use of the water weapon by the belligerents in the civil war in Syria and Iraq from 2012 to 2015 exceeds prior use by any nation or subnational group and it is unprecedented in modern conflict in many ways. Compared with smaller extremist organizations, the Islamic State was the main perpetrator taking advantage of all categories of the water weapon. In contrast, al-Shabaab in Somalia and Boko Haram in Nigeria wielded the weapon more selectively and less frequently. Their use of the weapon was constrained, to a certain extent, by ecological and tactical limitations, not the least of which was their relative inability to hold territory. It is a general lesson of history that terrorist and guerilla groups are poor at establishing durable governance structures. In any case, al-Shabaab and Boko Haram did not govern territory as effectively as IS because it was not their intention to do so based on their political aims and doctrine.

There are historical examples of limited use of water as a weapon by nation-states in conflicts, but scant evidence of its use by subnational actors until today. Still, something can be learned from a brief review of how nations have employed the water weapon and how these strategies and tactics may have provided ideas and inspiration to the VEOs waging war in the Middle East and Africa. Modern nation-states' use of the water weapon involves attacks on infrastructure and can be traced back to the seventeenth century and the Franco-Dutch War. In 1672, Louis XIV started the war, and the French overran the Netherlands. In defense, the Dutch opened their dikes and flooded the country, creating a watery barrier that was virtually impenetrable.[35]

Centuries later, during the Second Sino-Japanese War in 1938, Chinese forces destroyed the Huayuankow Dike on the Yellow River. Several thousand invading Japanese soldiers were washed away, and their advance was stemmed. However, as is often the case with the water weapon, the unintentional result was major floods that damaged parts of three Chinese provinces and destroyed several million hectares of farmland. The human death toll from the incident was also extraordinary. Several towns and cities were inundated, and hundreds of thousands of Chinese people drowned. Millions were left homeless. Not easily found in the historical record, this incident is nonetheless likely to have been the most destructive act of water weaponization ever recorded.[36]

The next decade saw a more notorious and more successful usage of strategic water weaponization by Allied forces in May 1943. During the Second World War, Allied air strikes destroyed two dams in Germany's Ruhr Valley that were impounding a massive 130 million and 200 million cubic meters of water, respectively, dealing a strong blow to Germany's military-industrial capability. Over a hundred factories were damaged. Bridges, coal mines, and farms were lost along with at least 1,300 German citizens' lives. This figure does not include the large number of enslaved workers who also perished in the attack.[37]

20   *Weaponizing Water*

The Korean Conflict was the next chapter in water weaponization, when use of the water weapon was more intrinsic. In 1952, US and allied forces strategically bombed dams in North Korea, an approach that some consider one of the more important aspects of the air war.[38] Successful allied attacks on North Korea's Sui-ho Dam on the Yalu River caused electricity outages in North Korea and parts of Chinese Manchuria for two weeks. The goal of this bombardment was to cut off the flow of hydroelectric power. The situation would have been more morally troublesome and more relevant to this book if the allies had intended to release the dammed water to wipe out soldiers or civilians, but because this was not their intent, significant political repercussions were lacking. Rather than applauding the restraint demonstrated, given the laws of war that renounce the water weapon, some US members of Congress complained that such successful actions had not been initiated earlier.[39] However, it was during the Korean Conflict that an international consensus around this indiscriminate form of warfare began to form consistent with coalition actions against the North Koreans.

Subsequent US strategic offensives against Vietnam served only to solidify the global consensus that clashed with US war-fighting strategy.[40] In 1966, as part of Operation Rolling Thunder, the US Department of Defense entertained the idea of breaching Vietnamese dikes, which had existed for centuries, in the high monsoon period to flood crops and so induce a food crisis. President Lyndon Johnson shut down the idea for fear that the North Vietnamese would exploit the situation for propaganda purposes.[41]

In subsequent years, as the war ground on, the morality of the decision to breach the dikes was the subject of vigorous debate between President Richard Nixon and his closest advisers, including Secretary of State Henry Kissinger. Nixon considered the strategic use of the water weapon as an option alongside the use of nuclear weapons. The question of whether the United States intentionally bombed dikes in Vietnam is still debated. The legal arguments against targeting civilian infrastructure during wartime were also mounting, as will be discussed in the next section.

It is notable that the United States established a cloud-seeding program during the Vietnam War, which broadly is considered meteorological warfare and more narrowly could be considered a type of water weaponization. Cloud seeding, or treating clouds with chemicals to induce rain, was conducted under Operation Popeye in 1967–1972. It was a highly secret attempt to extend the length of the monsoon season over the Ho Chi Minh Trail to soften the roads and create landslides that would make it impassable. The cloud-seeding technique may have been used widely in South Vietnam as well. The cloudbanks were also intended to obfuscate fire from anti-aircraft batteries to protect US bombing missions.[42]

Legal and Theological Constraints

Water weaponization violates international law as well as moral and religious norms. Use of the water weapon is a clear violation of the international body of law regulating armed conflict, and its use by Islamic extremist organizations is also problematic for a variety of reasons particular to Abrahamic faith traditions.

Charlotte Grech-Madin of Uppsala University identified the evolution of a water (weaponization) taboo that prescribes national military strategies. She asserts that at one time water was a standard weapon in conflicts between nation-states (including as recently as the Korean War), but the latter half of the twentieth century witnessed a remarkable strengthening of state consciousness against weaponizing water in conflict.[43]

Given Katzenstein's definition of norms as the "collective expectations for the proper behavior of actors with a given identity,"[44] Grech-Madin provides a convincing argument that a normative water taboo has evolved since World War II and that it rules out the use of water as a weapon in a range of conflicts since that time when it may have been strategically beneficial. However, she notes that there are limits to this taboo, especially in its application beyond international conflict.[45]

International Law

In 1863, US president Abraham Lincoln enacted the Lieber Code, also known as military General Orders No. 100, designed to regulate the actions of federal troops against opposing Confederate forces during the US Civil War. Widely held to be the first comprehensive codified law of war, it set out provisions for the ethical conduct of war, including protections for civilians and civilian property—defined in a sufficiently expansive way to include water infrastructure—and prohibited the use of poison. The code stated that use of poison in any manner, "be it to poison wells, or food, or arms, is wholly excluded from modern warfare."[46]

The Hague Conventions of 1899 and 1907 were the first multilateral treaties regulating the conduct of war and were largely based on the Lieber Code. The Hague Convention of 1899, with respect to the Laws and Customs of War on Land, as confirmed in 1907, also outlawed the use of poisons, looting of a town or place, and the bombardment of undefended towns. Article 25 of The Hague declarations of 1907 protects basic infrastructure such as water systems, undefended towns, villages, dwellings, and buildings. The vast majority of sovereign states at that time were party to these conventions.[47]

After the Second World War, the international community undertook new efforts to regulate armed conflict with some regard to water and infrastructure. The Fourth Geneva Convention of 1949 prohibits the destruction of property not justified by military necessity. However, the clearest international legal instrument against the use of water in wartime comes from the Additional Protocols of the Geneva Convention.

Protocol II, Article 49 (dated 1977), relates to the Protection of Victims of International Armed Conflicts:

> Starvation of civilians as a method of combat is prohibited. It is therefore prohibited to attack, destroy, remove or render useless, for that purpose, objects indispensable to the survival of the civilian population, such as foodstuffs, agricultural areas for the production of foodstuffs, crops, livestock, drinking water installations and supplies and irrigation works.[48]

Within the body of the conventions, Article 56 (Protocol I, 1977) is the most directly relevant to water weaponization, even unintentional:

> Works or installations containing dangerous forces, namely dams, and dikes, and nuclear electrical generating stations shall not be made the object of attack, even when these objects are military objectives, if such an attack may cause the release of dangerous forces and consequent severe losses among the civilian populations.

In the wake of the Vietnam War, the UN convened the Global Conference on the Human Environment in Stockholm in 1972. Above all, the aim of this conference was to protect and improve the environment for present and future generations. The 1972 Stockholm Declaration presented a common outlook for the environment based on preventing harm to natural resources expressly, including flora, fauna, and water. The declaration served as an early articulation of the concept of sustainability that later became an established principle of international customary law.[49]

Inspired partially by US military actions such as the meteorological warfare characterized by Operation Popeye, the international Convention on the Prohibition of Military or Any Hostile Use of Environmental Modification Techniques (ENMOD) was opened for signatories on December 10, 1976. In Article I, the convention prohibits the contracting parties from engaging in "military or any other hostile use of environmental modification techniques having widespread, long-lasting or severe effects as the means of destruction, damage or injury to any other State Party."[50]

Within the ENMOD treaty, the term *environmental modification technique* refers to "any technique for changing—through the deliberate manipulation of natural processes—the dynamics, composition or structure of the Earth, including its biota, lithosphere, hydrosphere and atmosphere, or of outer space." Water poisoning along with "interference with the hydrological balance" is prohibited.[51]

The convention has seventy-eight signatories. Therefore, its provisions only carry the force of customary international law with regard to regulating the actions of signatories. It is notable that, except for Syria, none of the state-level belligerents discussed in this volume, including the United States (as a combatant actor in some form in Iraq and Syria, Nigeria and Somalia), initially ratified the ENMOD treaty. However, Iraq, Syria, and Turkey are signatories as of 1977.[52]

At its Madrid Conference in 1976, the International Law Association (ILA) adopted the Resolution on the Protection of Water Resources and Water Installations in Times of Armed Conflict (Madrid Rules). These rules offer guidelines for protecting water to ensure that human consumption is protected. The resolution declares that water diversion, flooding, and poisoning, along with "interference with the hydrological balance," are prohibited.[53]

The ILA is an international nongovernmental organization founded for "the study, clarification and development of international law, both public and private, and the furtherance of international understanding and respect for international law."[54] Its long-established history and consultative status provide it the legitimacy to create guidance on water-related issues and make decrees. The ILA addresses the contamination of water, water as a target by militant organizations, and the overall protection of water and water installations, dams, dikes, and occupied territories and renders illegal any action that would cause disproportionate civilian suffering according to international law. Ultimately, the organization's focus remains on protecting civilians and it has prohibited the destruction or diversion of water

24 *Weaponizing Water*

that causes disproportionate suffering to civilians. The prolonged attention on international water law is a testimony to the complexity of the problems involved and the undeveloped state of this branch of the law.[55]

The actions of the Geneva Water Hub represent the most recent attempts to regulate the abuse of water and related infrastructure, including water weaponization. In 2015, fifteen countries[56] co-convened the Global High-Level Panel on Water and Peace with the task of developing a set of proposals aimed at strengthening the global framework to prevent and resolve water-related conflicts and facilitate the use of water as an important factor of building peace and enhancing the relevance of water issues in national and global policymaking.[57]

In July 2019, the panel endorsed twenty-eight draft principles on environmental protection in conflict.[58] The *Geneva List of Principles on the Protection of Water Infrastructure* expressly prohibits the deliberate destruction of water infrastructure. The panel members consulted existing laws of war, human rights law, water law, and environmental law to clarify the legal state of the environment in conflict.[59] The group cooperated with United Nations organizations such as UN Environment and UNICEF. Although, again, this declaration amounts to what is called soft international law, analysts and policymakers in the fields of development and water security are hopeful that implementation of these principles will further strengthen international prohibitions against weaponizing water.[60] This latest effort to prohibit the abuse of water is especially important. As water stress increases in the Middle East and Africa, the need for the community of nations to craft international legal responses will only grow more acute.

In cases where water weaponization is clearly considered to be a war crime or a crime against humanity and therefore a terrorist act, the United Nations and some regional and subregional organizations that enforce international criminal law may be relevant actors. They can provide the means to prosecute individuals who committed or ordered the weaponization of water. The mandate and law-making powers of international criminal enforcement organizations vary considerably. Some, such as the International Criminal Court (ICC) based in The Hague, Netherlands, have extensive legislative and supranational authority.

In 1998, the Statute of the International Criminal Court adopted in Rome led to the establishment of the International Criminal Court. The ICC Statute does not provide jurisdiction for prosecuting an offense of "terrorism," which describes many acts of water weaponization, but the ICC may prosecute terrorist acts if they amount to war crimes, crimes against humanity, or genocide within the definition provided in the statute.[61] The ICC is the only organization that has the power to, as it is politely described, "obtain individuals abroad" for purposes of putting them on trial. The other bodies possess only the power to adopt non-binding recommendations. Although this is the case, the ICC lacks universal territorial jurisdiction and may only investigate and prosecute crimes committed within member states, crimes committed by nationals of member states, and crimes in situations referred to the court by the UN Security Council.[62] A brief review of the cases of the forty-five leaders who have been indicted by the court for these crimes against humanity does not indicate that water weaponization has ever been among the counts of the indictment.

The UN Security Council also has the power to create ad hoc tribunals under Chapter VII of the UN charter, for crimes against humanity. These tribunals were established in the war in the former Yugoslavia in 1993 and the Rwandan genocide of 1994. Other tribunals tasked with adjudicating cases of war crimes, crimes against humanity, and genocide have been created, so it is also possible that water weaponization could fall within the scope of the crimes prosecuted by such tribunals. Again, there is no evidence that this has yet been the case.

Finally, at the most granular level of legal options, authorities have the power to prosecute individual terrorists who perpetrate acts of water weaponization under the national and local criminal laws. Governments that have territorial jurisdiction over such acts can bring charges for murder or even destruction of property, so terrorism need not be an explicit factor. Globally, it is unclear how often local criminal law has been used to regulate armed conflict under any circumstance let alone in relation to water weaponization.

Water and International Human Rights Law

Denial of water to an individual is a basic human security violation. Accordingly, the human right to water and sanitation (HRWS) has been recognized in international law through human rights treaties and UN resolutions. Most prominently, the right is stipulated in the International Covenant on Economic, Social and Cultural Rights (ICESCR), which is binding under international law.[63] The ICESCR recognizes the right of every human being to have access to sufficient water for personal and domestic uses (between 50 and 100 liters of water per person per day). This water supply must also be safe and affordable (not to exceed 3 percent of household income) and physically accessible (the source has to

26   *Weaponizing Water*

be within 1,000 meters of the home, and water collection time should not exceed thirty minutes).[64]

Furthermore, after protracted negotiations in the UN General Assembly, 122 countries formally acknowledged the human right to water and sanitation in Resolution 64/292 on July 28, 2010.[65] The General Assembly declared that clean drinking water is "essential to the full enjoyment of life and all other human rights."[66] In September 2010, the UN Human Rights Council adopted a resolution recognizing that the human right to water and sanitation forms part of the right to an adequate standard of living or freedom from want that is intrinsic to human security.[67]

Islamic Theology

As established above, weaponization of water is a clear violation of international law. It is also a violation of Islamic laws (*urf*) and inimical to some of the most prominent aspects of Muslim culture. It is therefore a remarkable hypocrisy that Islamic extremist organizations that espouse Sharia law would engage in the weaponization of water. Dating from approximately 1790 BC and considered the predecessor of basic Jewish and Islamic legal systems, the Babylonian legal Code of Hammurabi that enshrines the idea of proportionality through the doctrine of "an eye for an eye" is the first known written law to govern irrigation rights.[68] Sanskrit, Jewish, and Christian texts also contain provisions to protect civilians and the destruction of the natural environment.

The significance of water in Islam is reflected in the Quran, where it is mentioned sixty-three times. Islamic water use requirements are also found in the hadiths—reports or statements of action prescribed by the prophet Muhammad. First and foremost, they establish the characteristics of the relationship between humankind and nature. Humans are co-owners of three things: water, fire, and pastures and therefore must share them.

As indicated by the Quran, sharing water is the highest form of charity, and there will be a reward for sharing water with any living being, including animals.[69] *Sadaqah*, or the act of giving alms or charity, is one of the five pillars of Islam. Providing food or water is considered an act of *sadaqah*. Muslim children are often told that the act of providing water for their family or elders will result in *thawab*, spiritual merit or reward that accrues after performing a good deed. In addition to short-term giving, *Sadaqah Jariyah* is a type of charity that continues to benefit people over the long term and earns the giver rewards, even after death.

Developing a clean water system, as extremist groups often have done when attempting to curry favor with subject populations, is an example of an attempt to perform *Sadaqah Jariyah*.[70]

According to Islamic belief, the way in which a person has treated water is also an important consideration on the Day of Resurrection. This is detailed in a number of hadiths emphasizing that water should be freely available to all. A man who, having water in excess of his needs, refuses it to a traveler will be ignored.[71] The Quran states: "Whoever digs a well will receive reward for that from Allah (*swt*) on the day of judgment when anyone amongst jinn, men, and birds drink from it."[72] Likewise, general hoarding of water is described as a sin. The Quran admonishes: "Do not withhold the surplus of water, for that will prevent people from grazing their cattle," and "Do not withhold the surplus water in order to withhold the surplus grass."[73]

Islamic Water Law

Islamic law itself is essentially based on water. *Sharia*, as referred to before the advent of Islam in Arabia, stemmed from the *shuraat al-ma'a*, a series of rules that granted permits and rights for drinking water.[74] The meaning of the term was only later expanded to include the entire body of laws and rules given by God.[75] The conception of Sharia as "the watering source" or "the path that leads down to a source of water" is an allegorical demonstration that Divine law will quench the thirst for knowledge. It is the path leading to the source of truth.[76]

The basic principle of Islamic water law states that water, pasture, and fire—in their natural states—are res communes (common things), as are other "natural" resources such as land resources (grazing and minerals) and resources of the sea. "No legal person or ruler, therefore, may appropriate a river, for example, or try to sell or rent its water. Nor may tax be taken directly on such natural resources, only on the produce resulting from their exploitation (e.g. on crops, livestock, or on the profits of pearling expedition)."[77]

Islamic water law addresses allocation and precedence of use. The paramount rule in this legal system is *shafa*, the universal right of humans to quench their thirst and that of their animals. Second is *shirb,* the right of irrigation, which gives all users the right to water their crops.[78] Therefore, in places where an irrigation system passes through or under another village and the water remains in its pure, unpolluted state, people have the right to tap into it for drinking purposes so long as they do not pollute it. Above the ground, whoever has

28   *Weaponizing Water*

surface or riparian rights to water may do nothing to impede the flow of that water supply or prevent access.[79]

Water is also intrinsic to the active religious practice of Islam. *Zamzam* water is a key part of the hajj, the pilgrimage to Mecca, which is a responsibility of every Muslim. It is considered to be the water that sprang forth from the earth when Hajar—wife of the prophet Abraham— ran through the desert hills praying to God to bestow water upon her thirsty son, Ishmael.

Ablution, or ritual purification through hand washing, in preparation for prayers is an obligatory and deeply meaningful spiritual practice. Therefore, mosques are required to provide running water. Any form of water weaponization that denies water to areas where mosques are located is easily interpreted as a sin of great magnitude.

This description of the centrality of water to Islam exposes the heresy of using water as a weapon. This heresy is especially profound as applied to extremist groups. Al-Shabaab, Boko Haram, and the Islamic State are all adherents to a Salafist fundamentalist interpretation of Islam that requires literal interpretation of the hadiths. Yet the hadiths are unambiguous when it comes to the abuse of water.

Therefore, it is particularly ironic that IS relied on theology to justify the use of the water weapon. Muslim, Christian, and Jewish texts alike teach that depletion of the Euphrates, an outcome accelerated by IS's interference with water installations, portends the Day of Judgment. IS has used Islamic (and biblical) tradition to portray the Day of Judgment itself as a flood.

According to their argument, Noah as a prophet of Allah built the Ark in response to the flood that punished those who rejected his messengers. The flood was the consequence of opposing the truth, and the destruction it caused demonstrated that anyone who rejected the truth would be punished.

The story of the Ark, as portrayed by the Islamic State, seeks to proclaim that those who choose to embrace the truth are the righteous and the few and that those few, in their acceptance, save themselves from total destruction. In this way, IS propaganda, through *Dabiq*, the official magazine of the Islamic State, gives those deemed "nonbelievers" the metaphorical choice to be part of the few or the many—to choose between "the Islamic State or the flood."[80] Seen in this light, the use of the water weapon to eliminate opposing populations (which has, in many circumstances, mainly included other Muslims) gains legitimacy and is theologically supported as an inevitable actualization of IS's prophetic vision.

This propaganda is based on twisted logic. It also stands against the hadith and Sharia law as practiced even before the advent of Islam. In short, the use of the water weapon by all three Salafist groups examined in this volume is not only illegal, odious, and hypocritical but also arguably heretical.

Although it is predictable that VEOs will have little to no respect for international law, an interesting proposition is whether clearly identifying water weaponization as a profoundly heretical practice could be used as a way to pressure these extremist groups into altering their decisions to use the water weapon. This is an option that is at least worth exploring as part of a comprehensive counterinsurgency strategy in the war of ideas against extremism.

About the Book

The chapters that follow explore how the water and conflict cycle operates in various geographies and how the weaponization of water by violent extremists has played a role.

Chapters 2 through 4 trace the water and conflict cycle and water weaponization in the cases of Syria and Iraq, Nigeria, and Somalia, especially during the years 2011–2017 when drought swept across all of these countries. The focal actors in these conflicts are the Islamic State and other jihadists in Syria and Iraq, Boko Haram in Nigeria, and al-Shabaab in Somalia. Hausa-Fulani militants in Nigeria and the Kurdistan Regional Government (KRG) in Iraq are other subnational actors who play roles in the case studies. Although I argue that violent extremist organizations are responsible for the lion's share of the abuse of water resources during the relevant time frame, internal wars are notoriously messy, and all belligerents bear some culpability. Chapter 5 explores actions that national governments and the international community can take using the tools of defense, development, and diplomacy optimistically to stop water weaponization where it occurs or, at a minimum, to discourage normalization of its use in modern warfare.

Notes

1. Marcus King, "Water Security," in *An Introduction to Non-traditional Security Studies*, ed. Mely Caballero-Anthony (Thousand Oaks, CA: Sage, 2016), 156.
2. Willem Ligtvoet et al., *The Geography of Future Water Challenges* (The Hague: PBL Netherlands Environmental Assessment Agency, 2018).

30   *Weaponizing Water*

3. Jessica E. Tierney, Caroline C. Ummenhofer, and Peter B. deMenocal, "Past and Future Rainfall in the Horn of Africa," *Science Advances* 1, no. 9 (2015): e1500682.

4. Doyle Rice, "It Was 129 Degrees in Iran Thursday, Which Is One of the Earth's Hottest Temperatures Ever Recorded," *USA Today*, June 29, 2017.

5. Ibid.

6. Lisa Allen et al., "Summary for Policymakers," in *Climate Change 2013: The Physical Science Basis, in Contribution of Working Group I to the Fifth Assessment Report of the Intergovernmental Panel on Climate Change*, ed. T. F. Stocker et al. (Cambridge: Cambridge University Press, 2013), 22.

7. George Zittis et al., "Business-as-Usual Will Lead to Super and Ultra-Extreme Heatwaves in the Middle East and North Africa," *Climate and Atmospheric Science* 4, no. 20 (2021): 1–9.

8. Colin P. Kelley, "Climate Change in the Fertile Crescent and Implications of the Recent Syrian Drought," *Proceedings of the National Academy of Sciences* 112, no. 11 (March 7, 2015): 3241–3246, https://doi.org/10.1073/pnas.1421533112.

9. Martin Hoerling et al., "On the Increased Frequency of Mediterranean Drought," *Journal of Climate* 25, no. 6 (March 2012): 2146–2161, http://dx.doi.org/10.1175/JCLI-D-11-00296.1.

10. United Nations University, "Former National Leaders: Water a Global Security Issue, 3/20/2011," https://unu.edu/media-relations/releases/water-called-a-global-security-issue.html.

11. Ibid.

12. Philip A. Baumgarten, "Israel's Transboundary Water Disputes," Elisabeth Haub School of Law Student Publications, Pace Law School, May 14, 2009, https://digitalcommons.pace.edu/lawstudents/2.

13. "Water Conflict," Pacific Institute, accessed March 5, 2021, https://www.worldwater.org/water-conflict/.

14. Ibid.

15. Ibid.

16. Peter Schwartzstein, "Why Water Conflict Is Rising, Especially on the Local Level," Center for Climate and Security, February 26, 2021, https://climateandsecurity.org/2021/02/why-localized-water-violence-is-flourishing-even-as-transboundary-water-wars-are-not/.

17. Ashok Swain, "Water and Post-Conflict Peacebuilding," *Hydrological Sciences Journal* 61, no. 7 (2016): 1313–1322.

18. "Integrated Management and Negotiations for Equitable Allocation of Flow of the Jordan River Among Riparian States," Aquapedia, November 13, 2014, https://aquapedia.waterdiplomacy.org/wiki/index.php?title=Integrated_Management_and_Negotiations_for_Equitable_Allocation_of_Flow_of_the_Jordan_River_Among_Riparian_States.

19. Aaron T. Wolf, Annika Kramer, Alexander Carius, and Geoffrey D. Dabelko, "Water Can Be a Pathway to Peace, Not War," *Navigating Peace*, no. 1 (July 2006), https://grist.org/wp-content/uploads/2009/06/navigatingpeaceissue1.pdf.

20. Karin Aggestam, "Desecuritisation of Water and the Technocratic Turn in Peacebuilding," *International Environmental Agreements: Politics, Law and Economics* 15, no. 3 (2015): 327–340.

21. Marwa Daoudy, "Water Weaponization in the Syrian Conflict: Strategies of Domination and Cooperation," *International Affairs* 96, no. 5 (September 1, 2020): 1347–1366.

22. Idean Salehyan, "From Climate Change to Conflict? No Consensus Yet," *Journal of Peace Research* 45, no. 3 (2008): 315–326.

23. Carl-Friedrich Schleussner, Johnathan F. Donges, Reik V. Donner, and Hans Joachim Schnellnhuber, "Armed-Conflict Risks Enhanced by Climate-Related Disasters in Ethnically Fractionalized Countries," *Proceedings of the National Academy of Sciences* 113, no. 33 (2016): 9216–9221, https://doi.org/10.1073/pnas.1601611113.

24. Solomon M. Hsiang, Marshall Burke, and Edward Miguel, "Quantifying the Influence of Climate on Human Conflict," *Science* 341 (September 2013), https://doi.org/10.1126/science.1235367.

25. Halvard Buhaug et al., "One Effect to Rule Them All? A Comment on Climate and Conflict," *Climatic Change* 127 (December 2014): 391–397. https://link.springer.com/article/10.1007/s10584-014-1266-1.

26. Thomas F. Homer-Dixon, *Environmental Scarcity and Violence* (Princeton, NJ: Princeton University Press, 1999).

27. Paul Collier and Anke Hoeffler, "Greed and Grievance in Civil War" (Policy Research Working Paper no. 2355, World Bank, Washington, DC, May 2000).

28. Aaron Sayne, "Climate Change, Adaptation and Conflict in Nigeria" (Special Report 274, United States Institute of Peace, Washington, DC, June 2011), 5, https://www.usip.org/sites/default/files/Climate_Change_Nigeria.pdf.

29. Ibid.

30. Elizabeth Chalecki, "A New Vigilance: Identifying and Reducing the Risks of Environmental Terrorism," *Global Environmental Politics* 2, no. 1 (2002): 46–64, https://doi.org/10.1162/152638002317261463.

31. National Intelligence Council, *Global Water Security*, Intelligence Community Assessment ICA 2012-08 (Washington, DC: Office of the Director of National Intelligence, February 2, 2012), http://www.dni.gov/files/documents/Special%20Report_ICA%20Global%20Water%20Security.pdf.

32. Mark Zeitoun and Jeroen Warner, "Hydro-Hegemony: A Framework for Analysis of Trans-Boundary Water Conflicts," *Water Policy* 8, no. 5 (September 2006): 443.

33. *Encyclopaedia Britannica Online*, s.v. "weapon," accessed September 28, 2022, https://britanica.com/technology/weapon.

34. *Encyclopaedia Britannica Online*, s.v. "strategic weapons system," accessed May 1, 2020, https://www.britannica.com/technology/strategic-weapons-system.

35. "Dutch Flood Land to Repel French," World's Water, Pacific Institute, https://www.worldwater.org/conflicts/dutch-flood-land-to-repel-french-2/.

36. Arthur Westing, International Peace Research Institute, and United Nations Environment Programme, *Environmental Hazards of War: Releasing Dangerous Forces in an Industrialized World* (Thousand Oaks, CA: Sage Publications, 1990).

37. Ibid.

38. Ibid.

39. Charlotte Grech-Madin, "Water and Warfare: The Evolution and Operation of the Water Taboo," *International Security* 45, no. 4 (April 20, 2021): 84–125, https://doi.org/https://doi.org/10.1162/isec_a_00404.

40. Ibid.

41. Ibid.

42. Seymour M. Hersh, "Rainmaking Is Used as a Weapon by U.S.," *New York Times*, July 3, 1972.

43. Charlotte Grech-Madin, "The Water Taboo: Restraining the Weaponisation of Water in International Conflict" (PhD diss., Department of Peace and Conflict Research, Uppsala University, 2020), http://urn.kb.se/resolve?urn=urn:nbn:se:uu:diva-397700.

32   *Weaponizing Water*

44. Peter Katzenstein, "Introduction: Alternative Perspectives on National Security," in *The Culture of National Security*, ed. P. Katzenstein (New York: Columbia University Press, 1996), 1–32.

45. Ibid., 59.

46. *The War of the Rebellion: A Compilation of the Official Records of the Union and Confederate Armies,* series III (Washington, DC: Government Printing Office, 1899), 3:148–164.

47. "Convention for the Pacific Settlement of International Disputes," October 18, 1907, Netherlands Ministry of Foreign Affairs, no. 003316, https://archive.vn /20130616131806/http://www.minbuza.nl/en/key-topics/treaties/search-the-treaty -database/1907/10/003316.html#selection-47.0-47.63.

48. "Protection of Objects Indispensable to the Survival of the Civilian Population, Protocol Additional to the Geneva Conventions of 12 August 1949, and relating to the Protection of Victims of Non-International Armed Conflicts (Protocol II), 8 June 1977," International Committee of the Red Cross, https://www.icrc.org /applic/ihl/ihl.nsf/Article.xsp?action=openDocument&documentId=ACF5220D5853 26BCC12563CD0051E8B6.

49. "Report of the United Nations Conference on the Human Environment" (United Nations A/Conf.48/14/Rev1, Stockholm, June 5–16, 1972), https://documents -dds-ny.un.org/doc/UNDOC/GEN/NL7/300/05/IMG/NL730005.pdf?OpenElement.

50. "Convention on the Prohibition of Military or Any Hostile use of Environmental Modification Techniques (ENMOD), New York, 10 December 1976" (United Nations Treaty Series, vol. 1108, October 27, 1978), 151, https://treaties.un .org/Pages/ViewDetails.aspx?src=TREATY&mtdsg_no=XXVI-1&chapter=26&clang =_en.

51. Ibid.

52. International Law Association, "Resolution on the Protection of Water Resources and Water Installations in Times of Armed Conflict, Madrid, 1976" (report of the Fifty-Seventh Conference, Madrid, August 30–September 4, 1976), xxv–xxxvi.

53. Ibid.

54. "About Us," International Law Association, https://www.ila-hq.org/index .php/about-us.

55. Charles B. Bourne, "The International Law Association's Contribution to International Water Resources Law," *Natural Resources Journal* 36, no. 2 (1996): 155, https://digitalrepository.unm.edu/nrj/vol36/iss2/2.

56. Those countries are Cambodia, Colombia, Costa Rica, Estonia, France, Ghana, Hungary, Jordan, Kazakhstan, Morocco, Oman, Senegal, Slovenia, Spain, and Switzerland.

57. "Global High-Level Panel on Water and Peace—Secretariat," Hydropolitics Toward Peace and Security, Geneva Water Hub, https://www.genevawaterhub.org /resource/global-high-level-panel-water-and-peace-secretariat-0.

58. Geneva Water Hub, *The Geneva List of Principles on the Protection of Water Infrastructure* (Geneva: Geneva Water Hub and Platform for International Water Law, 2019), https://www.genevawaterhub.org/resource/geneva-list-principles -protection-water-infrastructure.

59. Global High-Level Panel on Water and Peace, *A Matter of Survival: Report of the Global High-Level Panel on Water and Peace* (Geneva: University of Geneva, 2017).

60. Personal communications with Dr. Mara Tingino (Lead Legal Specialist, Platform for International Water Law, Geneva Water Hub), August 5, 2019.

61. Gennady M. Danilenko, "The Statute of the International Criminal Court and Third States," *Michigan Journal of International Law* 21, no. 3 (2000): 445, https://repository.law.umich.edu/mjil/vol21/iss3/3.

62. "The International Criminal Court: An Introduction," archived from the original on March 3, 2013, accessed April 21, 2021, https://web.archive.org/web /20130602223510/http://aiic.net/page/1660.

63. UN General Assembly, "International Covenant on Economic, Social and Cultural Rights" (United Nations, Treaty Series, vol. 993, December 16, 1966), 3, https://www.refworld.org/docid/3ae6b36c0.html.

64. Ibid.

65. UN General Assembly, "Resolution 64/292: The Human Right to Water and Sanitation: Resolution," United Nations Digital Library, August 2010, https:// digitallibrary.un.org/record/687002?ln=en.

66. United Nations, "Right to water and sanitation is legally binding, affirms key UN body," UN News, October 1, 2010. https://www.un.org/en/?_gl=1*4cbv8y*_ga *ODMyMTc3NjcOLjE2NjUxNTUwNTY.*_ga_TK9BQL5X7Z*MTY2NTE1NTA1 Ni4xLjEuMTY2NTE1NTA5My4wLjAuMA

67. Office of the High Commissioner for Human Rights, www.ohchr.org [retrieved June 25, 2021].

68. Haleh Hatami and Peter H. Gleick, "Conflicts over Water in the Myths, Legends, and Ancient History of the Middle East," *Environment: Science and Policy for Sustainable Development* 36, no. 3 (1994): 10–11, https://doi.org/10.1080/00139157 .1994.9929156.

69. Distributing water hadith, Sahih Bukhari, https://www.sahih-bukhari.com /Pages/Bukhari_3_40.php.

70. "What Is Sadaqah Jariyah?" Islamic Relief USA, http://irusa.org/sadaqah -jariyah/.

71. Ibid.

72. "Clean Water for Deprived Communities in Africa," Islamic Ummah Relief (IUR), https://islamicummahrelief.org/cleanwater4africa/.

73. Distributing water hadith, Sahih Bukhari, https://www.sahih-bukhari.com /Pages/Bukhari_3_40.php.

74. Francesca de Châtel, "Drops of Faith: Water in Islam," *Water Resources IMPACT* 11, no. 6 (November 2009), https://www.jstor.org/stable/10.2307/wateresoimpa .11.6.0005.

75. Lucius O. Mendis, "Ancient Water and Soil Conservation Ecosystems of Sri Lanka" (paper presented at International History Seminar on Irrigation and Drainage, Teheran, Iran, May 2–5, 2007).

76. Saffet Catovic, "Islamic Sacred Texts Related to Water," GreenFaith Water Shield, https://faithinwater.org/uploads/4/4/3/0/44307383/islamic_sacred_texts-water -greenfaith.pdf.

77. John C. Wilkinson, "Muslim Land and Water Law," *Journal of Islamic Studies* 1 (1990): 60, https://www.jstor.org/stable/pdf/26195667.pdf?ab_segments=0%2Fbasic _SYC-4929%2Ftest&refreqid=search%3A07e28fa360d70d35277bf7f0f4b0fc6b.

78. de Châtel, "Drops of Faith."

79. Wilkinson, "Muslim Land and Water Law."

80. Al-Kinānī, Abū 'Amr, "It's Either Islamic State or the Flood." *Dabiq* 1435, Ramadan Issue no. 2. https://ia601805.us.archive.org/34/items/db-mgz/db02-flood.pdf.

2

The Islamic State of Syria and Iraq

AT THE TIME HE WAS INTERVIEWED IN 2016, MUSTAFA ABDUL Hamid was a thirty-year-old refugee from a town of outsized strategic importance in the north of Syria called Ayaz, near the Turkish border. He was one of many refugees interviewed by John Wendle of *Scientific American* in Kara Tepe, the main camp for Syrian refugees on the Greek island of Lesbos. Abdul Hamid landed in Greece having first fled to the Syrian capital Damascus. He was but one of hundreds of thousands of farmers displaced by the worst drought in instrumental record that had beset the country in 2010–2011.

His plight is emblematic of that of his compatriot farmers, whose anger about loss of livelihood erupted in the streets at the onset of the civil war. Speaking to Wendle, Mustafa observed: "Before this drought farming was very good and profitable for the farmers."[1] Before the drought, he used to harvest three-quarters of a metric ton of wheat per hectare, but later, Mustafa's wheat harvest fell to half of its prior level. He had no intention of returning to Syria because of the ongoing impossible situation there that had been brought on by a changing climate and the continuous violent social upheavals resulting from the warring factions in the civil war. Mustafa complained that these warring factions were stealing wheat reserves and, in effect, using food as a weapon to control populations. Mustafa fundamentally understood that water was the real underlying issue. "All I needed was water," he said, "and I didn't have water . . . land plus water equals politics, which is power."[2]

This chapter focuses on Syria and Iraq, the area that became the domain of the Islamic State (IS) during the Syrian Civil War. The time

36 *Weaponizing Water*

period covered by this chapter runs from approximately 2012 to 2016, when the Islamic State's strength and thus its ability to weaponize water were most intensive.[3]

Societal Context of Syria

Geography

Syria, formally the Syrian Arab Republic, is a Middle Eastern country that borders Lebanon to the southwest, the Mediterranean Sea to the west, Turkey to the north, Iraq to the east, and Jordan and Israel to the south. It is about one and a half times the size of the US state of Pennsylvania. Topographically, the country consists mostly of semiarid and desert plateau, although the coastal plains bordering the Mediterranean feature a more humid climate. In the east, high mountains and deserts are also prominent features.[4] The Euphrates, bisecting the country in the east, is Syria's major river, although there are also several lesser water bodies.

Since ancient times, the area has been known as the Fertile Crescent, and the northern part, called Mesopotamia, encompasses the Tigris and the Euphrates river basins in an area that straddles Syria and Iraq. The region is also known as the "cradle of civilization" because it is where settled agriculture first took hold as farmers cleared land and modified the natural environment. Syria is shown in the map in Figure 2.1.

Political History

Modern Syria is a polyglot nation riven with political divisions born out of a long history of colonial rule by the Ottoman Empire and a shorter period of rule by France. In 1916, near the end of World War I, Britain and France signed the Sykes-Picot Agreement, a secret treaty that divided the ailing Ottoman Empire into the spheres of influence of each signatory. In 1920, the area that is now Syria was administered under the French Mandate. In 1945, at the conclusion of the Second World War, the territory gained independence when the Republic of Syria joined the United Nations. The era following independence, roughly from 1949 to 1971, was characterized by political instability corresponding with a succession of coups.

Within the larger context of the Cold War alliance systems, Syria, which functioned as a socialist state under the Baath Party, fell into political alignment with the Union of Soviet Socialist Republics (USSR). The

Figure 2.1 Map of Syria

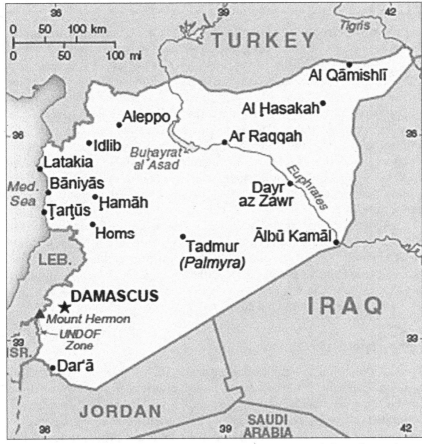

Source: US Central Intelligence Agency, "Syria," World Factbook, https://www.cia.gov/the-world-factbook/countries/syria/.

alliance was influenced by the 1956 Suez Crisis, when Egypt was invaded by Israel, France, and the UK after it blockaded the Suez Canal, a development that underscored the importance of strategic waterways in the Middle East. Opposition from Britain, Israel, and France as well as Syria's pan-Arab socialist affinity with Egypt were among the factors that led the two countries of Syria and Egypt to form a political union in 1958. The result was the sovereign state of United Arab Republic (UAR), led by the visionary Gamal Abdel Nasser of Egypt. The UAR

38   *Weaponizing Water*

was a short-lived experiment. In 1961, an uprising of disgruntled Syrian army officers restored the separate Syrian regime and held a constitutional referendum.

Shortly thereafter, in 1963, the Arab Socialist Baath Party fell under the control of its military wing and assumed control in Damascus. The coup caused a split in the party; one branch broke off to rule Iraq, and the other Syria. Hafez al-Assad, a Baathist military officer who participated in the 1963 coup, installed himself as leader of Syria in 1970. Hafez al-Assad ruled Syria for decades until 2000. That year, Bashar al-Assad was reluctantly selected by his father as the heir apparent and, upon his father's death, was installed in office following a one-party election. In a series of three nondemocratic elections up to 2014, Bashar al-Assad was sworn in for another seven-year term, continuing a brutal regime that has carried through the ensuing civil war until the time of this writing.

Although Bashar al-Assad is for all intents and purposes a dictator who has assumed war powers, the form of government in Syria that has evolved can be described as a dictatorial semi-presidential system. This arrangement features Bashar as president alongside the prime minister and the cabinet. The cabinet is named by the president but can be theoretically dissolved by the parliament.

Demographics and Economy

Syria's population is estimated to be nearly 22 million as of 2022.[5] The population density is highest along the Mediterranean coast in the three largest cities of Damascus, Aleppo, and Homs. In the last decade, the population of these cities has been significantly increased by migration due to such factors as declines in agricultural productivity of the land. The relatively fertile Euphrates River valley is also a significant population center.

Syria is characterized by religious and ethnic cleavages that have historically made the prospect of political integration problematic. The largest ethnic group is Syrian Arabs, making up roughly 74 percent of the population but not including at least 6 million refugees now outside the country. About 600,000 semipermanent Palestinian internal refugees are now counted among the overall population numbers.[6]

The second largest ethnic group in Syria is the Alawites. The Alawites are a people defined largely by their religion, which has historical and theological links to Shia Islam, though many of the Alawite beliefs differ markedly. Although some inhabit the three major cities,

The Islamic State of Syria and Iraq   39

the Alawites are the dominant sect in the coastal towns and the nearby mountainous Latakia region, where they were driven by persecution especially during Ottoman rule. They are considered heretics by many mainstream Sunni and Islamic extremist organizations.[7]

However, the al-Assad family hails from this community. Therefore, the Alawites possess outsized political power in the country. President Bashar al-Assad has filled many of his senior political posts with Alawites, and Alawites occupy many posts in the highest echelons of the state security apparatus. Recent surveys indicate that Alawites now represent 17.2 percent of the Syrian population, an increase from 11.8 percent in 2010. But this number has probably declined because the community has suffered heavy casualties during the civil war.[8]

The next largest ethnic group is the Kurds. The Kurdish people, who are in effect a nation spread among several countries, make up between 7 percent and 10 percent of the population.[9] Kurds reside primarily in the northeastern corner of Syria, where they have continually sought to create an autonomous state.

Finally, there is a significant Turkic or Turkish-speaking population. About a half dozen other minority groups are present, including Armenians and Greeks and other small communities with ancient roots. Levantine Arabic is the official language of Syria, although many other languages are widely spoken.

In terms of religion, those subscribing to Islam comprise 87 percent of the population. This estimate includes Sunni Muslims, who comprise 74 percent, and Shia (including the Alawites in this case) at 13 percent. Christians comprise 10 percent of the population. Finally, there is a Druze community present in the rugged mountain region of the southwest and the Israeli-occupied Golan Heights, and their population was estimated at 3 percent.[10] Like the Alawites, the Druze play a greater role in politics and security than their numbers alone suggest, largely owing to the legacy of their prominent role in the struggle against the French colonial rule.

As a socialist state since 1963, Syria has traditionally pursued what can be characterized as a command-and-control economy. Before the current war, the Assad regime had begun to liberalize the economy by taking measures such as consolidating multiple exchange rates and cutting state subsidies on some items. Also prior to the war, petroleum was the country's most important export, constituting 40 percent of export earnings, but production has declined during the war.

Agriculture is the largest sector in the domestic economy. About 25 percent of the land in Syria is arable and most of it is used for agriculture.

40 *Weaponizing Water*

In the prewar era, the agriculture sector contributed about 20 percent of GDP and 20 percent of employment.[11] Today, the economy is plagued by long-run economic constraints, including foreign trade barriers and sanctions, declining oil production, high unemployment, and rising budget deficits. As a result of these numerous economic factors and the civil war, most of Syria's population are now living below the poverty line.

The Syrian Civil War

Conditions for political-based violence have long been ripe in Syria because of the ethnic and sectarian cleavages. It is said that success has many fathers. Likewise, wars have many causes. Among these were the political uprisings known as the Arab Spring, a series of anti-government protests, uprisings, and armed rebellions that spread across much of the Middle East and North Africa in the early 2010s. The Arab Spring began with protests in Tunisia calling for political freedom in response to poor living conditions under mostly oppressive regimes. Inspired, in part, by the political aspirations of the Arab Spring, on the one hand, and grinding poverty, on the other, the demonstrations in Syria that began in several cities were violently repressed by the Syrian government. But then these localized protests escalated to armed conflict on the national level.

The main combatants are the Syrian armed forces and foreign allies, including Russian forces and Iranian-backed proxies, against an alliance of mostly Sunni opposition groups, including violent extremist organizations and the Syrian Democratic Forces composed mostly of Arabs. Various Kurdish militias also fought against the regime. A number of countries have provided support to one faction or another, including Iran, Russia, Turkey, and the United States. US involvement was primarily limited to an air campaign with the declared purpose of countering IS, although some ground forces and special operations units have been deployed to aid Kurdish fighters. Virtually all sides in the conflict have been accused of severe human rights violations, often against civilians. These actions, as well as displacement from the fighting itself, were major drivers of the outward flow of refugees that has caused great human suffering.

The war has taken a heavy toll on the Syrian population in many ways. According to estimates from the Syrian Observatory for Human Rights, the total number killed as of the summer of 2020 is between 380,000 and 850,000.[12] Within Syria, estimates in 2015 claimed that as many as 10.9 million people, or almost half of the population, have been displaced.[13] As stated, about 5.5 million Syrian refugees have fled the country. This figure includes 2 million moving to Egypt, Iraq, Jordan, and Lebanon, 3.5 million Syrians registered in Turkey, and more than 33,000 Syrian refugees registered in North Africa.[14] Thousands of these refugees have eventually made their way to Europe. Many European countries are beset with increased nativist sentiments that have created a politics that prevents the refugees' humane absorption into society.

A large percentage of the refugees were farmers. The role that agricultural declines, caused by drought and water stress, played in sparking the war itself is discussed in the following pages. First, it is important to better understand the overall status of water resources in Syria and their impacts on the economy at a national level.

Water Resources and Management

Syria is a semiarid country with numerous natural water challenges. These challenges, such as desertification, are exacerbated by climate trends including higher temperatures and drought. Other factors, such as overgrazing and soil erosion, are caused primarily by unsustainable agricultural practices. Anthropogenic (human) activity is also detrimental to water quality as Syrian surface water sources have been degraded by pollution, including through the disposal of raw sewage and chemicals associated with the refining of petroleum.

Water supply for agricultural uses is a perennial concern. Syria must share its major river, the Euphrates, with other countries, making estimations of the inflow rate necessary for maximizing agricultural production unreliable. This problem is compounded by the fact that transboundary water agreements with the other riparian nations, primarily Turkey, are largely outdated nonbinding memoranda of understanding, when up-to-date water agreements between states often can add predictability to water supply. Turkey's water withdrawals from the Euphrates for agricultural production in the Anatolian region and the accompanying challenges to regional water supply are undoubtedly the cause of a reduction in the surface water flows in Syria. Lack of quality data to support flow rate estimates makes the exact amount difficult to identify. Flow rate data, in addition to political will, is necessary to organize an informed international negotiation of a lasting treaty among the riparian nations about the allocation of shared water resources.

In addition to natural environmental forces, a growing population in the ten years before 2015 and a corresponding growth in water demand

42 Weaponizing Water

also put pressure on the already-stressed water supply in Syria. In 2014, it was estimated that 78 percent of all groundwater withdrawals were from unsustainable sources such as depleted aquifers.[15] A population that grew from 3.3 million in 1950 to approximately 19.4 million at the outbreak of the Syrian Civil War in 2011 was largely responsible.[16] Syria's average annual population growth rate was among the highest in the arid Middle East and North African region, reaching a prewar level of 2.94 percent.[17]

Syrian over-abstraction of groundwater and unpredictable river flows have diminished available water supplies. When the amount of water taken from groundwater is greater than the amount of water falling as rain, it is called over-abstraction. When water is taken from aquifers, groundwater levels fall. High population growth and urbanization of migration are localized threats to water resources. In Damascus, between 1993 and 2000 groundwater levels were drawn down by more than 6 meters per year in some areas.[18] It is estimated that 78 percent of all groundwater withdrawals in Syria are unsustainable.[19] Poor state water management policies extending back to the 1970s have contributed to this unsustainable groundwater usage. As with surface waters, making an overall estimation of groundwater resources is difficult because of the poor data available to the government in Damascus.

In Syria, the agricultural sector consumes the most water, with 90 percent of water usage dedicated to agriculture, the highest percentage of any country in the region. Important agricultural areas lie in the northeast and the south of the country. Most agricultural land is irrigated using a system of government-built open concrete canals, whose efficiency is low, with losses from canals as high as 60 percent.[20] Over 80 percent of farmland is irrigated using traditional flooding methods, which is similarly inefficient.

Before the onset of the civil war, measures indicated that the amount of irrigated land was also rising. Although these figures paint a general picture of the hydrological situation in Syria, it is important to understand that infrastructure may have been destroyed during the war, and farmers may have been displaced, further complicating the amalgamation of national-level statistics.

Water governance is a persistent cause for concern. Management of the Syrian water sector is dysfunctional. More than 140 laws dealing with water governance have been passed since 1924.[21] But because of a lack of enforcement, these water use laws effectively exist only on paper.[22]

Syrian water governance is highly centralized by the national government, on the one hand, but also fragmented among regional and local institutions with overlapping functions and responsibilities and lacking in power to enforce regulations, on the other. At the national level, the State Minister for Environmental Affairs is responsible for dealing with all main environmental issues, including water management. The Ministry of Housing and Construction is responsible for proposing, planning, and executing overall provision of water and sanitation services. Finally, the Ministry of Irrigation is responsible for supplying water for agriculture. Key structural factors prevent the implementation of an effective, integrated water resource management system.

The Ministry of Local Administration plans and implements governmental activities and maintains responsibility for issuing standards and monitoring the quality of water for all uses at the regional level. A General Commission for Water Resource Management is in charge of integrating water policies between various ministries.[23] The ministries also suffer from capacity issues, as most employees lack formal technical education.

Water resource management in Syria is not only inefficient but also corrupt. Water plans are created, but not implemented. Water laws that are on the books are not enforced, and targets for water supply are not met. According to Francesca de Châtel, who wrote in 2014 about the role of drought and climate change in the Syrian uprising, "Water and its management become almost abstract concepts that have little connection to reality and the rapidly worsening state of the country's water resources."[24]

To make matters worse, the policies that were enforced were largely detrimental. Subsidization of the diesel fuel that is used to pump water encouraged overirrigation, which depleted aquifers at an unsustainable rate. National water policies also encouraged cultivation of water-intensive crops such as cotton and wheat, while overplanting rendered the land unsuitable for future agricultural use.[25] Heavy subsidization of water itself encouraged inefficient irrigation techniques, including traditional flooding methods and open concrete irrigation canals that allow for rapid evaporation.

Observers have indicated poor governance was a significant factor in Syria's water crisis. The Assad regime has been quick to point to external factors affecting adequate water supply in order to deflect the blame for mismanagement. This is not to say that demand created by population growth, increased droughts, and Turkey's impoundment of water do not also play roles in creating water stress. These factors, compounded by an underlying legacy of poor water management, came to a head and created a crisis when another dynamic was introduced: Syria and Iraq experienced the worst drought in instrumental record from 2007 to 2010.[26]

Societal Context of Iraq

Geography

Iraq, also partly situated in what was ancient Mesopotamia, occupies the eastern wing (opposite Syria) of the Fertile Crescent, also referred to as the cradle of civilization. The country is bordered by Jordan, Kuwait, Iran, Saudi Arabia, Syria, and Turkey (see Figure 2.2) and remnants of human settlement in Iraq date back to the Sumerian civilization in 50,000 BC. The Sumerians were a hydraulic civilization, able to divert the Tigris and Euphrates Rivers for irrigation.

Iraq is divided into four geographical regions largely on the basis of hydrology: the Tigris–Euphrates alluvial plains in central and southeast Iraq; the Al-Jazīrah region in the north, between the Tigris and Euphrates Rivers; the western and southern deserts, which cover approximately two-fifths of the country; and the highlands in the north and northeast that form Iraqi Kurdistan. The agriculture supported by the Tigris–Euphrates river system is essential to Iraq's economy.[27]

Political History

Iraq arguably began to coalesce as a nation during a period known as the Arabization of Iraq, which started under the leadership of Ali ibn Abu Talib in AD 636, when the capital of the Rashidun Caliphate was moved from Medina in modern-day Saudi Arabia to the city of Kufa in Iraq. The ruling power structure shifted in 1258 when the Mongols attacked Baghdad, destroying the city and executing the remaining Abbasid dynasty family members. The dynasty had ruled for about a hundred years. Except for a brief sixteen-year interregnum during which the Safavid Empire ruled the country, Iraq was next governed by the Ottoman Empire from the fourteenth century until the end of World War I. The Treaty of Sèvres in 1920 established by mandate of the League of Nations the nation of Iraq, under British administration. In 1921, Faisal I was proclaimed king under the mandate, and this marked the beginning of the Hashemite monarchy. The Hashimi are any of the Arab descendants, either direct or collateral, of the prophet Muhammad. The mandate was terminated in 1932 when Iraq was admitted to the League of

The Islamic State of Syria and Iraq 45

Figure 2.2 Map of Iraq

Source: US Central Intelligence Agency, "Iraq," World Factbook, https://www.cia.gov/the-world-factbook/countries/iraq/.

Nations as an independent nation. In 1945, the country celebrated its status by joining the United Nations and served as one of the original founders of the Arab League. However, in 1958 the Iraqi army staged a coup to overthrow the rather weak monarchy.

The next major political shift came in 1968, when a young army officer named Saddam Hussein played a key role in a bloodless coup referred to as the July 17 Revolution, which formed the Arab Socialist Baath Party. From 1968 to 1979, Saddam served as the vice president

46   *Weaponizing Water·*

of Iraq, a term that revealed signs of his future brutality. During this time, he established a police state that suppressed opposition movements of the Shia and the Kurds. Saddam filled positions of power with his fellow Sunni Arabs, even though Shiites were a significant minority. In 1979, Saddam formally became Iraq's president, although he had by then been the de facto leader for many years. During his presidency, Iraq endured numerous wars, including the Iran-Iraq War (1980–1988) and the Gulf War (1991). In 2003, upon dubious accusations that Iraq possessed weapons of mass destruction, the United States invaded Iraq as part of its Global War on Terror and deposed Saddam Hussein.

In January 2005, Ibrahim al-Jaafari's United Iraqi Alliance coalition of Shiite parties won the election. The newly elected body was given a mandate to write a new constitution and exercise legislative functions until the new constitution came into effect. Iraq held an election under the new constitution that brought Jalal Talabani, a Kurd, to the presidency, and results were certified in February 2006. A compromise among the winning parties led Talabani to name Nuri al-Maliki, a Shiite member of the Islamic Dawa Party who was supported by the United States, to the post of Prime Minister. During the month of April, Iraqis endured 135 car bombings by Sunni insurgents.[28] Maliki, who also had strong ties to Iran, deepened the ethno-sectarian cleavages exposed by the violence that were pulling the country toward the brink of civil war.

Since the US invasion in 2003, Iraq has descended into chaos. A key trigger was what became known as the de-Baathification process of Iraq's government, military, and ruling institutions. When US Ambassador Paul Bremer, who became the regent over Iraq, dissolved Iraq's Sunni-led military in May of that year, 350,000 soldiers were left unemployed. Those who held the rank of colonel or higher were permanently banned from taking positions in Iraq's new government.

Military-age males with no prospect of employment are rarely a stabilizing factor in fragile states, to say the least. The resulting insurgency came quickly. Al-Qaeda in Iraq, emboldened by the Western presence in Iraq, increased the number of bombings and assassinations of the US military. The insurgency was fueled by the discovery of prisoner abuse carried out by the US military at Abu Ghraib prison. Sectarian violence escalated into the spring of 2004, with Shia militia targeting Coalition forces and Sunni insurgents seeking greater territorial control. In April, the US military launched the First Battle of Fallujah. The catalyst for the battle was the killing and mutilation of four military contractors

The Islamic State of Syria and Iraq   47

from the private military firm Blackwater and the deaths of five US soldiers a few days earlier.

The First Battle of Fallujah marked a turning point in public perception of the ongoing conflict because it was insurgents, not exclusively forces loyal to Saddam Hussein, who were the opponents, and the regular US military sustained casualties during the operation itself. Although it was technically a victory, the battle was seen as a significant setback by the US military.

Attempts to regain control of the city were unsuccessful until Operation Phantom Fury, also known as the Second Battle of Fallujah, occurred in December 2004. This operation also resulted in significant US casualties. The offensive, led by US Marines and including British and Government of Iraq forces, was ferocious. Accounts from US Marines described some of the heaviest combat since the Battle of Hue City in Vietnam in 1968.[29]

The damage to civilian infrastructure, including electric and water utilities, was grave, setting a precedent for the amount of damage that was to come in other urban areas in subsequent years of fighting. About 20 percent of the buildings in Fallujah were completely destroyed, and from half to two-thirds of the remaining buildings had notable damage. The fighting created roughly 200,000 internally displaced people, most of whom have never returned—another characteristic of the future wars in the region.[30]

In January 2008, Parliament began to allow former officials from Saddam's Baath Party to return to governmental positions and collect pensions, but infighting between the Iraqi army and militias continued. The following winter, the United States handed control of the Green Zone, the center of the Coalition Provisional Government, to the Iraqis. President Barack Obama announced the plan for withdrawal shortly thereafter.

In August 2010, President Obama oversaw the full withdrawal of US troops that left only US military advisers and trainers on the ground. Although a new government that included all major political and ethnic groups was formed by Prime Minister Maliki at the behest of President Talabani, Shia and Sunni militias continued to clash.

By the summer of 2013, coincident with the US withdrawal, IS had made inroads against the Iraqi government. Between 500 and 1,000 inmates were released from Abu Ghraib prison and IS was gaining significant territory with the seizure of Fallujah, Ramadi, Anbar, Mosul, and Raqqa. With a political gridlock taking hold of Parliament, the Iraqi government requested US assistance in fighting IS in June 2014.

48　*Weaponizing Water*

Between August 2014 and July 2017, the Iraqi government, the People's Mobilization Force, the Kurdish Regional Government, and the US Coalition were locked in a territorial face-off with the Islamic State, whose members continued to terrorize and massacre Iraq's minority groups.

Although the threat from IS has receded as the primary contenders for power have disbursed, sectarian tensions remain as the Iraqi government increasingly aligns with Iran.

During the May 2018 parliamentary elections, Shia cleric Muqtada al-Sadr's political bloc took the largest number of seats. Sadr was the leader of a militia known as the Mehdi Army. He capitalized on growing public resentment of the preceding Tehran-backed governments that had failed to improve basic public services and build hospitals and schools. Protests erupted over unemployment, corruption, and shortages of clean water and electricity. The protests continued until the end of 2019.

Following months of protests across Iraq and the resignation of Prime Minister Adel Abdul-Mahdi, in October 2019 Mustafa Al-Kadhimi became a leading contender for the premiership. He is a former director of the Iraqi National Intelligence Service who played a vital role in the fight against IS.

Al-Kadhimi is not affiliated with any of the Iraqi political parties and, perhaps as a result, he has few allies in government. Parliament is heavily dominated by pro-Iran MPs who have balked at his references to protester demands. In April 2020, Iranian proxy forces in Iraq published a statement that accused Al-Kadhimi of culpability for the deaths of their leader, Iranian general Qasem Soleimani, and charged him with conspiring with the United States.[31] Without solid sectarian or political durability, Al-Kadhimi's government is uncertain, at best, as Baghdad continues to strive for legitimacy.

Demographics and Economy

As of 2020, Iraq's population is estimated at 39 million concentrated in the northern, central, and eastern parts of the country, with many larger urban areas centered along the Tigris and Euphrates Rivers. The country's major urban areas are Baghdad, the nation's capital, Mosul, and Basra, though a large portion of the country's population also lives in the Kurdish-administered cities Kirkuk and Erbil.

Iraq is primarily ethnically Arab, but key differences exist between Sunni and Shia Islam. Ethnic Arabs comprise the majority (75–80 percent) of the country's population. The second largest ethnic group is the Kurds, who represent 15–20 percent of the population. The remaining 5 percent consists of an array of Turkmen, Yazidi, Shabak, Kaka'i, Bedouin, Romani, Assyrian, Circassian, Sabean Mandean, and Persian peoples.[32]

Sectarian tensions have long divided Iraqi society, and they are inseparable from daily politics. Although the country historically was ruled by Sunni Muslims, in recent years the tables have turned and the government has been led by a Shia majority. After the US-led invasion in 2003, the United States spearheaded the implementation of a concept known as the *Muhasasa Ta'ifia*—an attempt to manage religious diversity by providing proportional governmental representation for Iraq's various ethnosectarian groups. This principle has guided every election since then. However, many blame the *Muhasasa* for the increase in sectarian violence throughout the country and for creating the country's corruption, collusion, and patronage systems. The original goal of the *Muhasasa* was to establish equal representation of Sunni, Shia, and Kurdish groups by allocating access to the highest political offices. However, critics claim that the result of implementing this system is not equal representation, unity, or democracy but rampant corruption that fuels infighting.[33]

It certainly appears to the naked eye that the underlying hatred among groups is too strong for the *Muhasasa* to succeed. Under Saddam's rule, ethnic tensions were exploited with the mistreatment of the minority Kurdish and Shia populations. Residual resentment of Sunnis from the 1988 Operation Anfal, which killed scores of Kurds and destroyed 2,000 Kurdish villages, and from the more favorable treatment of Kurdish-controlled northern Iraq under the UN Oil-for-Food Programme solidified ethnosectarian cleavages. The US invasion in 2003 exacerbated the tensions—ostracizing Sunni nationalist forces in favor of compliant, seemingly religious representatives through the de-Baathification process.

Economic growth has stagnated. Iraq's unstable economy is largely dependent on oil resources, which provide approximately 85 percent of government revenue and 80 percent of foreign exchange earnings for the country's state-run economy. In 2017, Iraq's GDP growth slowed to 1.1 percent, partly because of an uptick in civil unrest and a slow global oil market. Iraq has received a significant amount in foreign aid to assist in the fight against terrorism, as well as for the country's reconstruction and rehabilitation initiatives in areas formerly controlled by the Islamic State. The Iraqi government seeks investors to boost the economy, but many are wary of the country's

50 *Weaponizing Water*

instability, wavering security, and dubious political system. Moreover, rampant corruption, failing infrastructure, and a lack of essential services have made it increasingly difficult for foreign investors to become involved in Iraq's economy.[34]

Water Resources

Whereas Syria experiences significant water stress, Iraq faces more of an absolute water shortage over wide swathes of the country, especially in the regions south of Iraqi Kurdistan. The Tigris and Euphrates Rivers account for 98 percent of Iraq's surface water. Therefore, Iraq is held hostage by dam projects initiated by neighboring states, which have caused water levels to fall by 40 percent in the last few years.

It is estimated that the Government of Iraq is unable to provide water regularly to a significant proportion of its approximately 39 million citizens. This failure results from a combination of exogenous factors that include climate conditions and unilateral infrastructure development by neighboring states. Within Iraq, the water infrastructure continues to deteriorate because of neglect, insufficient maintenance, and war damage from successive US invasions in 1991 and 2003 and the war against IS.

Current and reliable data is hard to obtain, but a 2013 study of Iraq's water supply estimated the quantity at 43 billion cubic meters (BCM) for 2015, which was then expected to drop to 17.61 BCM by 2025 as a result of the exogenous and interior issues mentioned. These quantities were unable to sustain water demand even at the time the projections were made, when demand was estimated to be between 66.8 and 77 BCM.[35] Meanwhile, overall conditions have worsened.

In 2015, the population of Iraq was 44.35 million, and it is expected to grow to 70 million by 2025, barring unforeseen warfare.[36] According to a 2012 UNICEF report, 90 percent of Iraq's population had access to potable water. However, in rural areas, only 77 percent of the population has access to improved drinking water sources compared to 98 percent in urban areas. Lack of access to improved water sources (likely protected from contamination) has contributed to dramatic increases in the number of waterborne illnesses in the country. As in Syria, projected population growth will further strain access to available water.

As the primary sources of surface water, the Tigris and Euphrates Rivers provide approximately 70 percent of Iraq's overall water supply. The headwaters of both rivers lie in Turkey. The Tigris flows in Iraqi

The Islamic State of Syria and Iraq 51

territory, whereas the Euphrates first passes through Syria. On the Tigris River upstream from Iraq, hydroelectric dams have been built that jeopardize water access for downstream populations. This is an ongoing problem. Hezha Abdulwahed, the water department director in the city of Dohuk, said that the Tigris River's water levels had dropped 8 billion cubic meters in 2020 and that it was flowing at around 50 percent below average levels.[37]

The most significant of these dams is Turkey's massive Southeastern Anatolia Project (Güneydoğu Anadolu Projesi, or GAP). The entire GAP consists of nineteen hydroelectric plants and twenty-two dams within the Tigris and Euphrates river basin, which will significantly decrease the availability of water for neighboring Syria and Iraq.

The Ilısu Dam is one of the largest projects in the GAP and will affect 90 miles of the Tigris and 150 miles of its related tributaries. The goal of the Ilısu Dam is to generate 12,000 megawatts of electricity for the southeastern part of Turkey. It began holding back water in June 2018.[38, 39] The massive Ilısu Dam will create a reservoir covering 190 square kilometers (74 square miles) in addition to displacing over 70,000 people when it is filled to capacity.[40] The project will flood the 12,000-year-old town of Hasankeyf, which is of high cultural and historical importance to the Kurds. Generally, the dam will have widespread negative impacts on ecology and biodiversity in the river while it reduces water availability for agriculture and irrigation. The Tigris River's capacity is already deteriorating as a result of natural factors, including declining precipitation and increasing desertification, and damming it will hasten its ruin.[41]

Tensions between Iraq, Syria, and Turkey over access to the Tigris and Euphrates Rivers have been high over at least the last forty years. Two major incidents have punctuated this period. In 1975, Syria and Iraq were brought to the brink of war upon Syria's completion of the Tabqa Dam, when Iraq sent troops to the border and threatened to bomb the structure. Nearly simultaneous with Syria's completion of the Tabqa Dam, Turkey began construction on the GAP, all while Iraq grappled with a drought that was significantly impacting the availability of water resources.

Then, in 1990, Turkey cut off access to the Euphrates to fill the Ataturk Dam—a decision that temporarily reduced the water flow into Syria and Iraq by 75 percent. This water shortage again led Iraq to threaten to blow up the dam, which angered the Turkish government to the point of threatening to cut off the water supply completely. As of today, Iraq

52 *Weaponizing Water*

has long sought a means other than saber rattling to influence Turkey's water policies; it has been unable to do so.

Water Resources Management

It is widely accepted that the oldest hydraulic civilization in the world arose about 7,500 years ago in Mesopotamia, which is modern-day Iraq. It was with great ingenuity that the Sumerians built canals to irrigate wheat and barley fields. Despite this noble heritage of innovation, modern water resource management in Iraq is often the victim of neglect and ignorance.

The majority of Iraq's agricultural products are grains irrigated primarily with the surface waters of the Tigris and Euphrates. The water available for irrigation depends on factors such as droughts, water supply from outside the country, and salinization rate. Salinization is the process by which water-soluble salts accumulate in the soil, making it inhospitable for plant growth. Salinization is caused by natural processes, such as mineral weathering or the gradual withdrawal of an ocean and farming practices inappropriate to arid regions. Salinity is a major cause of lowered crop yields, especially in southern Iraq. Generally, the water tables in southern Iraq are saline and so close to the surface that only a little overirrigation brings them up to plant root level and destroys the crop. High groundwater tables affect more than half of the irrigated land. Once severe salinization has occurred in soil, the rehabilitation process can take several years.

In Iraq, the maintenance of irrigation systems has been sporadic. Since 1992–1993, when the amount of land under irrigation reached its height, interruptions in maintenance due to factors such as warfare and political instability have caused these systems to fall into disrepair, also diminishing water availability.[42]

Failure to properly manage water resources is palpable in the southern city of Basra. A 2018 Human Rights Watch study reports that over the last thirty years, Iraqi authorities have been unable to effectively manage and regulate the country's water resources, which has left a lasting and significant impact. The report observes that in Basra "waterways including the Shatt al-Arab are replete with contaminants from human, animal, industrial, and agricultural waste. The conventional water treatment plants are not adequately removing the contaminants or testing the water quality, and in some cases are even failing to add enough chlorine during treatment."[43]

The Islamic State of Syria and Iraq   53

Current water problems in Basra can be traced in part to the policies of Saddam Hussein, who intentionally drained regional marshlands that were a vital part of the water ecosystem. In 1990, following the invasion of Kuwait, the US allies' strategic bombing campaign against Saddam's forces, undertaken in contravention of the laws of war, also damaged key regional water infrastructure, including hydroelectric dams, sewage treatment facilities, and water purification systems as well as other civilian infrastructure.

At the same time, in order to cope with the stringent international sanctions that were placed on Iraq, Saddam sought to boost domestic agricultural production. However, failure to increase agricultural yields in part resulted from the fact that the regime had not invested significantly in planning and maintaining irrigation infrastructure.[44] Under Saddam, poorly planned and constructed canal systems were just one of the ways that water was lost and water resources utilized inefficiently.[45] Water resource management took a backseat during the long period of violence and upheaval that followed the overthrow of Saddam's government in 2003.

Systemic Responses to Water Stress in Syria and Iraq

Iraq was especially unprepared for the water crises that came to a head in 2007–2010 as both it and Syria experienced the worst drought since meteorological measurements have been recorded. The high temperatures and desertification that resulted carried heavy consequences for Iraqi cereal harvests. A study commissioned by the UN states that between 2017 and 2026 periods of drought in Iraq are likely to persist and increase in severity, which in turn will increase the country's dependence on food imports. In 2014, UNESCO reported that Iraq was losing approximately 100,000 donum (1 donum equals slightly less than 1 acre) per year as a result of desertification and soil salinization.

Food Insecurity and Migration

Drought conditions had a strong impact on migration. A large number of Iraqis who had migrated to Syria, probably considering the move temporary before the drought, elected to remain in Syria. Given the environmental conditions in their home country, some 1.2–1.5 million Iraqi refugees had little incentive to return.

54   *Weaponizing Water*

In Syria, the impacts of the 2011 drought were perhaps felt most strongly in the northeast, where agriculture is the predominant economic sector. According to some estimates, pastoralists had already lost 70 percent of their livestock from 2006 to 2010, just before the worst of the drought. By 2011, the entire northeastern governorate of Hassakeh suffered crop failure rates of 75 percent.[46] In 2009, the UN reported that 800,000 people had lost their livelihoods as a result of the drought.[47] After 2011, the collapse of the agricultural sector pushed 2 million to 3 million people into conditions of extreme poverty, contributing to an untenable political atmosphere.[48]

The drought's impact on the agricultural sector in 2010–2011 was devastating. In Syria, it triggered mass migration. The internally displaced people (IDPs), many of whom were farmers and herders, relocated to cities in search of more productive work. When they reached their destinations, they were relegated to peripheral shantytowns, the Syrian government complicit in their neglect. These makeshift settlements lacked basic water and sanitation services, among other necessities. The UN estimated that 50,000 Syrian families migrated from rural to urban areas in 2010 alone.[49] A rising tide of 1.5 million people flowed from the agricultural northeast to urban areas in the south.[50] But by this time, many areas in the south, such as the city of Homs, were already overrun by Iraqi war refugees. On the precipice of the Syrian popular uprising in 2011, the total number of displaced Syrian and Iraqi people in Syrian urban areas peaked at 3 million.

Some environmental migrants settled in the Syrian countryside and outside smaller towns in areas including the Daraa Governorate, an agriculturally dependent area that experienced a particularly large influx of farmers and young unemployed men.[51] Daraa City, the capital of the governorate, lies on the Jordanian border about 100 miles south of the Syrian capital of Damascus. With a population of 100,000 mostly Sunni Muslims, Daraa City gained notoriety as the host of the events many see as the proximate spark of the Syrian uprising.

In March 2011, the residents of Daraa initially took to the streets to protest the arrest of fifteen children who had scrawled anti-government slogans on a wall. The slogan THE PEOPLE WANT TO OVERTHROW THE REGIME was common to the Arab Spring uprisings. This and subsequent protests in the city were met by Syrian security forces opening fire on the protesters; in the March protest, security forces killed three people. The daily protests that followed caused significant unrest and property damage in Daraa and several other cities, including Al-Hasakah, Deir ez-

Zor, and Hama. By April, the Assad regime had blockaded the city and assaults by his forces were eventually met with armed resistance.

The ongoing protests shifted focus from anger over local conditions and government suppression, and people began to direct their ire toward the more systemic issues of the Assad regime's general corruption. One corrupt practice that fell under scrutiny was the allocation of licenses regulating groundwater usage in a system that favored certain elite constituencies who supported the regime.[52]

It has been observed that the Syrian uprising was different from other Arab Spring uprisings in countries that were undergoing (often violent) political transitions at the time. In Syria, more marginalized social groups rose up, with poorer segments of society, particularly rural and rural-to-urban migrants, playing a leading role. It is clear that protests broke out in Daraa and, subsequently, other urban locations in areas that had experienced large influxes of impoverished rural environmental migrants.[53]

Climate change in the form of increasing drought was also a driver for the movement of refugees not only from rural to urban areas in Syria but also across borders. These included people from the northern and northeastern parts of Syria who fled to Lebanon's Bekaa Valley, a large agricultural area in eastern Lebanon. Interviews with these Syrian refugees who now live in Lebanon reveal that climate is a major obstacle for many people when they consider returning to their homeland. The drought and the war's destruction, which includes damage to water infrastructure, mean it is unlikely that many of these refugees will leave Lebanon anytime soon. If they were to return, they would face not only the environmental and economic hardships of farming but also the need to repair war-damaged wells and irrigation canals. As of 2019, the Assad regime had repaired very little of this infrastructure.[54]

National Policy Failures

As stated, the drought that caused acute economic and social disruption was only one factor in the mix. It must be seen in the context of fifty years of failed governmental policies in Syria attempting to liberalize the economy.[55] During the decades leading to the war, the Assad regime implemented rapid economic liberalization as part of the planned transition to a market economy away from its socialist central planning roots. Among these reforms, the Syrian government abruptly canceled energy and fertilizer price subsidies and state purchase guarantees for

56 Weaponizing Water

commodities. The subsidies on diesel fuel used to power water pumps were also removed.[56]

Seen in the larger context of the political events that occurred, the drought of 2011 was an untimely blow that culminated in a growing humanitarian catastrophe that was itself based in poor water policy and other endemic social structural factors. It was a threat multiplier. But, though it was significant, the role of the drought was indeed overplayed, providing the Assad regime with a convenient fig leaf to disguise the structural inequities it had perpetrated and its lack of policy planning. Climate change and the drought played into the hands of the Assad regime as a "false opportunity to blame external factors for its own inability and failings to reform or to promote more inclusive economic policies."[57] The regime's inability or unwillingness to address food insecurity brought about by the aforementioned factors fomented political discontent beyond the boiling point.

Sectarian issues have long plagued Syria. In the early 2000s, shifts in the political economy resulting from economic liberalization redistributed wealth into the hands of a new political and economic elite that had unique access to global markets through political ties. This elite is dominated by Assad's Alawite sect.[58] The dominant narrative about the Syrian Civil War tends to emphasize the underlying sectarian cleavages.[59] There is no doubt that the prominent insurgent and rebel groups drew from the Sunni majority, which was considered an underclass. However, the narrative fails to recognize the complex web of factors that triggered and accelerated the Syrian Civil War, such as demographic change, poor policies, and environmental change. In the milieu of governance deficiencies and other structural factors that contributed to the Syrian Civil War, water stress can be seen as a necessary but not sufficient variable. At this point, it is fair to say that Syria is not on a path toward either better water management or more favorable climatic conditions.

Popular Radicalization

Climate change–driven drought was clearly one factor that ultimately motivated people to violence in both Syria and Iraq, although the sociopolitical impacts of the drought played out differently in each country. The wars in Iraq started much earlier. It can be argued that Iraq has been in one phase of war or another going back to the Iran-Iraq War in the 1980s, and certainly since the Gulf War of the 1990s. The roots of

Islamic radicalization run deeper in Iraq than in Syria, and the non-state belligerents have been at war in Iraq since 2003, because they are, arguably, part of a cycle of conflict that began with the US invasion in 2003. These events transpired well before the drought of 2011, making it difficult to isolate the drought as a factor driving extremist violence. Though the drought might not have been a root cause of conflict in Iraq, it might have acted as a conflict accelerant. In Syria, the drought's impacts caused more discernible and detrimental second- and third-order effects on human security, including agricultural systems. Ultimately, it is more likely that dislocation and loss of livelihood resulting from environmental change created the conditions for radicalizing disaffected populations in Syria.

A few observers have searched for the link between the drought and extremist recruitment. This is a complicated puzzle. It is clear that in Syria, like in Iraq, only some of the forces opposing the regime gravitated toward violent extremism. Syrian rebels who formed the popular base of the uprising did not espouse Islamic fundamentalism. The conflation of Alawite chauvinism, lack of rainfall, malice, neglect, and incompetence led to the catastrophic conditions that fomented anti-regime militancy.

Nonetheless, it is true that Islamic State membership, when it emerged in Syria, drew disproportionately from the populations of Syria's east and northeast, where the drought hit especially hard. It is notable that the drought-affected area is near the Iraqi border, which made it easier for IS to infiltrate across the frontier undetected.[60] Although many of the people in this region of Syria were devout Sunni Muslims, the formation of an Islamic caliphate was not necessarily as important of a project for them as it was for their Iraqi brethren. The increasing misery of the population, caused by many factors including environmental forces and migration, provided fertile ground for sympathy for extremist groups such as IS rather than providing the direct motivation to join.

For IS itself, grievances against Assad and his failed water policies were not a prime motivating factor. In fact, at the time of its inception, IS did not have a specifically anti-Assad agenda other than its general opposition to any regime that could stand in the way of the establishment of the caliphate. Instead, IS spent most of its energy fighting against mainstream Syrian rebel groups and subduing local populations in areas where it had influence.

However, it is interesting that estimates indicate 60–70 percent of IS fighters in Syria were actually Syrian, even though the group was projecting from Iraq. A number of these Syrian fighters were victims of

58   *Weaponizing Water*

the drought, so it is plausible that they were more susceptible to recruitment as IS fighters for that reason. Attempts to systematically interview former IS fighters to determine their motivations have been limited because many are now either dead, detained and inaccessible, or still in hiding. However, the anecdotal narratives of refugees in Jordan's Zaatari refugee camp, which houses the highest number of Syrian displacements as of this writing, are telling. A journalist who had access to the population conducted many interviews and found that some refugees were indeed farmers who had fallen victim to drought and were later recruited into extremist organizations.[61]

Some new recruits for the Assad regime's forces faced the same desperate conditions as their displaced rebel counterparts. Syrian army recruits often came from rural areas that were the same as or adjacent to those affected by the drought. However, on balance, a decision to join Assad's forces rather than the "Free Syrian Army" opposition or extremist groups was more strongly based on religious, sectarian, or tribal loyalties, factors that alienated these fighters from the Sunni majority. The drought created the context of deprivation in which all combatants made their choices to join a faction, whether it was pro- or anti-Assad.[62]

Climate change–induced migration was a destabilizing factor in Iraq. The Al-Nusra Front, an offshoot of al-Qaeda in Iraq (AQI), and IS both initially recruited heavily from Iraq. Former Iraqi military leaders formed the backbone of the Al-Nusra leadership structure. However, others in the rank and file were motivated by the political and economic exclusion they faced under the Shiite-dominated government of Prime Minister Nouri al-Maliki, who was a divisive figure. The drought of 2010–2011 threatened the livelihoods of both Sunni military professionals and farmers who had returned to climate-stressed rural areas and felt the impacts of exclusion intensifying underlying grievances.

It was at this time that IS opened a new front in Syria's northeast, where societal resilience had been diminished by the drought. This cleared a corridor for IS combatants traveling from Iraq and provided an area where they mixed with Syrian refugees already arrived. IS grew and gained momentum in part through the support of internally displaced Sunnis who had migrated from the south.

Taking several complicated factors in turn, the drought of 2011 led directly to acute water stress. However, it is the second- and third-order effects of the drought, such as food insecurity and migration to areas that could not absorb additional population, that led to desperate living conditions for these migrants. The greatest difficulty lies in understanding to what extent the drought was a trigger for or an aggravator of conflict.

The Water Stress and Conflict Cycle in Syria and Iraq

It is useful to think of the relationship between water stress and conflict in Syria as a cyclical pattern. The conflict cycle leads from ecological impacts to radicalization and violence. Ecological changes in the form of droughts and their attendant consequences such as water stress affect key human systems such as agriculture. These impacts then lead to second-order consequences, including environmentally induced migration, anti-government sentiment that could manifest as adherence to extremist ideologies, and the birth or intensification of existing conflict.

This cycle is characterized by a strong feedback mechanism that intensifies the previous pattern. The collapse of human food and governance systems precludes the stability necessary for governments to (re)gain legitimacy by making and implementing policies that improve human conditions and ultimately stem the impact of ecological changes.

Figure 2.3 summarizes the dynamics described in this chapter, sorting the process into a cycle with four distinct stages. By 2011, the

Figure 2.3 Water Stress and Conflict Cycle in Syria and Iraq

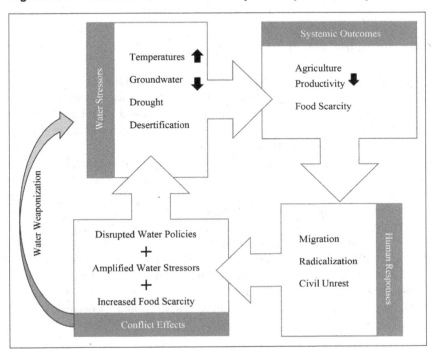

60   *Weaponizing Water*

drought's impacts on the physical environment, probably exacerbated by climate change, caused cascading effects on ecological and human systems, such as agriculture. Large populations, including newly impoverished farmers, migrated to urban centers while poor water management policies systematized political marginalization of impacted populations on a sectarian basis. Water as a factor leading to war surfaces again because the Syrian government (in particular) was unable to provide reliable water resources to these displaced peoples. Finally, the figure illustrates the feedback mechanism, showing how conditions of conflict, including water weaponization, exacerbated the initial ecological impacts of water stress in both Syria and Iraq.

In conclusion, water stress resulting from climate change, among other factors, played a meaningful and underlying role in creating the harsh conditions that led to political unrest and, ultimately, the choice for Iraqis and Syrians to migrate or take up arms.

If droughts across the region worsen as predicted, human suffering will rise on a similar trajectory. This will continue unless a durable peace prevails and the governments of Syria and Iraq find the political will and capability of providing food security to their populations. Because of the relatively advanced state of peace there, Iraq is facing just this challenge today.

Weaponizing Water

Moving beyond the questions of causality and linkages between water stress and the rise of violent conflict, the rest of this chapter contextualizes water's role in the conduct of war in Syria and Iraq. I explain how water became a primary weapon and detail the circumstances and characteristics of its usage primarily by IS.

As a point of departure, it is important to understand that, from a historical perspective, water weaponization in Syria and Iraq is not new. As mentioned, the land area of Syria and Iraq constitutes part of ancient Mesopotamia. This region hosted the earliest recorded conflict over water approximately 4,500 years ago. A dispute over access to irrigation water led King Urlama of the city-state of Lagash to cut off the water supplied to the neighboring city of Umma by the Shatt al-Gharraf River.[63]

In accordance with this history were the actions of a far more recent despot, Saddam Hussein. He used water as a strategic weapon against a Shia population known as the Marsh Arabs, or Madan, who reside in the

The Islamic State of Syria and Iraq   61

swampy but fertile area near the confluence of the Tigris and Euphrates in the south of Iraq, the traditional location of the Garden of Eden. This area is the largest wetland ecosystem in the Middle East.

The Marsh Arabs did not support Saddam's annexation of Kuwait and rebelled against the regime in the wake of the 1991 US invasion. In response, Saddam's purposeful and systematic diversion of the water that fed the marshes drove more than 100,000 people from their homes, destroying a unique way of life that relied on fishing, harvesting cane reeds, and raising water buffalo, and causing an environmental disaster of "epic proportions," according to US intelligence sources.[64] Iraqi actions were under international scrutiny. The ostensible reason the marshes were drained was to create new agricultural land, but salinization destroyed the usefulness of the area. Restoration efforts were 75 percent successful by 2008, but this improving trend substantially reversed by July 2015 because of greatly reduced water flow and salinization of the two major rivers that fed the marshes. The area was made a UNESCO World Heritage Site in 2016.[65]

More recently, history has repeated itself. IS used its control of the upper Euphrates River to once again reduce flow to the Marsh Arabs, whom it considers enemies.[66] This chapter builds upon these precedents to explain how water is being used by combatants in the contemporary conflicts in Syria and Iraq.

The scale and frequency of the Islamic State's use of the water weapon in Syria and Iraq—widespread and systematic—is unprecedented and surprising to many. Which characteristics of IS motivated them to weaponize water? A greater understanding of the IS's ideology, historical development, methods, and structure is necessary to seeing how those characteristics facilitated the use of water as a weapon. No other subnational actors, including other violent extremist organizations (VEOs), have crossed the threshold to water weaponization with the same zeal and level of success.

Islamic State of Iraq and Syria

The Islamic State of Iraq and the Levant (ISIL) is also known as the Islamic State of Iraq and Syria (ISIS). The full name of ISIL in Arabic translates to al-Dawla al-Islamiya fi Iraq wa al-Sham, which produces the acronym DAIIS, also known as Daesh. But the organization considers the term *Daesh* derogatory because it can mean "to trample down

62   *Weaponizing Water*

and crush" or "a bigot." Thus, IS forbade the use of the term in its territory, although it is no doubt flattering in some respects. The brief chronology of IS names is illustrated in Table 2.1.

The roots of the Islamic State can be traced to the group Jama'at al-Tawhid wal-Jihad (JTWJ), which ensconced itself in Jordan in 1999 under the leadership of Abu Musab al-Zarqawi. Seen in retrospect, JTWJ's initial objective was modest. It intended to overthrow the secular government of Jordan. Al-Zarqawi had traveled to Afghanistan to fight in the Soviet-Afghan War in the 1980s, but to his dissatisfaction, he arrived after the Soviet troops had departed. He had a chance to return to Afghanistan after the US invasion in 2001, where he established a jihadist training camp funded by al-Qaeda leader Osama bin Laden near Herat. Al-Zarqawi relocated to Iraq sometime in 2002 to recover from wounds he had suffered fighting the American-led forces. In Iraq, al-Zarqawi pledged formal allegiance to al-Qaeda. At that time, al-Qaeda in Iraq was part of the Mujahideen Shura Council (Majlis Shura al-Mujahideen), a coalition of six Sunni Islamist groups formed to resist the American and Iraqi authorities' efforts to gain Sunni support.[67]

By 2006, al-Zarqawi's group had been established and he changed the organization's name to Islamic State of Iraq, or ISI. On June 7, 2006, a US strike killed al-Zarqawi. Abu Ayyub al-Masri, an Egyptian, initially took his place in October 2006 but quickly deferred to Abu Omar al-Baghdadi as leader. By 2014, al-Baghdadi made it known to all

Table 2.1   Chronology of IS Names

Group Name	Years in Use
Jama'at al-Tawhid wal-Jihad (JTWJ)	1999–2004
Al-Qaeda in the Land of Two Rivers (also known as al-Qaeda in Iraq, or AQI)	2004–2006
Majlis Shura al-Mujahideen (MSM)— Mujahideen Shura Council	2006
Al-Dawla al-Islamiya fi al-Iraq— Islamic State of Iraq (ISI)	2006–2013
Al-Dawla al-Islamiya fi al-Iraq wa al-Sham— Islamic State of Iraq and al-Sham	2013–present

Source: Aaron Y. Zelin, "The War Between ISIS and al-Qaeda for Supremacy of the Global Jihadist Movement," Research Notes: Washington Institute for Near East Policy, no. 20, June 2014, https://www.washingtoninstitute.org/media/2714.

that he intended to reestablish a caliphate, a united Islamic community, under one political ruler.

Ideology

The ideology of the Islamic State is rooted in a fundamental, radical interpretation of Salafi (Sunni) Islam. Its members see a theocratic proto-state as the restoration of the Caliphate of Islam's seventh-century "Golden Age." Those who fail to adhere to or obey the strict interpretation of Sharia law face persecution and are labeled as *kafir* (infidels). To gain and maintain power, IS engages in a physical form of enforcement—the *Jihad al-Asghar* (the lesser jihad). IS has dedicated itself to "Holy War" against "crusaders." The Islamic State's narrative is based on an apocalyptic vision of the total defeat of Western powers, which it construes as the Army of Rome.[68]

Since losing control of its major stronghold in Mosul, Iraq, and its self-declared capital city of Raqqa, Syria, in 2017, IS transitioned from a proto-state to an insurgency. Because of this significant loss of territory, IS shifted toward a "long-war" narrative—encouraging sustained acts of terrorism in a war of attrition. The group redirected its propaganda to send the message that, although its fighters are less visible, its presence in Syria and Iraq would endure.

Even so, establishing an Islamic caliphate is an enduring goal. Director of External Operations Abu Muhammad al-Adnani underlined the importance of the caliphate to the central IS narrative: "Without [the caliphate], authority becomes nothing more than kingship, dominance and rule, accompanied with destruction, corruption, oppression, subjugation, fear, and the decadence of the human being and his descent to the level of animals."[69]

The 2003 US invasion destroyed Iraq's existing social, political, and military structures. Paul Bremer, the US regent, formally disbanded the Iraqi army. This action, along with underlying sectarianism, drove many unemployed soldiers to join a Sunni insurgent movement that would evolve into IS. The United States tried to reestablish a viable Iraqi military, but it was, in some ways, too little too late.

The US invasion marked the humiliation of a Muslim—albeit highly secular—state. This humiliation fed into IS's narrative. Parliamentary elections held in 2005 resulted in a Shia-controlled Parliament for the first time. Marginalization of Sunni men led to increased sectarian violence. Iraq's Shias, facing the brunt of reprisals, turned to Iran.[70] The

64   *Weaponizing Water*

Shiite United Iraqi Alliance Party consolidated several factions and named Nouri al-Maliki, who had been a dissident under Saddam, prime minister in 2006.[71] The United States was closely involved in the election. From this perspective, it is understandable that almost all of the IS leaders are former members of Iraq's Sunni-dominated military or intelligence services, many of whom were members of former dictator Saddam Hussein's Baathist Party. In short, these men had nothing more to lose after they had been stripped of their positions and pensions during the imposition of the post-Saddam restructuring process.[72]

Leadership

Abu Bakr al-Baghdadi was not a member of Saddam's regime. His path to extremism was more traditional. Until his death at the hands of US forces on October 30, 2019, he was the self-proclaimed caliph of the Islamic State. The term *caliph* implies that he was a successor of the prophet Muhammad. This proclamation was rejected by the overwhelming majority of the world's Muslims.

Details of al-Baghdadi's early years are scant, but what is known is that al-Baghdadi was born in 1971 in Samarra, Iraq. In 1999, at the age of twenty-eight, he received a master's degree and enrolled in a doctoral program for quranic studies at Saddam University for Islamic Studies. There, al-Baghdadi read publications of the Muslim Brotherhood and joined the organization, a controversial but essentially political movement that advocated a moderate approach to pan-Islamism. Al-Baghdadi was quickly frustrated with what he saw as the Brotherhood's prioritization of theory over action. In response, al-Baghdadi founded the Jamaat Jaysh Ahl al-Sunnah wa'l Jamaah (Army of the People of the Sunnah and Communal Solidarity). The organization's primary mission was to combat US forces in response to the US invasion of Iraq in 2003. As a result, al-Baghdadi was captured by US forces and detained at the notorious facility called Camp Bucca, which housed up to 100,000 suspected jihadists and members of the overthrown Baathist regime. Although reports of his incarceration vary, al-Baghdadi was present there for ten months in 2004.[73]

Surprisingly, given his radical and extreme views, al-Baghdadi gained some measure of trust from his captors and he became one of the few inmates allowed to roam "freely" within the confines of the prison. Although some inmates saw him as aloof and opaque, he made a name for himself as a preacher and footballer, gaining the nickname

The Islamic State of Syria and Iraq   65

"Maradona" after the famous Argentinian sports hero.[74] Ironically, jailers also saw al-Baghdadi as a conciliatory and calming influence and turned to him for help in resolving conflicts among the inmates.[75] The fact that he was always near the center of conflicts might have raised alarm bells to the astute observer. All the while, al-Baghdadi was recruiting and developing a structure for governance of the Islamic State. Nonetheless, by December 2004, his jailers reached the conclusion that al-Baghdadi no longer posed a risk and they released him.[76]

Upon release, al-Baghdadi formally joined the Islamic State of Iraq (ISI), successor of al-Zarqawi's AQI. He assumed leadership in April 2010, after a joint US-Iraqi operation killed ISI's leaders Abu Omar al-Baghdadi (no relation) and Abu Ayyub al-Masri. Abu Bakr al-Baghdadi subsequently relocated from Iraq to Syria. There, he announced a merger with another faction, the Al-Nusra Front, under the control of Abu Muhammad al-Julani. The Islamic State in Iraq and Syria (ISIS), as we have come to understand it, was born.

The birth was, however, premature because al-Julani rejected the alliance with al-Baghdadi's faction and instead declared allegiance to al-Qaeda. Ayman Zawahiri, second emir of al-Qaeda, also opposed the merger. Al-Baghdadi ignored Zawahiri's wishes and by 2014 had consolidated control within IS. Shortly thereafter, on July 5, 2014, al-Baghdadi appeared at Mosul's Grand Mosque and made his infamous if not entirely ingenuous public declaration:

> I was appointed to rule you but I am not the best among you. . . . If you see me acting truly, then follow me. If you see me acting falsely, then advise and guide me. . . . If I disobey God, then do not obey me.[77]

Methods

Media manipulation. As IS matured, the organization used the media for spreading propaganda, recruiting sympathizers, and undermining rivals. Although IS's use of social media was not unique among jihadists, it used it more pervasively. The Islamic State became highly adept at using the internet and social media to recruit new members and to gain global support.[78] The organization switched with relative ease between platforms to avoid suspension.

As would be expected of a group with its objectives, IS's highly refined and curated media products ignored defeats and highlighted vivid images of the capture of villages, tactical counterattacks, and

66 *Weaponizing Water*

attacks against government or sectarian targets. IS's propensity for documentation made the task of tracking its tactics such as water weaponization much easier. IS's actions even at the most localized level were codified on platforms such as Twitter.

Terrorist tactics. The Islamic State is infamous for torture and execution of prisoners. The group released videos of the brutal executions of American journalists James Foley, Steven Sotloft, and British aid worker Alan Henning, among others. In 2017, IS was responsible for killing 1,568 prisoners. It adhered to a strict list of offenses (*hudud*), implementing punishments frequently and severely on subjugated populations. Some of the *hudud* were punishable by death.[79]

The Islamic State also perpetrated grave war crimes on a much larger scale. In August 2014, IS launched a surprise offensive against Iraqi Kurdistan and seized control of Sinjar, where it commenced waging a systematic ethnic-cleansing campaign against the minority Yazidi population. Sinjar was home to approximately 400,000 Yazidis, members of a non-Muslim religious and ethnic minority deemed heretics by IS.[80] After IS forces captured the city, they systematically executed the men and kidnapped and trafficked thousands of women and children. As a result, 200,000 residents fled from the city and surrounding villages. Some 50,000 took refuge on Mount Sinjar, where IS laid siege for days.

The attack on the Yazidis set the standard for IS's propensity to siege an area and create widespread human suffering. The Yazidis were trapped without food, water, or medical care, causing dozens to die from dehydration alone. At the request of the Iraqi government, the United States responded by conducting air strikes against IS militants and air-dropping humanitarian aid, including massive quantities of water. Supported by US airstrikes, between August 9 and August 13, Kurdish forces opened a safe corridor, allowing most of the surviving Yazidis to flee.[81, 82]

Battlefield tactics and weapons. At the height of its territorial reach, IS fielded a force that resembled a conventional army and employed a strategy centered on seizing and holding territory. IS always retained the capacity for guerilla-style tactics.[83] In combat, IS preferred its forces to be in a defensive posture, which allowed them to suddenly seize the initiative, mount fast counterattacks, and infiltrate the adversary's rear areas. Like those of other extremist organizations, IS tactics are characterized by a willingness to endure high casualties on the assumption that IS soldiers will relish the opportunity to achieve martyrdom.

In 2016, the battle for Mosul in Iraq marked a turning point. IS experienced large setbacks and could sense the tide of the conflict turning. The group then began transitioning back to asymmetrical strategies and insurgent tactics. The overriding consideration was to avoid direct confrontation with superior military forces. Sabotage of infrastructure, isolated suicide attacks, and hit-and-run operations were favored approaches.[84] In 2015, there were 411 IS-led suicide attacks in Iraq and Syria that killed 2,200 people.[85] The majority of attacks occurred in 2017, with an average of 20 suicide attacks a month in Iraq and Syria.[86]

The Islamic State also made widespread use of improvised explosive devices (IEDs), including roadside bombs, larger landmines, and car bombs. As a defensive measure, IS used landmines to cut off access to cities and villages. During the confrontation in 2016, the inner-city terrain of Mosul was conducive to defense through the innovative pairing of car bombs and drones, though these tactics were less successful in the outskirts of the city.

Improvised explosive devices were IS's most deadly weapon. The group manufactured them from fertilizers and other precursors, such as ammonium nitrate, on a quasi-industrial scale characterized by mechanized production, long supply chains, and funding lines.

According to data from the US Joint Improvised-Threat Defeat Organization (JIDO), in 2015, 11,500 IED explosions in Iraq resulted in nearly 35,000 casualties. This places Iraq at the top of the list of countries with the highest mortality globally.[87] In urban areas, such as the cities of Fallujah and Mosul, that were under siege by Coalition forces, the Islamic State used tunnels. As a means of protecting fighters, IS also employed the use of human shields—housing civilians on the ground floors of buildings while fighters remained on the roofs. But this tactic backfired in an unknown number of instances when Coalition airstrikes destroyed entire buildings with the civilians inside. The indiscriminate nature of "warfare by IED," the use of human shields, and IS's lack of concern about collateral damage to civilian populations foreshadowed the ways in which the organization would weaponize natural resources, including water.

Traditional weapons. During its peak of power, IS deployed weapons for numerous ground battles. Individual fighters carried assault rifles, machine guns, and handheld rocket launchers.[88] The Islamic State obtained anti-armor ammunition from captured Syrian stockpiles. They fielded a variety of tanks, armored vehicles, and towed artillery, including an astonishing 2,300 US-made High-Mobility Multipurpose Wheeled

68 *Weaponizing Water*

Vehicles (HMMWVs) and dozens of Soviet-made T55 main battle tanks.[89] SA-7 surface-to-air missiles, a ubiquitous Soviet-designed system, were used to blast Coalition helicopters out of the sky.[90] By 2015, IS had shifted away from large-scale combat operations, and drones became central to its warfighting strategy. Success in drone-based warfare was proof that IS was more tech-savvy than other jihadist groups at that time. Recognizing that a few-thousand-dollar investment could disrupt the plans of powerful global militaries, IS developed its drone programs without evident external support.[91]

IS might have started using drones to film propaganda videos, but the group soon expanded its arsenal to include grenade-dropping drones, quadcopters, kamikaze and decoy bombers, and surveillance drones.[92] Coalition forces considered drones important enough to target them explicitly in airstrikes, and in 2016 they became one of the most daunting problems for US operations in Iraq. At this time, the tempo of drone attacks against Coalition forces was about once a day.

Combatants. By 2017, some 40,000 foreign fighters from 120 countries had joined IS (see Table 2.2).[93] The terrorist group maintained a network of roughly twenty affiliate groups from around the world and ranging in strength. Some affiliates have as few as hundreds of fighters, while others, such as ISIS-Khorasan, the affiliate in South and Central Asia—which was active in the Afghan conflict—have thousands. ISIS-Khorasan has recruited many fighters from the Taliban.[94]

In Syria and Iraq, foreign fighters played an important role in ISIS's combat structure. An apparent paradox is the number of foreign fighters that originated from countries with high levels of economic development, low income inequality, and highly developed political institutions. Many foreign fighters also hailed from western Europe. Generally, the foreign fighters are highly ethnically and sociologically diverse. The majority of the rank-and-file IS recruits came from the Middle East and Arab world.[95] At that time, the organization's foreign contingent was approximately 14,000 members strong, mainly concentrated in Iraq but with an estimated 2,000 in Syria from foreign countries.[96]

By 2019, the fortunes of IS were crumbling and approximately 10,000 suspected members of the Islamic State were held in prisons in Syria's northeast. With IS defeated in Iraq and Syria, at least on the surface, a diaspora of foreign fighters trained in terrorist tactics with new connections have returned home. If and when these fighters develop cells and commit attacks in third countries, it is an open question of

The Islamic State of Syria and Iraq **69**

Table 2.2   Origin of IS Foreign Fighters

Country	Number of Foreign Fighters
Tunisia	6,000
Saudi Arabia	2,500
Russia	2,400
Turkey	2,100
Jordan	2,000
France	1,700
Germany	760
UK	760
Belgium	470

Source: Richard Florida, "The Geography of Foreign ISIS Fighters," CityLab newsletter, Bloomberg, August 10, 2016, https://www.citylab.com/equity/2016/08/foreign-fighters-isis/493622/.

how they will deploy the skills and tactics learned on the battlefields of Iraq and Syria, including attacks on key civilian infrastructure.[97]

Administrative organization. At the height of its influence, the Islamic State's administrative structure, which included separate branches of government, resembled that of many republics. The Islamic State was led by a caliph, also called emir, who ruled from Raqqa, Syria, the de facto capital. When IS was fully intact, there were several levels of delegated authority. Two chief deputies sat beneath the emir and supervised IS territory in Syria and Iraq, respectively. These two deputies and a cabinet of advisers comprised IS's executive branch, called *Al-Imara*, or "the Emirate."

The legislative branch was composed of the Shura and Sharia Councils, which reported directly to the caliph. The nine-member Shura Council was responsible for approving lower local councils' decisions and ensuring that they adhered to religious doctrine. The Shura was also responsible for relaying al-Baghdadi's orders through the rest of the organization.

The six-member Sharia Council was the more powerful body, in part because it was theoretically responsible for selecting the caliph, although this was not the case with al-Baghdadi. A main enforcement body for Sharia law flowing from the Quran and the Hadith, the Sharia Council acted through a police force and courts. IS also created other councils to deal with finance, legal, intelligence, and even media issues.

70   *Weaponizing Water*

In addition to governing bodies, IS operated a secret service, referred to as the Emni, that served as both an internal police force and a unit for conducting operations abroad. The unit has deployed operatives to Europe to connect with local sympathizers and plot domestic attacks.[98]

Financing. At the height of its power in Iraq and Syria, IS was easily the richest jihadist organization in the world. A large factor in IS's success was its diversity of funding sources. Analysts estimated that in 2014 the group had $1.3–$2 billion in assets, with a daily income of $3 million.[99]

Between 2014 and 2017, IS derived income from a variety of sources, including direct taxation, looting, and extortion. By December 2015, IS's reported annual earnings were $45 million through kidnapping ransoms and more than $360 million from tax collection.[100] Natural resources in the form of oil revenues also played a large role in IS finances. By 2017, ISIS's oil revenues declined to $4 million per month from a peak of $40 million per month in 2015.[101]

While IS controlled oil fields in eastern Syria and northern Iraq, it commandeered the crude and smuggled it by truck to Turkey and Syrian government-controlled lands in exchange for cash and refined petroleum. IS employed similar overland routes to export antiquities. In May 2015, the UN estimated that IS earned as much as $100 million annually from the illegal sale of antiquities looted from captured territories.[102]

The Fall of al-Baghdadi

On October 26, 2019, US Special Forces Operational Detachment-Delta, commonly known as Delta Force, along with soldiers from the Army 75th Ranger Regiment, were airlifted through airspace controlled by Russia and Turkey into the rebel-held Idlib province of Syria near the Turkish border. Their mission was to capture al-Baghdadi.[103] US president Donald Trump later stated that al-Baghdadi was hunted by American military canines and cornered in a tunnel, where he died by self-detonating a suicide vest that also killed three young children, reportedly his own.[104]

Despite IS's defeat on the battlefield and al-Baghdadi's death, the extremist group has reemerged, albeit extremely weakened, from the ashes. The Shura Council convened to elect Abu Ibrahim al-Hashimi al-Quraishi as the new leader.[105] Al-Quraishi's IS was essentially reduced to scattered sleeper cells.[106]

As of 2020, Turkey joined the war against IS as an active belligerent. The Turks launched a military operation to root out Kurdish militants in northern Syria. At that time, IS's number of self-reported attacks rose, exceeding sixty a month.[107] The veracity of these figures, though, was contested by military officials with Operation Inherent Resolve and US Central Command (CENTCOM). However, both CENTCOM and the US Defense Intelligence Agency agree that al-Baghdadi's death had a deep psychological but limited immediate operational impact. According to Iraqi Kurdish leader Barzani, IS members are now "acting as insurgents, and as you know, covert operations and mainly just trying to blend in."[108] However, IS's global footprint is still considerable.[109]

The Islamic State is like nothing that has come before it. It is clear that IS has opened new ground for terrorist groups in terms of organizational capability, savagery, and ingenuity. Therefore, it is not surprising that an organization that relies on indiscriminate killings, terrorism on a grand scale, and strategic propaganda would seize upon a resource as universal for survival as water to achieve these ends. Water was precious yet readily at their disposal. The Islamic State's status as a proto-state allowed it to exploit water on a scale so massive it has rarely been seen in the history of conflict. The Islamic State wielded the water weapon in both predictable and unique ways. The next section provides a deep analysis of how IS involved water at both the strategic and the tactical level in the conflict in Syria and Iraq.

Wielding the Water Weapon

The Islamic State established a record of natural resource exploitation with its use of hydrocarbon resources as a chief means of financing military operations and raising funds and administering the caliphate. Although water's direct monetary value compared to that of oil is small, water was an opportune target. It served as an effective means of raising revenue from subjugated populations. Weaponizing water also suited IS's military modus operandi on all levels of the insurgency and fit the group's disregard for civilian suffering and its penchant for strategic propaganda.

Strategic Water Weaponization

During the Syrian Civil War, IS eventually gained control of all major dams on the Tigris and the Euphrates in Iraq upstream from Baghdad, with the exception of the Bekhme in Iraqi Kurdistan. The Islamic

72 Weaponizing Water

State's ability to seize and destroy major dams raised the specter of floods that could wipe out population centers as well as enemy forces distributed over wide areas. Also, when a hydroelectric dam that provides power to vast regions—as many on the Tigris, Euphrates, and Mosul Rivers do—is disabled, electricity supplies can also be cut off, establishing an effective zone of control over the population in the dam's service area. The array of forces opposing IS, primarily the Coalition led by the United States, was compelled to take this reality into account in decisions about occupying physically vulnerable territory, positioning forces, and executing counteroffensives.

Seizure of dams had high propaganda value, and the practice exemplified the use of water as a strategic weapon. It was an act that efficiently achieved virtual control over large areas by threatening large populations with inundation, loss of electric power, and loss of potable water. Weaponization is thus multidimensional and has distributed and varied economic consequences across wide spatial areas. But it is a blunt technique because affected areas might not be overtly hostile. This consideration comes into play in the following examples of warfare based on the seizure of dams.

Tabqa (Euphrates) Dam. The Islamic State captured the Tabqa Dam, most commonly known as the Euphrates Dam, in 2013. The Euphrates Dam is Syria's largest and it lies 40 kilometers north of the city of Raqqa, which served as the capital of the IS caliphate at the height of its power. The dam's construction took place from 1968 to 1973 and, with the help of Soviet engineers, it created Lake Assad, Syria's largest water reservoir.

The Euphrates Dam is 60 meters (200 feet) high and 4.5 kilometers (2.8 miles) long, with an installed hydropower capacity of 824 megawatts, which has never been met in part because of the reductions in anticipated water flow from Turkey, which lies upstream.[110] The Euphrates, Baath, and Tishrin Dams form a chain of hydroelectric power stations that together supplied around 70 percent of Syria's needs for water and electricity.[111] Therefore, when IS seized the Euphrates Dam in February 2013, its leadership saw the need for the dam to remain operational as a way to curry favor with the people who depended on it for electricity. Accordingly, IS retained engineering staff at the dam site, as it did not have the expertise to keep the generators running.

Later in the conflict, when it was clear that the tide of the war had turned, IS threatened to destroy the dam in retaliation for an offensive on the nearby city of Raqqa by Coalition forces. In January 2016, IS leaders took refuge inside the dam, gambling that the United States would not bomb them there, and reportedly set detonators inside the dam themselves. This action might have been a factor in the anti-IS Coalition's hesitation and slowed advance on the city. What ensued was a six-week standoff where IS and the Coalition each held opposing control towers on the dam. Coalition military planners determined that aerial bombing would have led to a favorable outcome but that the risk to the structure was too great.

IS was able to weaponize the dam during its tenure as custodian. The dam's seizure certainly provided IS with strategic capabilities, including the ability to release approximately 11 million cubic meters of water into Syria to inundate farmlands and cut the electricity supply to Damascus.[112] To gain military advantage, IS had already started pumping water into the Al Jer canal to flood all of the villages near Kwaires Airfield in Syria, a key base for Assad's forces.[113] IS also used the area protected by the threat of inundation as a cordon sanitaire, where it was able to establish two prisons.

In March 2017, the Euphrates Dam hydroelectric power station was compromised after heavy fighting damaged the main control panel. The Islamic State warned of the dam's imminent collapse. It blamed American airstrikes as the cause of damage and spread the claim that the lives of 90,000 downstream residents were in jeopardy. Syria's ally Russia was also instrumental in amplifying this narrative of American negligence of the lives of civilians.

In response to these allegations, the Syrian rebel forces and the Coalition halted operations to allow for inspection of the dam. The delay gave IS the tactical opportunity to reinforce its positions and deploy an additional 900 fighters to the battlefield. In the final stages of the siege, after the rest of the city had been liberated by the Coalition, the dam effectively became the last bridge into nearby Raqqa.[114] Again, there was concern about damaging the structure, so IS was able to negotiate a safe conduct withdrawal after the United States dedicated a substantial deployment of Special Operations Forces to clear the dam.[115] Shortly thereafter, Syrian Democratic Forces (SDF), an alliance of Arab fighters and Kurds allied with the Coalition, announced they had finally captured the dam on May 10, 2017.[116]

Baath Dam. The Baath Dam, Syria's third largest, lies downstream of the Euphrates Dam and is also one of the chain of facilities that regulates the flow of water supplying electricity to the region. The dam impounds 90 million cubic meters of water and is 3 kilometers long

(1.86 miles), 60 meters (196 feet) wide at its base, and 10 meters (33 feet) high, with a generation capacity of 375 million kilowatts (or 375 gigawatts) of electricity a year. The Baath Dam also maintains the reservoir that provides irrigation to Syria's Al-Hasakah province.[117]

The timing of taking control of the Baath Dam was opportune. IS seized the structure in February 2013, a week before the capture of the Euphrates Dam. Control over this much electricity-generating capacity acted as a force multiplier, marking a significant milestone in IS's fight for control of Syria and firmly establishing its ability to weaponize water at the strategic level. Upon its recapture by SDF on June 4, 2017, the structure was renamed the Freedom Dam. This occasion was a milestone for the SDF because it marked the recapture of all three dams on the Euphrates and broke IS's stranglehold on a vast swath of territory. Two years later, Turkey invaded this section of northern Syria. By the time the dam was returned to the Syrian government in 2019, it had sustained severe damage and was less effective than before the hostilities.[118]

Tishrin Dam. The Tishrin Dam in Manbij, a city 22 kilometers from Raqqa, also holds a great deal of strategic value because it generates power for towns and villages across the countryside of the eastern Aleppo province. It is the farthest downstream of the chain of dams that produces electric power for Syria. Its six massive generators produce 6 billion kilowatts (6,000 gigawatts) per year, while behind the dam lay a massive 1.8 billion cubic meters of water.[119]

The strategic weaponization campaign around dams can be said to have started here when Syrian rebels first took the dam from Assad's forces in 2012. In September 2014, IS captured the dam from rebel forces. A combination of the SDF and Kurdish forces and US-led Coalition forces recaptured the Tishrin Dam from IS on December 26, 2015, in an action also known as the Southern Kobanî offensive.[120]

Shortly before the offensive, IS had called on communities living east of the Euphrates River in Syria to evacuate their homes out of fear that the dam might collapse at any moment, although there was no evidence to support this claim. SDF took over the dam at a time when there was a sudden rise in water levels and localized floods were spreading. The situation posed a crisis that was exacerbated by the fact that some of the dam operators had fled.[121]

The correlation of forces was unclear, and the military situation remained somewhat in flux. There were rumors that even after the SDF took control of the dam, for several days an IS cell remained hidden in

The dam and had planted explosives as a means to destroy it. These rumors proved to be false, and foreign experts tried to provide reassurance by stressing the fact that although such explosive charges might damage part of the dam, they were very likely not powerful enough to destroy it entirely. Explosive power was a constant limiting factor for IS; only specific types of explosives that emitted enormous blasts could destroy a structure as large as a dam. Such logistical constraints left IS with the opportunity for only a more modest breach, which would limit the downstream damage.

Mosul Dam. It was the Islamic State's operations at the Mosul Dam in Iraq that epitomized water weaponization on the strategic level. On August 7, 2014, IS seized control of the 3.2-kilometer-long structure situated on the Tigris River upstream of Mosul City and Baghdad. At that time, Nadhir al-Ansari, an engineer involved in the building of the dam, said that if the dam were breached, the floodwaters would take four hours to reach Mosul and forty-five hours to reach Baghdad. More than a million people would be killed if a "good evacuation plan" were not in place.[122] This threat to such a large population created a much higher level of concern for the Coalition than previous IS actions against dams.

Accounts suggest that IS seizure of the dam provided the primary motivation for the United States to instigate a series of airstrikes on August 8, 2014, an event that marked a major escalation of the war. Thereafter, on August 17–18, Iraqi and Kurdish forces fought a pitched battle that reclaimed the dam with the support of about thirty-five US airstrikes.[123] In a letter to Congress justifying the escalation of the war, the White House explained that "failure of the Mosul Dam could threaten the lives of large numbers of civilians, threaten US personnel and facilities—including the US Embassy in Baghdad—and prevent the Iraqi government from providing crucial services to the Iraqi populace."[124] In this way, it was IS's use of the dam and water as a strategic instrument that accelerated the conflict in a monumental way. It brought a new actor (the United States) and a new type of warfare (the aerial campaign) into the fray in a way that would permanently shape the outcome of the war.

The stability of the Mosul Dam, even without interference by IS, was a constant worry to those who were paying attention. A contemporary news account explained that the dam sat on soluble rock and hundreds of employees had to work around the clock pumping a cement mixture into the earth below to keep it stable. Azzam Alwash, an Iraqi American civil engineer who is a leading water expert in Iraq, called the situation tantamount to "a nuclear bomb with an unpredictable fuse."[125] An Italian construction and engineering firm that had been contracted by the Iraqi government to make repairs on the dam confirmed that constant maintenance would be necessary because the rocks at the foundation of the dam were prone to dissolution. As of 2017, a team of experts has been assigned to monitor the status of the dam at all times, and so far, it remains stable.[126]

Fallujah Dam. In Iraq, the Fallujah Dam distributes water from the Euphrates River to irrigation projects throughout Anbar Province and is important for electricity generation.[127] After gaining control there, IS closed the gates to the dam in the first week of April 2014, which reduced water flow.[128] However, IS subsequently reopened five gates on April 10, realizing that the reservoir could flood its upstream stronghold in Fallujah. Iraqi officials stated that previous flooding from the dam had already caused families in the area to flee, and the flooding provided a battlefield advantage for IS by impairing the Coalition troops' ability to maneuver.[129]

Decline of water levels due to the impoundment of the dam's waters was also an effective weapon against the Coalition because it resulted in power outages in Baghdad, which lies downstream.

However, in this case the water weapon proved to be a double-edged sword. By closing the floodgates, IS also diverted water behind the dam over an irrigation channel and flooded land with up to 4 meters of water up to 100 kilometers away, including the city of Abu Ghraib, where the notorious prison that held IS prisoners is located. More than 10,000 houses and 200 square kilometers of fertile farmland, important to the annual harvest, were destroyed in the area between Fallujah and Abu Ghraib, and over 60,000 residents were displaced. This destruction of land and livelihood was a clear example of the massive power of the water weapon. A list of Iraqi dams, including the dates that they fell under IS control, is illustrated in Table 2.3.

In addition to seizing dams that posed a serious virtual threat if they were breached, IS also diverted waterways to its advantage in Iraq through other means. The group's actions at the Khalis tributary of the Tigris River provide a key example. In October 2014, IS diverted the tributary to flood parts of the town of Mansouriya in Diyala Province. According to a local official, this action flooded over 3,000 donum (781 acres) of agricultural land and inundated homes with up to 2 meters of water, causing hundreds of families to flee. The Islamic State also cut off water from the Khalis tributary for ten days, suspending supply to

The Islamic State of Syria and Iraq   77

Table 2.3   Dams Occupied by Islamic State

Dam	Dates Occupied
Syria	
Tishrin Dam	11/2012–12/2015
Euphrates Dam	2/2013–5/2017
Baath Dam	2/2013–6/2017
Iraq	
Mosul Dam	August 2014
Samarra Dam	5/2015–1/2016
Ramadi Dam	5/2015–1/2016
Fallujah Dam	2/2014–6/2016

Source: Tobias von Lossow, "Weaponizing Water in the Middle East: Lessons Learned from IS," in *Water and Conflict in the Middle East,* ed. Marcus DuBois King (New York: Oxford University Press, 2020), 156.

local villages and the towns of Mansouriya, Salam, and Sarajiq, which made them easier prey for the militants.[130]

Tactical Water Weaponization

As opposed to seeking virtual control over large areas or populations, tactical water weaponization is the use of water as a weapon on the battlefield in direct or immediate support of military operations and against targets usually of military value. Therefore, water weaponization in confined spaces in support of military objectives is generally characterized as tactical. For example, in September 2014, IS diverted waters from rivers in the Shirwain basin area in Diyala Province, Iraq, to inhibit an advance by Iraqi Security Forces. The decision collaterally flooded nine nearby villages in an act of unintentional weaponization where the primary intent was nonetheless to achieve a military objective.[131]

Tactical-level water weaponization can be as basic as disposing of decomposing bodies in a water well used by adversaries, a practice associated with warfare in the Middle Ages, although it was almost certainly used earlier. The twelfth-century Holy Roman emperor Frederick Barbarossa is said to have dumped human corpses down wells during a military campaign in Italy in 1155 to thwart his enemies by poisoning.[132] This technique has not been widely used, and there are relatively few examples in twenty-first-century conflicts. However, poisoning water in such a way was not unheard of in Syria and Iraq. On December 11, 2016, Iraqi Security Forces found fifteen decomposed bodies of

78 Weaponizing Water

civilians strewn inside a well south of Mosul in the village of Saf al-Tout; they were presumably executed by Islamic State militants. It is unknown whether this tactic was intended to taint the water supply because a number of mass graves were found nearby.[133]

A clearer example of tactical use of the water weapon is to deny the enemy's forces, rather than civilians, proximate, immediate access to potable water on the battlefield. This slows down the enemy owing to the logistics of transporting water across desert environments. On several occasions, IS destroyed pumping stations to deny water to Iraqi forces, forcing them to wait for water to be shipped into the area.

Water can be an instrument of psychological warfare or terrorism when the threat of withholding or contaminating it is leveraged to create fear among noncombatants. This form of weaponization is classified by Chalecki as "hydro-terrorism."[134] In the Iraqi and Syrian conflict, IS operationalized hydro-terrorism to achieve both strategic and tactical objectives.

Events associated with the Wadi Barada River Valley offensive of 2016–2017 are an example of the tactical use of the water weapon as psychological terrorism. On December 23, 2016, Syrian government forces conducted airstrikes and shelled Wadi Barada in response to the rebels' alleged pollution of the water spring with diesel fuel. The UN Independent International Commission of Inquiry on the Syrian Arab Republic claimed that it found no evidence of deliberate contamination of the Wadi Barada water supply by rebels. It instead accused the Syrian Air Force of deliberately attacking the area, which subsequently contaminated water sources. The commission said that "the attack amounts to the war crime of attacking objects indispensable for the survival of the civilian population and further violated the principle of proportionality in attacks."[135]

In a subsequent siege, as ordered by the Syrian rebels the Wadi Barada Shura Council cut off water from the Ayn al Fijah spring, which supplies drinking water to Damascus. The council then demanded the cessation of military operations after the Syrian army's Fourth Mechanized Division and the Iranian proxy Hezbollah's incursion against anti-government militants in Zabadani, a nearby city on the border with Lebanon. The incursion occurred after days of indiscriminate "barrel bombings."[136] Barrel bombs, sometimes described as flying improvised explosive devices (IEDs), are made from metal canisters filled with high explosives and possibly shrapnel that are dropped by aircraft; they have poor accuracy and are often used indiscriminately against civilian targets by the Assad regime in Syria. The rebels' weaponization of water can be

The Islamic State of Syria and Iraq   79

seen as quid pro quo for the equally indiscriminate use of barrel bombs by Syrian forces. The water weapon is also a useful tool of extortion and incentivization. The Islamic State used the water weapon to establish credibility as a legitimate governing authority in occupied Syria. IS's modus operandi upon capturing a municipality was to assume total control over the core needs of a civilian population while spending significant resources on providing social services. These actions encompass monopolization not just of water resources but also of all industries and municipal services facilities, including electricity and gas supplies, local factories, and even bakeries. IS's goal was to take advantage of popular discontent and to distribute resources in what can be perceived as a more efficient and egalitarian provision of services.[137] These actions show that IS quickly adapted to the challenges of governing in some areas. In the Middle East, these methods were pioneered by Hezbollah, the Shiite militia that in Lebanon has evolved into a recognized political party by providing goods to a wide swath of the population.[138]

What IS provides, it could take away, as it did on more than one occasion. In June 2014, IS captured the cities of Mosul and Tikrit and cut off water to surrounding villages. Water distribution was suspended from Mosul's water purification plant to Christian-minority villages on the outskirts, including Qaraqosh and Bartalla. This compelled residents to buy water at the inflated rate of US$6.25 per cubic meter, a cost that was unaffordable to most residents. IS restored water service to Mosul by mid-June and offered it at discounted prices to the Sunni residents who returned to the city after IS's seizure and formed the base of the group's support.[139] When IS restored the water supply, some of the Sunni population who already supported the group viewed them as liberators.[140]

The Islamic State's ability to provide water was a significant factor in its ability to retain territory and legitimize its presence. IS used manipulation of the water supply and water prices as part of an economic stranglehold to persuade people to join its ranks. The high costs of utilities, including water, that existed to some extent before the occupation coupled with higher food prices and unemployment made people desperate and increased their susceptibility to recruitment. This approach was most successful in areas IS controlled for a significant period. As many as 1,200 fighters joined IS between May and September of 2015 in Palmyra, Syria, which was subject to these conditions.[141]

However, intentionally raising water prices to create misery and gain recruits who had no other options for survival had costs and risks. A population's confidence in IS's beneficence, shown through its provision of basic services such as electricity and water, could quickly be lost.

80   *Weaponizing Water*

We need only look at the events in Baghdad in the sweltering summer of 2015, where a heat wave provoked mass demonstrations over lack of access to electricity and water. In response to the public pressure, Iraqi prime minister Abadi implemented comprehensive structural reforms and declared a long weekend.[142] In a video posted by the Scenes from Mosul YouTube channel but since deleted, locals seethed as they described a city beset by electricity cuts and exorbitant water prices.[143] The social contract between the government and its constituents was stressed by these extreme events; governments that are responsive to constituents in the face of such stresses are likely to strengthen the social contract, whereas those that are unresponsive are likely to weaken it.

Delegitimization of the aggressor is also an outcome that frequently results in cases of unintentional water weaponization. Unintentional water weaponization is characterized by collateral damage to civilians or the ecological environment. Water weaponization—including the deliberate destruction of water-related infrastructure, no matter how intentionally it is targeted—can easily shift into a relatively crude and indiscriminate weapon. As of December 2015, 35 percent of all water treatment facilities in Syria had been damaged by various combatants. Presumably, the overwhelming percentage of this destruction was unintentional, in part because each side was not sure how long it would hold a given area and thus need access to its water sources to sustain its own combatants. The contamination of drinking water supplies as a by-product rather than an intended outcome of war was pervasive in Syria and Iraq.[144]

Patterns of Weaponization

The Islamic State was not the exclusive water weaponizer. As of 2016, water was either weaponized or at least viewed or experienced as a weapon by all major combatants in the theater of war, including the governments of Syria and Iraq. It can also be argued that the United States and its partners were not immune. The Coalition air warfare campaign against IS weaponized water to the extent that they damaged civilian water infrastructure. However, there are countless examples of collateral damage to water infrastructure in modern air warfare and scant evidence that the Coalition programmed destruction of water infrastructure into their combat operations.

The research in this volume indicates that in the context of the conflicts in Iraq and Syria national regimes used the water weapon far less frequently than substate actors, particularly extremists. Notably, there were only five incidents of water weapon usage by state-level actors in Syria and Iraq from 2012 to 2015, when IS was at the height of its power. Researchers such as von Lossow have found that use of the water weapon by state actors, including the Assad regime and its Russian allies, increased after 2015.[145] Table 2.4 demonstrates the frequency of water weapon usage by combatant group (other than Coalition forces) from 2012 to 2015.

This chapter's appendix (pp. 91–98) provides more details, including forty-four water weaponization incidents from August 2012 to July 2015 sorted by date, location, and nature of the body of water. Details of these incidents were gleaned from a variety of primary and secondary sources in English and Arabic such as articles, IS publications, newsfeeds, and social media, including Twitter.

Analysis makes it clear that the Islamic State was responsible for most deployments of the water weapon. Incidents attributed to IS nearly equal the total of all other incidents combined. IS's frequent weaponization of water is understandable in consideration of its declared strategic objectives. Territorial expansion through the establishment of a caliphate was the group's primary goal. Therefore, engaging the water weapon on the strategic level, such as through the seizure of a dam or the administration of water resources, was a ready and effective means for expanding control of vast swathes of territory.

The time series mapping of the weaponization data by researcher Sire Allers at George Washington University's Elliott School in 2015 also provides insight into how IS used the water weapon. Allers found

Table 2.4 Summary of Water Weaponization Incidents in Syria and Iraq (2012–2015)

Combatants	Attributed Incidents
Islamic State (IS)	21
Free Syrian Army (FSA)	2
Syrian regime	3
Iraqi Kurds	1
Jabhat al-Nusra	3
Islamist Sharia Council	2
Iraqi Security Forces (ISF)	4
Other	4
Nonattributable	6

82 *Weaponizing Water*

that the frequency of weaponization incidents reached a high point in December 2014, coincident with the time when IS held the greatest amount of land-based territory in Iraq, and declined thereafter. The summer of 2015 marked the peak of strategic weaponization, when IS managed to briefly consolidate virtual control over both the Tigris and Euphrates Rivers and their tributaries.

The Water Weapon and the Islamic State, a Coherent Strategy?

The frequency and widespread locations of IS's use of the water weapon indicate that water weaponization was integral to a larger warfighting strategy. There is no evidence that this has been the case in previous conflicts.

The Pacific Institute, a US think tank, maintains the highly regarded Water Conflict Chronology database that catalogs worldwide water conflicts from 3000 BC to AD 2010. It categorizes incidents by type of conflict and notes where water could be a trigger, a weapon, or a casualty in the conflict. Previous to the conflicts in Iraq and the Syrian Civil War, of the 343 entries, no more than a handful of conflicts occurred in which water was used as a weapon.[146]

Use of the water weapon is essentially problematic from legal, ethical, and theological standpoints. But these limitations were no impediment to IS. The possibility exists, however, that these considerations did inhibit other belligerents, including state actors, from weaponizing water.

Although the use of water as a weapon between nation-states may have roots in ancient Mesopotamia, where modern-day Iraq is, IS's systematic and sustained deployment of the water weapon is unprecedented in the history of modern conflict. From 2012 to 2015, the Islamic State was the only actor in the Syrian and Iraqi battlespace that displayed evidence of a truly strategic approach to water weaponization. Notably, one factor that separates IS from other extremist groups such as al-Qaeda-inspired Jabhat al-Nusra is the group's superior ability to frame their actions within the context of a larger cause and implement a military strategy to support that vision.[147] That vision was the establishment of a caliphate that would assume the attributes of statehood such as static control of territory and provision of municipal services to its populace. Therefore, control of water sources and selective use of the water weapon were integral to the fulfillment of that vision.

The Islamic State of Syria and Iraq   83

Water weaponization was a critical enabler of IS's successful strategic military campaign. With it, waging war was more efficient. Along with numerous factors, including high morale among its cadre and support from the Sunni population, water enabled IS to create an asymmetrical economy of force to exercise virtual control over disproportionate amounts of territory with small numbers of combatants.

The use of water as a tactical weapon in Iraq and Syria has caused few battlefield casualties. However, the water weapon has certainly taken a toll on vulnerable noncombatants. Cutting people off from potable water caused mass migration to refugee camps, and water issues continue to plague these displaced people. The camps in Syria, Iraq, Jordan, and Lebanon have experienced outbreaks of waterborne disease due to water contamination and the lack of sufficient water for basic sanitation and hygiene, among other factors.

So, from IS's perspective, the water weapon proved relatively useless as a tactical weapon on the battlefield but was much more effective as a tool of political control. This control has come at great cost to humanity. The lasting human suffering from water weaponization is palpable. Water weaponization is somewhat analogous to a weapon of mass destruction such as nuclear warheads, which release radiation, or chemical munitions, which contaminate the battlefield. The long-term human health consequences such as malnourishment, underhydration, and waterborne diseases will be visible for generations whatever the ultimate outcome of the war in Syria and Iraq that lingers to this day.

Finally, although use of the water weapon was integral to IS's warfighting strategy, it backfired on the group and acted as a harbinger of the organization's ultimate failure. Seizure of the Mosul Dam was the key accelerant that precipitated US involvement in the aerial campaign against IS. It prompted the United States to commit more deeply to the war and sweep the Islamic State off the battlefield in a way that could possibly lead to IS's demise.

As noted, recent research has shown that most of the belligerents in the Iraqi and Syrian conflict, including the Assad regime, relied on the water weapon at some point. What, then, made its use by IS so notable and odious in comparison to that of other actors? First, IS's systematic and sustained deployment of the water weapon is unprecedented in the history of modern conflict. Second, water weaponization was a critical enabler of IS's strategic campaign of actual and virtual territorial acquisition. Third, once territory was secured, controlling the water supply was a major factor in achieving the political objective of winning (at least some of) the hearts and minds of the Iraqi and Syrian people.

84   *Weaponizing Water*

Use of the water weapon by any party to the conflict in Iraq and Syria is especially troubling when viewed in the context of climate change and its resulting heat waves, desertification, and ever-dwindling water supplies. Refugees fleeing the war are relegated to living in camps where access to potable water is not assured. Despite attempts by the Iraqi government to control the situation, the destruction of water infrastructure and the near nonexistence of water conservation and distribution policies in Iraq and Syria also apply pressure to water supplies. Water subsidies often create perverse incentives for use.

Direct use of the water weapon takes a grand toll on human security, especially in vulnerable areas where lack of access to potable water has already caused human health crises. The targeting of electric power and water infrastructure compromises sanitation facilities, which increases waterborne diseases and jeopardizes hygiene. A lack of safe drinking water and washing water drastically increases people's susceptibility to waterborne and hygiene-related diseases such as cholera, typhoid, polio, hepatitis, and diarrheal diseases. As a result, civilians in affected areas are plagued with diarrhea, dehydration, malnutrition, and gastrointestinal diseases. Diarrhea is the most widespread of these issues and is the leading cause of death in camps for refugees and internally displaced peoples. For example, a reliable supply of clean water is key to recovery from cholera and diarrheal diseases, and this is often unavailable.

The devastation of the Iraqi health system that ensued after the Persian Gulf War of 1991 is instructive. Child mortality and disease incidence increased dramatically resulting from a combination of factors: the complete destruction of water infrastructure by US bombing raids, which violated international laws and norms; and the imposition of crushing economic sanctions, which restricted importation of chlorine for water purification and vaccines and other medical supplies. The incidence of waterborne diseases in Iraq increased again after the invasion of 2003, with large-scale cholera outbreaks in northern Iraq occurring reliably every few years. Today, organizations such as the International Committee of the Red Cross, UNICEF, and the World Health Organization are struggling to secure clean water sources and provide medical aid to people in Iraq. Internally displaced persons and refugees are at higher risk for waterborne diseases. According to the International Organization for Migration (IOM), in 2019 more than 20,000 Iraqis in the country's south were displaced by lack of access to clean water.[148]

The Islamic State of Syria and Iraq   85

Finally, water weaponization not only creates immediate human suffering but also perpetuates a protracted cycle of poverty and gender inequality. As is the case in areas of Africa and the Middle East where extremist groups are active and water is scarce, it is the children—particularly girls—who are forced to spend their days searching for essential resources, such as water, fuel, and food, instead of attending school.

Climate change will continue to be a major cause of water stress in Iraq and Syria. Climate modeling predicts severe and persistent regional droughts throughout the Mediterranean region are probable.[149] The UN body that assesses regional climate and socioeconomic vulnerability has found that higher temperatures and longer dry seasons are virtually guaranteed in the Middle East and North Africa to the year 2100.[150]

Desperate environmental conditions underscore the need for regional coordination of water resources. Regulation of new dam construction and water withdrawals is necessary to prevent the worst outcomes for human health and security. But the current political picture is grim. As of this writing, Turkey, the country who holds the cards as the upper riparian on both the Tigris and the Euphrates, has severed relations with Syria.

Iraqi Kurdistan, the semi-autonomous region which is relatively blessed with abundant water sources and sits upstream of water-hungry Iraq, is exerting more political power in postconflict Iraq. Riparian states will have to take the equities of Iraqi Kurdistan into account to reach a sustainable solution to regional water scarcity. This is a watershed moment for the Kurdistan Regional Government (KRG). It must map a difficult course to preserve the quality and quantity of its water resources while ensuring that federal Iraq, which lies downstream, receives an adequate flow from the Tigris and other tributaries that pass through its territory.[151] Dam development within the footprint of Iraqi Kurdistan has already led to tension with Baghdad that could erupt into intense conflict.

Conclusion

It is clear that the water weapon was deployed by more than one actor in the warring in Syria and Iraq. However, no group deployed the weapon as often and as systematically as IS. The Islamic State's water weaponization falls into all of the categories used to assess the phenomenon as

86 *Weaponizing Water*

identified in this chapter. An appreciation of how IS used the water weapon should inform any integrated strategy to stabilize and rebuild Iraq and permanently suppress the organization.

From a US military perspective, the use of the water weapon by IS in Syria and Iraq should be a wake-up call. It should inform engagement and counterinsurgency strategies in other areas of national security concern where water stress is prevalent and violent extremist organizations are active. These areas include but are not limited to Nigeria and Somalia, the subjects of the next two chapters of this volume.

Understanding water weaponization is key to rebuilding Iraq. (Syria is a different story because the Assad regime maintains a grip on power.) Those who are designing counterinsurgency strategies in Iraq should especially take into account how IS used water to reward subject populations for their obedience. Therefore, a key aspect of stabilization and reconstruction activities should be to provide access to water and to build related infrastructure for populations susceptible to extremist recruitment.

Military planners should also consider the possibility that a key factor in the defeat of IS may have been the degradation of the organization's ability to wield the water weapon. It goes without saying that future military action against IS or other emerging substate adversaries should always be taken in a way that prevents or minimizes damage to the water supply and infrastructure.

For a variety of reasons, the Iraqi government has been largely inept at managing the water sector, and the consequences are becoming more severe. Riots over lack of electricity provided by hydropower have been one of the population's responses to deteriorating water conditions. Take the situation that has developed in the southern, predominantly Shiite Iraqi city of Basra as an example.

This city faces a raft of water challenges. Upstream damming projects have decreased water levels in the Tigris and Euphrates Rivers, which converge near Basra and form the Shatt al-Arab, a waterway that continues to the Persian Gulf. Water scarcity paired with decades of water mismanagement, climate-induced heat waves, increased pollution, and saline intrusion from sea level rise have combined to create a desperate situation. Residents already depended on private carriers for access to clean water for drinking and sanitation. Then the supply of hydroelectric power—the responsibility of the government—was curtailed by low inflow.

Tensions exploded in the summer of 2018, and violent street protests erupted after about 118,000 people fell sick from polluted waters. The

The Islamic State of Syria and Iraq 87

pollution may have been caused by algal blooms and oil and chemicals that found their way into the Shatt al-Arab waterway. Saline intrusion from the Persian Gulf, related to lower water levels because of upstream dams, may have also played a role.[152] What is certain is that the Iraqi federal government failed to warn Basra residents about the danger.

Protests continued into 2019. Although the summer protests were mainly in the southern region of the country, including in Baghdad, where water quality issues and electricity shortages were also present, they were part of a larger cross-sectarian, nationwide upheaval. Protests stretched into the autumn and became part of a groundswell of discontent. This nationwide grassroots movement demanding major reforms became known as the Tishreen (October) movement.

Tishreen protesters had various objectives. Besides the lack of public services like water and electricity, protesters had grievances about the widespread corruption, unemployment, and sectarianism. The violent response to the Tishreen movement ultimately led to the resignation of Prime Minister Adil Abdul-Mahdi in November 2019, followed by six months of political stalemate while a new government was being formed.

In some areas, the Tishreen protests escalated into 2020 and 2021 and led to calls to overthrow the Iraqi government that were quickly and violently suppressed by government forces and allied Iranian-backed militias. Scores were injured and arrested, and some were subjected to torture in custody.[153] In all, the Tishreen protests were incredibly significant. They are the largest examples of civil unrest since the 2003 US invasion of the country.

In 2022, the water problem in Basra lingers and the potential for violent uprising presents a continuing threat to stability. Promised government projects to improve water quality have not materialized as a result of mismanagement and corruption.

At the time of this writing, as Iraq experiences summer heat waves, the pattern is being repeated and is continuing to create popular doubt about the legitimacy of the Iraqi government. Violence in Basra makes a stronger case for incorporating water into any strategy to rebuild the Iraqi state. Developing water infrastructure would foreground the legitimacy of the federal government as it provides reliable and badly needed water.[154]

The United States is the indispensable actor in Iraqi reconstruction. Targeted development assistance can be a vehicle for improving water conditions in Iraq. The US Agency for International Development (USAID) is supporting the return of Iraqis to their homes in areas freed from IS occupation. Pursuant to this overall mission, USAID plays a

88   Weaponizing Water

key role in the restoration of water infrastructure. In 2015, at the request of the Global Coalition to Defeat Daesh/ISIS, the United Nations, the Government of Iraq (GOI), the United States, and other international donors created the Funding Facility for Stabilization (FFS). The FFS restores essential services in the liberated provinces of Anbar, Diyala, Kirkuk, Ninewa, and Salah al-Din through the rehabilitation of public infrastructure—water, electricity, education, health, and others—damaged or destroyed by ISIS.

As of April 2021, twenty-eight donors, including the Government of Iraq, have contributed over $1.4 billion to the fund. USAID is the largest donor, contributing over $405 million since 2015. Rehabilitation efforts have been concentrated in western Anbar Province, one of the driest regions of Iraq, where $1.38 million was spent to restore water treatment facilities in an area where residents had access to running water for only a few hours a day during the IS occupation.[155]

One issue to consider in the area of development is that the United States is supporting the maintenance of electricity generators on dams as part of a restabilization program. The reconstruction plan currently in place aims to renovate water infrastructure such as boreholes and water treatment plants that, for the most part, provide drinking water. This plan, however, falls short of the larger goal of stabilization, especially of agricultural areas that rely on irrigation systems that also need repair. It is worth recalling that the deterioration of the farming sector led to widespread loss of livelihood and pushed more than a million people to migrate and some to take up arms in the ranks of extremists. Environmental peacebuilding is the concept that improved governance of natural resources can provide models for more effective and equitable governance of wider issues. The US experience provides an example. In postconflict areas, there is precedent for achieving stability through investment in environmental infrastructure, including water. The US military and private relief agencies worked together to replace water and sanitation infrastructure after the cessation of NATO-led airstrikes during the Kosovo conflict in 1999. Water restoration was among the highest priorities voiced by the local citizens. These actions contributed to a lasting peace there.[156]

Investment in desalinization technology is promising and warrants more attention from international donors. The Japan International Cooperation Agency (JICA) has invested in the Basra Water Supply Improvement Project. When complete, it will be the second largest plant in the Middle East (after the Jubail Plant in Saudi Arabia) that can theoretically supply potable water to over 3 million people.[157] Thus far, implementation of the project has been described as somewhat of a nightmare because timely payments by Iraq's Ministry of Municipalities are lacking and there are security concerns.

Desalinization is part of a larger water governance strategy in Iraq, but it is no silver bullet. Desalinization facilities, which have been successfully implemented in Saudi Arabia and Israel, are extremely energy- and capital-intensive for use in agriculture. For example, the Saudis use up to 20 percent of all domestically consumed oil and gas to power the country's facilities.[158]

Foreign investment and assistance could also be directed toward technical and financial support for more efficient water management. Such techniques might include, for instance, the introduction of drip irrigation systems to improve efficiency over surface canal distribution. Iraqi water governance, generally, and any restoration or construction of facilities should be based on the best available information and technology. High-quality hydrological data as well as reliable forecasts of the future impacts of climate change should be considered.

Collecting these hydrological data falls within the existing mission of some US governmental organizations. For example, the Army Corps of Engineers (USACE), the National Geospatial-Intelligence Agency (NGA), and the United States Geological Survey (USGS) are involved in the assessment of regional water resources in the United States and abroad. The NGA understands climate change in fragile states as a threat multiplier. These organizations may be able to provide data to the Government of Iraq and other public and private actors. This approach is feasible if the methods and technologies used are not too sensitive to disclose for reasons of US national security.

The reduction of upstream water flow in the Tigris and Euphrates water system is a perennial and growing challenge for Iraq. Regional coordination, including regulation of new dam construction and water withdrawals by riparian states, is necessary to avoid the escalating impacts of water scarcity in Iraq and to prevent the worst outcomes for human security. Less is known about the water supply situation in Syria partly because of the ongoing war. A successful US strategy should include commitment to hydro-diplomacy among the riparian states. Without immediate intervention, Turkey plans to continue its Southeast Ilısu Dam project, which jeopardizes the long-term security of downstream residents in Syria and Iraq.

Hydro-diplomacy is an important approach. Various stakeholders in the region have suggested a postconflict river issues commission be created. This commission would be composed of all of the interested riparians, including Turkey, Iraq, Syria, and Iraqi Kurdistan. Although Iraqi Kurdistan is not currently recognized as a fully sovereign political

90　Weaponizing Water

entity, it still must be considered a stakeholder because it contains abundant water resources. A commission made up exclusively of nation-states would bypass the opportunity for a fruitful dialogue with this regional authority.

While hostilities are ongoing in Syria, for example, this forum, if established, could provide a contingent mechanism for coordinating the allocation of surface waters necessary for human survival in the short term. Syria has signed written agreements with its neighbors about the allocation of water from transboundary rivers, but none of these agreements is an international treaty that carries legal weight. Such agreements would have to be ratified by the parliaments of the respective countries.

Yet, ongoing hostilities need not prevent cooperation over water. India and Pakistan or Israel and Jordan have conducted talks on water sharing and have adhered to existing water treaties even during wartime. The Indus Water Treaty, negotiated with the assistance of the World Bank in 1962, is one such durable agreement. The United States and other nations with vested interests in Iraqi stability should provide support for the establishment of a river commission and technical and financial assistance as needed. A river issues commission could be a significant positive step toward reallocation of water resources to satisfy immediate needs as well as sustainable regional water allocation agreements that would replace current practices, which are sorely out-of-date.

Finally, beyond hydro-diplomacy, the United States should use its diplomatic leverage in Iraq to encourage the Iraqi government to adhere to and support the application and enforcement of the existing body of international law that prohibits the use of water as a weapon. These laws and treaties might include inter alia the Convention on the Prohibition of Military or Any Other Hostile Use of Environmental Modification Techniques (ENMOD), Additional Protocol II of the Geneva Conventions Relating to the Protection of Victims of Non-International Armed Conflicts, and the Geneva List of Principles on the Protection of Water Infrastructure outlined in Chapter 1 of this volume.

The US government and other international actors must be willing and adept at using the foreign policy tools at their disposal to work in concert with the Iraqi government to resolve water challenges in Iraq. Water scarcity amplifies the impacts of water weaponization. It is equally important to engage with Syria if political conditions allow. If collaboration attempts are unsuccessful, it will not only facilitate future water weaponization but also provide non-state actors, including Sunni extremists, the opening to radicalize dissatisfied people and involve them in renewed jihadist struggles against the state.

Appendix

Incidents of Water Weaponization in Iraq and Syria (2012–2015)

Militant Group	Date	Location	Country	Affected Water Body	Affected Provinces	Action/ Summary	Intentions of Use
NA	Aug. 2012	Aleppo	Syria	NA	Aleppo	Water pipeline damaged and two water pumps sabotaged	Unintentional weaponization, Tactical weaponization
NA	Oct. 2012	Aleppo	Syria	NA	Aleppo	As-Safira road bridge blown up, irrigation canals to Aleppo outskirts (As-Safira, Tall Awn, and Al-Wahah) destroyed	Tactical weaponization
IS	Nov. 2012	Tishrin Dam	Syria	Lake Assad, Euphrates River	Aleppo, Al-Raqqah	Seized control of dam	Strategic weaponization
Free Syrian Army	Dec. 2012	NA	Syria	NA	NA	Video of militants poisoning rabbit; threatened to poison water supply	Psychological terrorism
Free Syrian Army/ rebels	Feb. 2013	Tabqa Dam	Syria	Lake Assad, Euphrates River	Al-Raqqah	Rebels seized control of dam and neighborhoods housing dam workers	Strategic weaponization
NA	Feb. 2013	Damascus	Syria	NA	Damascus	Water pumping reduced by 20 percent as a result of damage	Unintentional weaponization

continues

Appendix continued

Militant Group	Date	Location	Country	Affected Water Body	Affected Provinces	Action/ Summary	Intentions of Use
NA	Feb. 2013	Dayr az Zawr	Syria	NA	Dayr az Zawr	Water pumping reduced by 90 percent as a result of damage	Unintentional weaponization
ISIS	June 2013	Tabqa Dam	Syria	Lake Assad, Euphrates River	Al-Raqqah	Seized control of dam	Strategic weaponization
Syrian regime	Aug. 2013	Damascus	Syria	NA	Damascus	Unconfirmed fears of water contamination as a side effect of chemical weapons (chlorine)	Psychological terrorism
Jaysh al-Adiyat, ISIS	Jan. 2014	Nuaimiya Dam (aka Fallujah Dam)	Iraq	Euphrates River	Anbar	ISIS seized control of dam	Strategic weaponization
ISIS	Jan. 2014	Tabqa Dam	Syria	NA	Al-Raqqah	ISIS supporters spread rumors that they planted bombs on Euphrates River dam	Psychological terrorism
Syrian regime	Feb. 2014	Aleppo	Syria	NA	Aleppo	City water pipeline damaged	Unintentional weaponization
Iraqi Kurds	Feb. 2014	Dukan Dam	Iraq	Tigris River	Salah al-Din, Baghdad, Diyala, Tameem	Kurdish Regional Government refuses Baghdad request to increase Tigris water flow to north and central areas of Iraq	Strategic weaponization

continues

Appendix continued

Militant Group	Date	Location	Country	Affected Water Body	Affected Provinces	Action/ Summary	Intentions of Use
ISF	Mar. 2014	Haditha Dam	Iraq	Euphrates River, Lake Qadissiya	Anbar	Flooded areas where militants were positioned	Tactical weaponization
IS	Apr. 2014	Nuaimiya Dam (aka Fallujah Dam)	Iraq	Euphrates River	Anbar	Closed eight floodgates to cause upstream flooding and to cut downstream water supply	Tactical weaponization
IS	Apr. 2014	Tikrit	Iraq	Tigris River	Salah al-Din, Baghdad	Bombed gas pipelines to Tikrit contaminated Tigris River water supply, covering western half of Iraq	Unintentional weaponization
Islamist Sharia Council/ Jabhat al-Nusra	May 2014	Aleppo	Syria	NA	Aleppo	Tampered with water pumps/pipes to prevent flow to regime-controlled areas	Tactical weaponization
NA	May 2014	Al-Khafsah	Syria	NA	Aleppo	Stopped water pumping station from flowing to half of Al-Khafsah city	Tactical weaponization
Jabhat Al-Nusra	May 2014	Aleppo	Syria	NA	Aleppo	Cut water to parts of Aleppo; took control of water authority	Strategic weaponization

continues

Militant Group	Date	Location	Country	Affected Water Body	Affected Provinces	Action/ Summary	Intentions of Use
IS	June 2014	Mosul	Iraq	NA	Ninewa	Captured Mosul and Tikrit and cut off water to some parts; stopped water flowing from Mosul's water purification plant to villages on the outskirts of the city; restored water service to Mosul by mid-June and offered discounted prices	Strategic weaponization, Incentivization
Islamist Sharia Council	June 2014	Aleppo	Syria	NA	Aleppo	Bombed pipes from a water plant in Aleppo, damaging three to four water pipes and a sewage pipe, affecting 2 million, and poisoning "hundreds"	Strategic weaponization
IS	July 2014	Samarra Barrage	Iraq	Lake Tharthar, Lake Habaniya, Tigris River	Salah al-Din	Gained control of Samarra Barrage	Strategic weaponization
IS	July 2014	Qaraqosh	Iraq	NA	Ninewa	Cut off water to Christian-minority town	Strategic weaponization

continues

Appendix continued

Militant Group	Date	Location	Country	Affected Water Body	Affected Provinces	Action/Summary	Intentions of Use
IS	Aug. 2014	Mosul Dam	Iraq	Tigris River	Ninewa	Gained then lost control of Mosul Dam from Peshmerga from August 3 to 18; US airstrikes hit ninety targets to support Peshmerga offensive	Strategic weaponization
Syrian regime	Aug. 2014	Al-Raqqah	Syria	NA	Al-Raqqah	Government airstrikes hit city water plant, cutting water to residents and businesses	Tactical weaponization
IS	Aug. 2014	Haditha Dam	Iraq	Euphrates River, Lake Qadissiya	Anbar	Attempted to seize dam but was held off by US airstrikes; expelled by Iraqi forces from surrounding areas in September	Strategic weaponization
IS	Aug. 2014	Shirwain Basin	Iraq	Diyala	Diyala	Flooded nine villages by diverting water from rivers to inhibit ISF advance	Tactical weaponization
IS	Sept. 2014	Sudur Dam	Iraq	Tigris River	Diyala	Cut off water to Baladrooz, a Shiite area, and lined entrance road with IEDs	Strategic weaponization
IS	Sept. 2014	Ba'aqubah	Iraq	Tigris River	Diyala	Cut off Mahroot irrigation canal to Ba'aqubah	Strategic weaponization

continues

Militant Group	Date	Location	Country	Affected Water Body	Affected Provinces	Action/ Summary	Intentions of Use
ISF	Sept. 2014	Adhaim Dam	Syria	Adhaim Lake	Diyala	Seized control from ISIS	Strategic weaponization
IS	Oct. 2014	Mansouriya Township	Iraq	Tigris River	Diyala	Diverted streams, flooding over 3,000 donum (781 acres) of farmland, homes up to 2 meters, and causing hundreds of families to flee	Strategic weaponization
IS	Oct. 2014	Samarra Barrage	Iraq	Euphrates River	Salah al-Din	Samarra Barrage flooding plan thwarted by ISF	NA
IS	Nov. 2014	Lake Hims Dam	Syria	Orontes River, Lake Hims	Hims	Seized control of areas around Lake Hims	Strategic weaponization
NA	Dec. 2014	NA	Syria	NA	NA	35 percent of water treatment plants in Syria have been damaged	Unintentional weaponization
Jabhat al-Nusra	Dec. 2014	Idlib	Syria	NA	Idlib	Cut water to parts of Syrian state-run Idlib to demand release of thirty prisoners	Strategic weaponization
IS	Dec. 2014	Haditha Dam	Iraq	Euphrates River, Lake Qadissiya	Anbar	Threatened to bomb Haditha Dam with suicide bomber (causing security measures to be tightened)	NA
ISF	Jan. 2015	Sudur Dam	Iraq	Tigris River	Diyala	Seized control of dam from ISIS and restored water flow to Baladrooz	Strategic weaponization, Incentivization

continues

Militant Group	Date	Location	Country	Affected Water Body	Affected Provinces	Action/ Summary	Intentions of Use
ISF	Feb. 2015	Adhaim Dam	Syria	Adhaim Lake	Diyala	Foiled ISIS attack on dam	Tactical weaponization
IS	Apr. 2015	Tharthar Dam	Iraq	Lake Tharthar, Lake Habaniya, Tigris River	Anbar	Seized control of a dam and overran a military barracks in the Tharthar area of Anbar	Strategic weaponization
IS	May 2015	Ramadi Dam	Iraq	Euphrates River	Anbar	Seized the Ramadi dam; closed floodgates	Strategic weaponization, Tactical weaponization
IS	June 2015	Warar Regulator (aka Warar Dam)	Iraq	Euphrates River	Anbar	Reduced flow in Euphrates by closing several dam gates (the UN reported that IS reduced water through Warar Dam); reopened some gates after six days	Strategic weaponization, Tactical weaponization
Nour al-Din al-Zenki Movement	July 2015	Aleppo	Syria	NA	Aleppo	Targeted main electricity conversion station, collaterally damaged water pipelines from the Suleiman al-Halabi Water Pumping station	Unintentional weaponization

continues

Appendix continued

Militant Group	Date	Location	Country	Affected Water Body	Affected Provinces	Action/ Summary	Intentions of Use
Wadi Barada Shura Council	July 2015	Damascus	Syria	Wadi Barada, Ayn al-Fijeh spring	Damascus	Threatened to cut off water to Damascus if Zabadani operation was not halted	Psychological terrorism
Aleppo Conquest Operations Room	July 2015	Aleppo	Syria	NA	Aleppo	Seized control of water tanks and residential buildings in the Jamiyat Al Zahraa neighborhood of Aleppo	Strategic weaponization

Source: Compiled from English and Arabic media sources and Islamic State sources, including publications, videos, and social media postings.
Note: IED, improvised explosive device; ISF, Iraqi Security Forces; NA, not applicable.

The Islamic State of Syria and Iraq   99

Notes

1. John Wendle, "Syria's Climate Refugees," *Scientific American* 314, no. 3 (March 2016): 55.

2. Ibid.

3. This chapter is based on my review of English-language and Arabic sources, including academic literature, reports by think tanks and international organizations, and news accounts. I performed discourse analysis on Islamic State propaganda publications, such as the magazine *Dabiq*, and social media posts. Water weaponization incidents presented in this chapter's appendix were located and mapped using these sources and geospatial data.

4. US Central Intelligence Agency (CIA), "Syria," *World Factbook*, https://www.cia.gov/the-world-factbook/countries/syria/.

5. CIA, "Syria," *World Factbook*, https://www.cia.gov/the-world-factbook/countries/syria/#people-and-society.

6. CIA, "Syria," *World Factbook*, https://www.cia.gov/the-world-factbook/countries/syria/#transnational-issues.

7. "Syria's Alawites, a Secretive and Persecuted Sect," Reuters, January 21, 2021, https://www.reuters.com/article/us-syria-alawites-sect-idUSTRE80U1HK201 20131.

8. Michael Izady, "Syria: Ethnic Shift, 2010–mid 2018," https://gulf2000.columbia.edu/images/maps/Syria_Ethnic_Shift_2010-2018_lg.png.

9. "Who Are the Kurds?" BBC News, October 15, 2019, https://www.bbc.com/news/world-middle-east-29702440.

10. CIA, "Syria," *World Factbook*. https://www.cia.gov/the-world-factbook/countries/syria/#people-and-society.

11. Ibid.

12. Syrian Observatory for Human Rights, https://www.syriahr.com/en/.

13. Diana Al Rifai and Mohammed Haddad, "What's Left of Syria?" Al Jazeera, March 17, 2015.

14. "Syria Regional Refugee Response," United Nations High Commissioner for Refugees, https://data2.unhcr.org/en/situations/syria.

15. Yoshihide Wada, L. P. H. van Beek, and Marc Bierkens, "Nonsustainable Groundwater Sustaining Irrigation: A Global Assessment," *Water Resources Research* 48 (January 2012), cited in Peter Gleick, "Water, Drought, Climate Change, and Conflict in Syria," *Weather, Climate and Society* 6, no. 3 (February 2014): 331–340, https://www.jstor.org/stable/24907379.

16. Max Roser, Hannah Ritchie, Esteban Ortiz-Ospina, and Lucas Rodes-Guirano, "World Population Growth," OurWorldInData.org (2013), https://ourworldindata.org/grapher/population?time=0..latest&country=~SYR.

17. Francesca de Châtel, "The Role of Drought and Climate Change in the Syrian Uprising: Untangling the Triggers of Revolution," *Middle Eastern Studies* 50, no. 4 (2014): 524, https://doi.org/10.1080/00263206.2013.850076.

18. Francesca de Châtel, "Mining the Deep," *Syria Today*, January 2010.

19. Gleick, "Water, Drought, Climate Change, and Conflict in Syria."

20. de Châtel, "The Role of Drought and Climate Change."

21. "Country Profile—Syrian Arab Republic," AQUASTAT—FAO's Global Information System on Water and Agriculture, Food and Agriculture Organization, https://www.fao.org/aquastat/en/countries-and-basins/country-profiles/country/SYR.

22. de Châtel, "The Role of Drought and Climate Change," 532.

100 *Weaponizing Water*

23. "Country Profile—Syrian Arab Republic," AQUASTAT.

24. de Châtel, "The Role of Drought and Climate Change."

25. Gleick, "Water, Drought, Climate Change, and Conflict in Syria."

26. Colin P. Kelley et al., "Climate Change in the Fertile Crescent and Implications of the Recent Syrian Drought," *Proceedings of the National Academy of Science* 112, no. 11 (March 7, 2015): 3241–3246, https://doi.org/10.1073/pnas.1421533112.

27. "Geography," Embassy of the Republic of Iraq, May 29, 2020, http://www.iraqiembassy.us/page/geography.

28. Sarhang Hamasaeed and Garrett Nada, "Iraq Timeline: Since the 2003 War," United States Institute of Peace, May 2020, https://www.usip.org/publications/2020/05/iraq-timeline-2003-war.

29. Thomas E. Ricks, *Fiasco: The American Military Adventure in Iraq, 2003–2005* (New York: Penguin, 2007), 399.

30. "Still Locked Down, Fallujah Slow to Rebuild," NBC News, April 14, 2005.

31. "Who Is Mustafa al-Kadhimi, Iraq's New Prime Minister?" Al Jazeera, May 7, 2020.

32. CIA, "Iraq," *World Factbook*, https://www.cia.gov/the-world-factbook/countries/iraq/#people-and-society.

33. Arwa Ibrahin, "Muhasasa, the Political System Reviled by Iraqi Protesters," Al Jazeera, December 2019, https://www.aljazeera.com/news/2019/12/4/muhasasa-the-political-system-reviled-by-iraqi-protesters.

34. CIA, "Iraq," *World Factbook*, https://www.cia.gov/the-world-factbook/countries/iraq/#economy.

35. UN Iraq Joint Analysis and Policy Unit, *Water in Iraq Factsheet* (United Nations, March 2013), https://www.iraqicivilsociety.org/wp-content/uploads/2014/02/Water-Factsheet.pdf.

36. Jonathan Burden, "Water Shortage and Unrest in Iraq," Global Risk Insights, November 24, 2019, https://globalrisksinsights.com/2019/11/water-shortage-and-unrest-in-iraq/.

37. Samya Kullab and Rashid Yahya, "Minister: Iraq to Face Severe Shortages as River Flows Drop," *Washington Post*, July 17, 2020, https://www.washingtonpost.com/world/middle_east/minister-iraq-to-face-severe-shortages-as-river-flows-drop/2020/07/17/7054535a-c842-11ea-a825-8722004e4150_story.html.

38. Ahmed Aboulenein and Ali Kucukgocmen, "Turkish Dam Project Threatens Rift with Iraq over Water Shortages," Reuters, June 5, 2018, https://www.reuters.com/article/us-iraq-turkey-dam/turkish-dam-project-threatens-rift-with-iraq-over-water-shortages-idUSKCN1J11YL.

39. Ali Kucukgocmen, "Turkey Starts Filling Huge Tigris River Dam, Activists Say," Reuters, August 2, 2019, https://www.reuters.com/article/us-turkey-dam/turkey-starts-filling-huge-tigris-river-dam-activists-say-idUSKCN1US194.

40. "Slowly Flooding History," Earth Observatory, NASA, February 2019, https://earthobservatory.nasa.gov/images/146439/slowly-flooding-history.

41. UN, *Water in Iraq Factsheet.*

42. FAO STAT Food and Agriculture Organization, United Nations, https://www.fao.org/faostat/en/#search/Land%20area%20equipped%20for%20irrigation.

43. "Basra Is Thirsty: Iraq's Failure to Manage the Water Crisis," Human Rights Watch, July 22, 2019, https://www.hrw.org/report/2019/07/22/basra-thirsty/iraqs-failure-manage-water-crisis#.

The Islamic State of Syria and Iraq   101

44. Lina Eklund and Darcy Thompson, "Differences in Resource Management Affects Drought Vulnerability Across the Borders Between Iraq, Syria, and Turkey," *Ecology & Society* 22, no. 4 (2017): 9, https://www.ecologyandsociety.org/vol22 /iss4/art9/.

45. Ryan Wilson, "Water-Shortage Crisis Escalating in the Tigris-Euphrates Basin," *Future Directions International*, August 2012.

46. Wadid Erian, Bassem Katlan, and Ouldbdey Babah, *Global Assessment Report on Disaster Risk Reduction: Drought Vulnerability in the Arab Region: Special Case Study: Syria* (United Nations Office for Disaster and Risk Reduction, 2010), http://www.preventionweb.net/english/hyogo/gar/2011/en/bgdocs/Erian_Katlan_& _Babah_2010.pdf.

47. "Syria: Drought Driving Farmers to the Cities," IRIN News, September 2, 2009, http://www.irinnews.org/report/85963/syria-drought-driving-farmers-to-the -cities.

48. Robert F. Worth, "Earth Is Parched Where Syrian Farms Thrived," *New York Times*, October 13, 2010, http://www.nytimes.com/2010/10/14/world/middleeast /14syria.html?r=0.

49. Caitlin E. Werrell, Francesco Femia, and Troy Sternberg, "Did We See It Coming? State Fragility, Climate Vulnerability, and the Uprisings in Syria and Egypt," *SAIS Review* 35, no. 1 (Winter–Spring 2015): 29–46, https://doi.org /10.1353/sais.2015.0002.

50. Shahrzad Mohtadi, "Climate Change and the Syrian Uprising," *Bulletin of the Atomic Scientists*, August 16, 2012, http://thebulletin.org/climate-change-and -syrian-uprising.

51. Gleick, "Water, Drought, Climate Change, and Conflict in Syria," 331– 340.

52. de Châtel, "The Role of Drought and Climate Change," 521–535.

53. Shamel Azmeh, "The Uprising of the Marginalised: A Socio-economic Per-spective of the Syrian Uprising" (LSE Middle East Center Paper Series, November 2014), http://eprints.lse.ac.uk/60243/?from_serp=1.

54. Hussein A. Amery, "Climate, Not Conflict, Drove Many Syrian Refugees to Lebanon," The Conversation, December 3, 2019, https://theconversation.com/climate -not-conflict-drove-many-syrian-refugees-to-lebanon-127681.

55. de Châtel, "The Role of Drought and Climate Change," 521–535.

56. Azmeh, "The Uprising of the Marginalised."

57. Ibid.

58. "The 'Secretive Sect' in Charge of Syria," BBC News, May 17, 2012, http://www.bbc.com/news/world-middle-east-18084964.

59. Azmeh, "The Uprising of the Marginalised."

60. Juan Cole, "Did ISIL Arise Partially Because of Climate Change?" The Nation, July 24, 2015, https://www.thenation.com/article/archive/did-isil-arise-partly -because-of-climate-change/.

61. Jamal Halaby, "Syria Rebels Recruit at Refugee Camp," Associated Press, November 11, 2013.

62. Azmeh, "The Uprising of the Marginalised."

63. Ibid.

64. "Saddam Drives 100,000 Marsh Arabs from Homes," *The Times*, London: September 9, 1994.

65. "Iraq's Marshes, Once Drained by Saddam, Named a World Heritage Site," Reuters, July 17, 2016, https://www.reuters.com/article/us-un-heritage-iraq/iraqs -marshes-once-drained-by-saddam-named-world-heritage-site-idUSKCN0ZX0SN.

102 Weaponizing Water

66. Peter Schwartzstein, "Iraq's Famed Marshes Are Disappearing—Again," *National Geographic*, July 9, 2014, https://www.nationalgeographic.com/science/article/150709-iraq-marsh-arabs-middle-east-water-environment-world.

67. "Mujahideen Shura Council (Islamic State of Iraq)," Terrorism Research and Analysis Consortium, 2020, https://www.trackingterrorism.org/group/mujahideen-shura-council-islamic-state-iraq.

68. "ISIS," Counterextremism Project, 2020, https://www.counterextremism.com/threat/isis.

69. Michael Munoz, "Selling the Long War: Islamic State Propaganda After the Caliphate," Combating Terrorism Center at West Point, *CTC Sentinel* 11, no. 10 (November 2018), https://ctc.usma.edu/selling-long-war-islamic-state-propaganda-caliphate/.

70. Tim Arango et al., "The Iran Cables: Secret Documents Show How Tehran Wields Power in Iraq," *New York Times*, November 18, 2019, https://www.nytimes.com/interactive/2019/11/18/world/middleeast/iran-iraq-spy-cables.html.

71. Michael Eisenstadt, Michael Knights, and Ahmed Ali, "Iran's Influence in Iraq," Washington Institute, April 26, 2011, https://www.washingtoninstitute.org/policy-analysis/view/irans-influence-in-iraq-countering-tehrans-whole-of-government-approach.

72. Isabel Coles and Ned Parker, "How Saddam's Men Help Islamic State Rule," Reuters, December 11, 2015, https://www.reuters.com/investigates/special-report/mideast-crisis-iraq-islamicstate/.

73. Beatrice Dupuy, "President Obama Did Not Free Islamic State Leader al-Baghdadi from Prison," AP News, October 30, 2019, https://apnews.com/afs:Content:8037620747.

74. Ali Hashem, "The Many Names of Abu Bakr al-Baghdadi," Al Monitor, March 23, 2015, https://www.al-monitor.com/pulse/originals/2015/03/isis-baghdadi-islamic-state-caliph-many-names-al-qaeda.html.

75. Orlando Crowcroft, "Abu Bakr al-Baghdadi: How an Obscure Iraqi Academic Became the Leader of the Islamic State," Euronews, October 27, 2019, https://www.euronews.com/2019/10/27/how-abu-bakr-al-baghdadi-became-the-leader-of-isis.

76. Martin Chulov, "Isis: The Inside Story," *The Guardian*, December 11, 2014, https://www.theguardian.com/world/2014/dec/11/-sp-isis-the-inside-story.

77. "Abu Bakr al-Baghdadi," Counterextremism Project, 2020, https://www.counterextremism.com/extremists/abu-bakr-al-baghdadi.

78. Majid Alfifiet et al., "Measuring the Impact of ISIS Social Media Strategy" (Texas A&M University, 2018), https://snap.stanford.edu/mis2/files/MIS2_paper_23.pdf.

79. "Islamist Extremist Strategy: Executions," Tony Blair Institute for Global Change, September 13, 2018, https://institute.global/policy/islamist-extremist-strategy-executions.

80. Valeria Cetorelli et al. "ISIS' Yazidi Genocide," *Foreign Affairs*, August 14, 2019, https://www.foreignaffairs.com/articles/syria/2017-06-08/isis-yazidi-genocide.

81. Simona Foltyn, "Iraq's Yazidis Still Haunted by Sinjar Massacres," France 24, June 28, 2019, https://www.france24.com/en/20190628-revisited-iraq-yazidis-still-haunted-sinjar-massacres-islamic-state-group-nadia-murad.

82. "Remembering the Sinjar Massacre," Voice of America, August 3, 2018, https://editorials.voa.gov/a/remembering-the-sinjar-massacre/4512154.html.

The Islamic State of Syria and Iraq   103

83. Rukmini Callimachi, "Described as Defeated, Islamic State Punches Back with Guerilla Tactics," *New York Times*, January 21, 2019, https://www.nytimes.com/2019/01/21/world/middleeast/isis-syria-attack-iraq.html.

84. Michael P. Dempsey, "How ISIS' Strategy Is Evolving: What the US Can Do to Counter the Group's Shifting Tactics," *Foreign Affairs*, January 18, 2018, https://www.foreignaffairs.com/articles/syria/2018-01-18/how-isis-strategy-evolving.

85. Tony Blair, "The Depth of the Challenge," Tony Blair Institute for Global Change, December 4, 2015, https://institute.global/policy/depth-challenge.

86. Ibid.

87. Fatima Bhojani, "How ISIS Makes IEDs: The Supply Chain of Terrorism," *Foreign Affairs*, March 2, 2016, https://www.foreignaffairs.com/articles/2016-03-02/how-isis-makes-ieds.

88. "Weapons of the Islamic State," Conflict Armament Research, December 2017, https://www.conflictarm.com/reports/weapons-of-the-islamic-state/.

89. "Isis Captured 2,300 Humvee Armoured Vehicles from Iraqi Forces in Mosul," *The Guardian*, May 31, 2015, https://www.theguardian.com/world/2015/jun/01/isis-captured-2300-humvee-armoured-vehicles-from-iraqi-forces-in-mosul.

90. "PM Says Iraq Lost 2,300 Humvee Armored Vehicles in Mosul," Naharnet, May 31, 2015, http://www.naharnet.com/stories/en/180602.

91. Kirk Semple, "Missiles of ISIS May Pose Peril for Aircrews," *New York Times*, October 24, 2015, https://www.nytimes.com/2014/10/27/world/middleeast/missiles-of-isis-may-pose-peril-for-aircrews.html.

92. Alex Ward, "Guess Who Has Drones Now? ISIS," Vox, May 30, 2017, https://www.vox.com/world/2017/5/30/15686240/drones-isis-iraq-syria.

93. Karen Parrish, "Stopping Flow of Foreign Fighters to ISIS 'Will Take Years,' Army Official Says," US Army, April 6, 2017, https://www.army.mil/article/185550/stopping_flow_of_foreign_fighters_to_isis_will_take_years_army_official_says.

94. Paul D. Shinkman, "ISIS Remains Potent, Deadly Despite Baghdadi's Death, Top Spy Says," *US News & World Report*, October 30, 2019, https://www.usnews.com/news/world-report/articles/2019-10-30/isis-remains-potent-deadly-despite-baghdadis-death-top-spy-says.

95. Les Picker, "Where Are ISIS's Foreign Fighters Coming From?" National Bureau of Economic Research, *The Digest*, no. 6 (June 2016), https://www.nber.org/digest/jun16/w22190.html.

96. Miriam Berger, "Here's What We Know About the ISIS Prisons Controlled by the Syrian Kurds," *Washington Post*, October 19, 2019, https://www.washingtonpost.com/world/2019/10/12/inside-isis-prisons-controlled-by-syrian-kurds/; Kathy Gilsinan and Mike Giglio, "What ISIS Will Become," *The Atlantic*, November 22, 2019, https://www.theatlantic.com/politics/archive/2019/11/evolution-of-isis/602293/.

97. Richard Barrett, *Beyond the Caliphate: Foreign Fighters and the Threat of Returnees* (The Soufan Center and The Global Strategy Network, October 2017), https://thesoufancenter.org/wp-content/uploads/2017/11/Beyond-the-Caliphate-Foreign-Fighters-and-the-Threat-of-Returnees-TSC-Report-October-2017-v3.pdf.

98. "ISIS," Counter Extremism Project, 2020, https://www.counterextremism.com/threat/isis.

99. Martin Chulov, "How an Arrest in Iraq Revealed ISIS's $2bn Jihadist Network," *The Guardian*, June 15, 2014, https://www.theguardian.com/world/2014/jun/15/iraq-isis-arrest-jihadists-wealth-power.

100. Jose Pagliery, "Inside the $2 Billion ISIS War Machine," CNN Money, December 11, 2015, http://money.cnn.com/2015/12/06/news/isis-funding/.

104 *Weaponizing Water*

101. Patrick B. Johnston, "Oil, Extortion Still Paying Off for ISIS," The RAND Blog (blog), RAND Corporation, October 27, 2017, https://www.rand.org/blog/2017 /10/oil-extortion-still-paying-off-for-isis.html.

102. "ISIS," Counter Extremism Project, 2020, https://www.counterextremism .com/threat/isis.

103. "Al-Baghdadi Killed in Idlib, a Hotbed of Terror Groups, Foreign Fighters," VOA News, October 27, 2019, https://www.voanews.com/a/extremism-watch_al -baghdadi-killed-idlib-hotbed-terror-groups-foreign-fighters/6178342.html.

104. "Statement from the President on the Death of Abu Bakr al Baghdadi" (press release, The White House, October 27, 2019), https://trumpwhitehouse.archives.gov /briefings-statements/statement-president-death-abu-bakr-al-baghdadi/.

105. Gilsinan and Giglio, "What ISIS Will Become."

106. "ISIL Confirms Death of al-Baghdadi, Names New Chief," Al-Jazeera, November 1, 2019, https://www.aljazeera.com/news/2019/10/isil-confirms-death -leader-al-baghdadi-names-chief-191031151709004.html.

107. Shawn Snow, "DIA Says ISIS Took Advantage of Turkish Invasion of Northern Syria, Baghdadi Death Did Not Degrade Jihadi Group," *Military Times*, February 4, 2020, https://www.militarytimes.com/flashpoints/2020/02/04/dia-says -isis-took-advantage-of-turkish-invasion-of-northern-syria-baghdadi-death-did-not -degrade-jihadi-group/.

108. Loveday Morris and Louisa Loveluck, "Killing of ISIS Leader Has Not Hurt Group's Operations Says Iraqi Kurdish Leader," *Washington Post*, February 15, 2020, https://www.washingtonpost.com/world/killing-of-isis-leader-has-not-hurt -groups-operations-says-iraqi-kurdish-leader/2020/02/15/d3e7303a-4ff8-11ea-a4ab -9f389ce8ad30_story.html.

109. Vira Mironova, "The Year the Islamic State Lost Its Last Strongholds," *Foreign Policy*, December 27, 2019, https://foreignpolicy.com/2019/12/27/the-year-the-islamic -state-lost-its-last-strongholds/.

110. Carla Hunt, "Last Boat to Tabqa," *Saudi Aramco World* 25, no. 1 (1974): 8–10.

111. Feras Hanoush, "Raqqa's Water War," Atlantic Council, August 11, 2017, https://www.atlanticcouncil.org/blogs/syriasource/raqqa-s-water-war/.

112. Marwa Daoudy, "Water Weaponization in the Syrian Conflict: Strategies of Domination and Cooperation," *International Affairs* 96, no. 5 (September 1, 2020): 1347–1366.

113. Clionadh Raleigh, Andrew Linke, Håvard Hegre, and Joakim Karlsen, "Introducing ACLED: An armed conflict location and event dataset: Special data feature," *Journal of Peace Research 47*, no. 5 (2010): 651–660. https://doi.org/10.1177 /0022343310378914.

114. "US-Backed Forces 'Capture' Tabqa Airbase from ISIL," Al Jazeera, March 27, 2017, https://www.aljazeera.com/news/2017/3/27/us-backed-forces-capture-tabqa -airbase-from-isil.

115. Daoudy, "Water Weaponization in the Syrian Conflict," 1361.

116. Ellen Francis, "US-Backed Syria Militias Say Tabqa, Dam Captured from Islamic State," Reuters, May 10, 2017, https://www.reuters.com/article/us-mideast -crisis-syria-tabqa/u-s-backed-syria-militias-say-tabqa-dam-captured-from-islamic -state-idUSKBN1862E4.

117. Hanoush, "Raqqa's Water War."

118. "Syria Revives Important Dam in Al-Raqqa," Al Masdar News, December 4, 2019, https://www.almasdarnews.com/article/syria-revives-important-dam-in-al-raqqa/.

The Islamic State of Syria and Iraq   105

119. Hanoush, "Raqqa's Water War."

120. Suleiman Al-Khalidi, "US-Backed Alliance Pushes Toward Islamic State-Held Dam in Northern Syria," Reuters, December 24, 2015, https://www.reuters.com/article/us-mideast-crisis-us-syria-idUSKBN0U719520151224.

121. "Fears That Syria's Tishrin Dam May Collapse Amid Rising Water Levels," Middle East Eye, December 31, 2015, https://www.middleeasteye.net/news/fears-syrias-tishrin-dam-may-collapse-amid-rising-water-levels.

122. Julian Borger, "Mosul Dam, Engineers Warn It Could Fail at Any Time, Killing 1 M. People," *The Guardian*, March 2, 2016.

123. Vivian Salama and Diaa Hadid, "Obama: Iraq Forces Retake Mosul Dam from Militants," Associated Press, August 18, 2014, http://news.yahoo.com/iraqi-forces-reclaim-control-mosul-dam-085110244.html#.

124. Khalid Mohammed, "Obama Applauds Recapture of Mosul Dam, Says Iraq Must Unite Because 'the Wolf's at the Door,'" *Globe and Mail*, August 18, 2014, http://www.theglobeandmail.com/news/world/latest-round-of-us-airstrikes-aimed-at-helping-iraqis-reclaim-mosul-dams/article20091967/.

125. Dexter Filkins, "A Bigger Problem than ISIS," *The New Yorker*, January 2, 2017.

126. Hussein Rikar, "Mosul Dam No Longer on the Brink of Catastrophe," Voice of America, May 5, 2017, https://www.voanews.com/a/mosul-dam-no-longer-brink-catastrophe/3839850.html.

127. "Iraq Insurgents Use Water as a Weapon After Seizing Dam," Reuters, April 11, 2014, https://www.reuters.com/article/us-iraq-security/iraq-insurgents-use-water-as-weapon-after-seizing-dam-idUSBREA3A0Q020140411.

128. Tobias von Lossow, "Water as Weapon: IS on the Euphrates and Tigris," German Institute for International and Security Affairs, January 2016, https://www.swp-berlin.org/en/publication/water-as-weapon-is-euphrates-tigris/.

129. *Physical Protection of Critical Infrastructure Against Terrorist Attacks*, CTED Trends Report (United Nations Security Council Counter-Terrorism Committee. March 2017), https://www.un.org/securitycouncil/ctc/sites/www.un.org.securitycouncil.ctc/files/files/documents/2021/Jan/cted-trends-report-march-2017-final.pdf.

130. "داعش يشن حرب المياه في ديالى شمال شرق العراق" (Daesh Wages Water War in Diyala in Northeastern Iraq), YouTube video, 4:00, Al Aan TV, October 5, 2014, https://www.youtube.com/watch?v=6pGBtNbCkik.

131. Erin Cunningham, "Islamic State Jihadists Are Using Water as a Weapon in Iraq," *Washington Post*, October 7, 2014, https://www.washingtonpost.com/world/middle_east/islamic-state-jihadists-are-using-water-as-a-weapon-in-iraq/2014/10/06/aead6792-79ec-4c7c-8f2f-fd7b95765d09_story.html.

132. Peter Schwartzstein, "The History of Poisoning the Well," *Smithsonian Magazine*, February 13, 2019, https://www.smithsonianmag.com/history/history-well-poisoning-180971471/.

133. Raleigh et al., "Introducing ACLED."

134. Ibrahim Al Marashi, "The Dawning of Hydro-terrorism," Al-Jazeera, June 19, 2015, https://www.aljazeera.com/indepth/opinion/2015/06/dawning-hydro-terrorism-150617102429224.html.

135. "Human Rights Abuses and International Humanitarian Law Violations in the Syrian Arab Republic, 21 July 2016–28 February 2017" (paper presented at Independent International Commission of Inquiry on the Syrian Arab Republic, A/HRC/34/CRP.3, United Nations Human Rights Council, March 10, 2017), https://

106 *Weaponizing Water*

reliefweb.int/report/syrian-arab-republic/human-rights-abuses-and-international
-humanitarian-law-violations-syrian.

136. "Rebels Threaten Damascus Water over Zabadani Assault," NOW News, July 8, 2015, https://now.mmedia.me/lb/en/NewsReports/565548-rebels-threaten -damascus-water-over-zabadani-assault.

137. Charles Lister, *Profiling Islamic State* (Brookings Doha Center Analysis Paper, no. 13, November 2014), http://www.brookings.edu/~/media/Research/Files /Reports/2014/11/profiling-islamic-state-lister/en_web_lister.pdf?la=en.

138. Yochi Dreazen, "From Electricity to Sewage, US Intelligence Says That Islamic State Is Fast Learning How to Run a Country," *Foreign Policy*, August 19, 2014, http://foreignpolicy.com/2014/08/19/from-electricity-to-sewage-u-s-intelligence -says-the-islamic-state-is-fast-learning-how-to-run-a-country/.

139. "ISIS Cuts Off Water, Electricity, Destroys Churches," Assyrian International News Agency, July 18, 2014, http://www.aina.org/news/20140618172333.htm.

140. John Vidal, "Water Supply Key to Outcome of Conflicts in Iraq and Syria, Experts Warn," *The Guardian*, July 2, 2014, http://www.theguardian.com/environment /2014/jul/02/water-key-conflict-iraq-syria-isis.

141. Joanna Paraszczuk, "The ISIS Economy: Crushing Taxes and High Unemployment," *The Atlantic*, September 2, 2015, https://www.theatlantic.com/international /archive/2015/09/isis-territory-taxes-recruitment-syria/403426/.

142. Sardar Sattar, "KRG Announces Public Holiday Due to Heat Wave," BasNews, July 30, 2015, http://www.basnews.com/index.php/en/lifestyle/health/288389.

143. "Are You Provided Electricity, Water or Basic Services Under the Oppression of the Daesh Caliphate?" (Arabic translation), YouTube video, Witness from Mosul, August 19, 2015, https://www.youtube.com/watch?v=2imQZdyI5Z8.

144. "Syria in Crisis," Oxfam Hong Kong, December 5, 2014, https://www.oxfam .org.hk/en/news-and-publication/syria-in-crisis.

145. von Losslow, "Weaponizing of Water in the Middle East."

146. "Water Conflict Chronology," Pacific Institute, https://www.worldwater.org /water-conflict/.

147. Ahmed S. Hashim, "The Islamic State: From al-Qaeda Affiliate to Caliphate," *Middle East Policy* 21, no. 4 (Winter 2014), http://www.mepc.org/journal/middle -east-policy-archives/islamic-state-al-qaeda-affiliate-caliphate.

148. Amali Tower, "Climate Change Displacing Already Vulnerable Iraqis; Spells Trouble for the Region," Climate Refugees, January 13, 2022, https://www.climate -refugees.org/spotlight/iraq.

149. Kelley et al., "Climate Change in the Fertile Crescent," 3241–3246.

150. *Extreme Climate Indices for the Arab Region* (factsheet, United Nations Economic and Social Commission for Western Asia, August 2014), http://haqqi.info /en/haqqi/research/projected-extreme-climate-indices-arab-region.

151. Marcus DuBois King, "Assessing the Hydropolitics of Iraqi Kurdistan," in *Water and Conflict in the Middle East*, ed. Marcus DuBois King (New York: Oxford University Press, 2020).

152. "Basra is Thirsty," https://www.hrw.org/report/2019/07/22/basra-thirsty/iraqs -failure-manage-water-crisis#.

153. "Iraq: Protest Death Toll Surges as Security Forces Resume Brutal Repression," Amnesty International, January 23, 2020, https://www.amnesty.org/en/latest/news /2020/01/iraq-protest-death-toll-surges-as-security-forces-resume-brutal-repression/.

154. Marcus D. King, with Rianna LeHane, "Drought Is Leading to Instability and Water Weaponization in the Middle East and North Africa," Center for Climate

and Security, April 30, 2021, https://climateandsecurity.org/2021/04/drought-is-leading-to-instability-and-water-weaponization-in-the-middle-east-and-north-africa/.

155. "Stabilization in Iraq," USAID, updated March 24, 2021, https://www.usaid.gov/iraq/fact-sheets/stabilization-iraq.

156. Marcus DuBois King, "Water, US Foreign Policy and American Leadership" (Institute for International Economic Policy Working Paper Series no. IIEP-WP-2013-11, Elliott School of International Affairs, The George Washington University, October 2013), https://www2.gwu.edu/~iiep/assets/docs/papers/2014WP/KingIIEPWP201311.pdf.

157. "Basra Desalination Plant—Iraq," Arab Contractors, June 9, 2022, https://www.arabcont.com/english/project-629.

158. M. B. Baig et al., "Water Resources in the Kingdom of Saudi Arabia: Challenges and Strategies for Improvement," in *Water Policies in MENA Countries*, ed. S. Zekri, Global Issues in Water Policy series, vol. 23 (New York: Springer, Cham, 2020), https://doi.org/10.1007/978-3-030-29274-4_7.

3

Extremist Violence in Nigeria

ALTHOUGH NIGERIA IS NOT A COUNTRY WHERE THE INTENSITY of conflict rivals that in Iraq or Syria, it is still riven with regional conflict, including against a jihadist group that intends to establish a caliphate. Conditions in Nigeria mirror those in Syria in other important ways, too. The simultaneous existence of water stress, demographic growth, climatic variability, and myriad social cleavages and economic divisions is a familiar story.

The overall intensity of conflict is lower than in Syria and Iraq because the Nigerian government's engagement with Boko Haram, the jihadist group, is less than a full-scale civil war. However, internal confrontations between farmers and herders in the Middle Belt region over access to resources are at least as deadly. In short, there are very few places on earth where water stress and conflict conflate to a greater extent than in Nigeria. Figure 3.1 presents a map of Nigeria that includes its major bodies of water.

Previous conflict analysis has focused largely on potential disputes over water allocation among the ten riparian nations of the Niger River basin. Although it is safe to assume that allocation of waters in the Niger River basin inevitably causes disagreements and will continue to do so, if history is a guide, the possibility of interstate violence is relatively remote. Therefore, it is prudent to focus attention on water-driven internal instability in Nigeria that is perpetrated by non-state actors in a country already ranked among the most fragile on the globe.[1]

Conflicts over natural resources are endemic to Nigeria. Policies that encourage inefficient or exclusionary allocation of natural resources

110　*Weaponizing Water*

Figure 3.1　Political Map of Nigeria

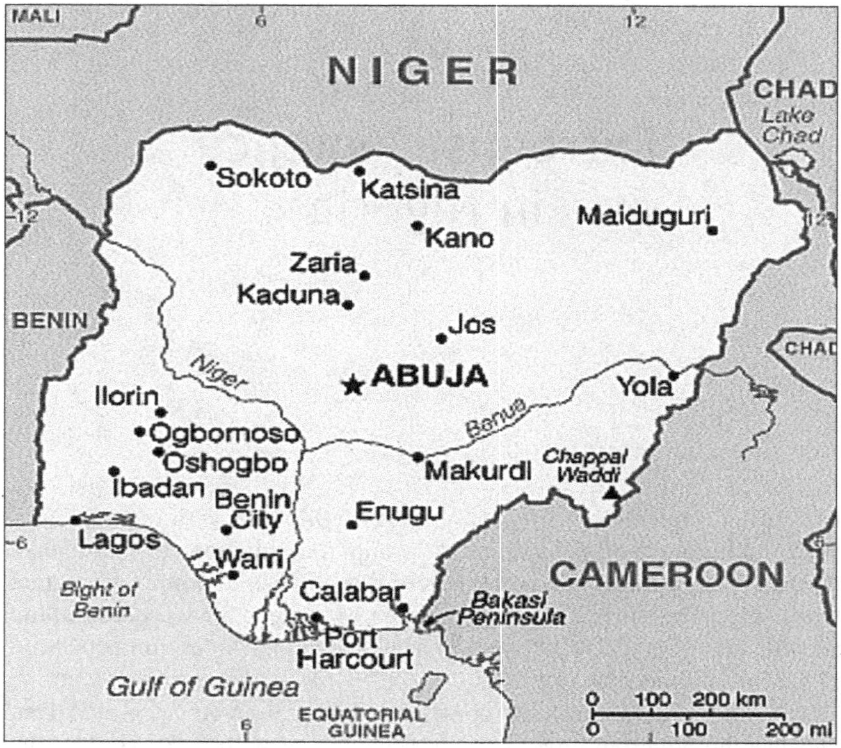

Source: US Central Intelligence Agency, "Nigeria," World Factbook, https://www.cia.gov/the-world-factbook/countries/nigeria/.

led to a civil war that raged from 1967 to 1970. Today, new grievances, stemming from similar policies but over water distribution, in this case, are also leading to violence. These underlying grievances are accentuated by the degradation of ecological and social systems.

Characteristics of Nigerian Society

Nigeria has experienced a tumultuous political history. Until the Second World War, the Federal Republic of Nigeria remained under British control. Under Britain, Nigeria grew exponentially, becoming the most populous country on the African continent during the nine-

Extremist Violence in Nigeria 111

teenth century. Following the end of World War II, successive constitutions granted the country greater levels of autonomy until 1960, when Nigeria achieved independence.

Since independence, Nigeria has vacillated between elected governments and military dictatorships. After a brief period of democratic rule known as the First Republic, Major Chukwuma Kaduna Nzeogwu staged a coup and served as head of state until 1979. The Second Republic, led by Shehu Usman Aliyu Shagari, lasted until 1983. Nigeria was once again subject to military rule as a result of a series of coups from 1993 to 1998, which ended in political transition following the death of General Sani Abacha. In 1999, Nigeria adopted a third constitution, transitioning from military rule to a civilian government, which spearheaded efforts toward institutionalizing democracy, undoing years of corruption, and reforming a petroleum-based economy.

Efforts toward democratization continued while ethnic and religious tensions simmered under the surface and then erupted in conflict during the presidential elections between 2003 and 2007. However, in 2007, the first civilian-to-civilian transfer of power occurred, marking the beginning of the longest period of civilian rule in Nigeria since the nation gained independence. The success of this civilian rule was visible in the outcome of the 2011 presidential elections, which were determined by international observers to be legitimate and credible. As a result of the election, the All Progressive Congress Party came to power in 2015, defeating the People's Democratic Party, which had held power since 1999. The current Nigerian government structure has carried through to the newest presidential and legislative elections conducted in 2019.[2]

Nigeria is by all accounts a critical actor in global affairs. It is Africa's most populous country, with the seventh-largest population in the world, and it is expected to become the third most populous country by 2050.[3, 4] Nigeria also has an outsized economy that accounts for nearly 20 percent of continental GDP and is relatively wealthy largely because of revenues from oil production.[5]

Despite these obvious strengths, Nigeria remains in many ways an aspirant geopolitical power. It wields considerable influence in regional institutions such as the African Union, but it is somewhat of a sleeping giant. Some indicators point to governance as the culprit. Better universal education and a more equitable distribution of wealth could unlock some of the massive potential of the Nigerian people.

Since assuming the presidency in 2015, Muhammadu Buhari, a former major general, has shifted Nigeria's focus inward rather than toward international relations because of internal challenges. These

112   *Weaponizing Water*

challenges include internal conflict involving extremists and insurgents in several regions, poverty, and increasing environmental degradation resulting from climate change. It is most likely that preoccupation with these issues preempts a coherent foreign policy strategy that would more effectively project Nigeria's influence. However, Nigeria's campaign to join the UN Security Council is a testament to the nation's ambitions and potential significance. Its quest to join the UN Security Council began in 1991, when the country's head of state, General Ibrahim Babangida, addressed the UN General Assembly. This request was reaffirmed when President Goodluck Jonathan enlisted UK support, arguing that Nigeria handles more than 75 percent of the security challenges in the West Africa subregion. Although Nigeria served as a nonpermanent member of the Security Council from 2014 to 2015, it continues to pursue a permanent seat.[6]

Buhari's inward focus carries repercussions for global security. Nigeria's military, the fourth largest in the region, historically has made large contributions to regional peacekeeping missions even as its home nation struggles to manage three distinct conflicts within its borders. Nigeria's enthusiasm for UN peacekeeping has waned notably in the last few years and it is unclear what sort of contribution Nigeria would make if called upon again by the United Nations today. Close to home, Nigeria participates in the Multinational Joint Task Force (MNJTF), which includes military units from Cameroon, Chad, Niger, and Benin and is responsible for securing the shared border region around Lake Chad. The MNJTF was created under the aegis of the Lake Chad Basin Commission to counter the regional threat from Boko Haram.

The basis of Nigeria's economic power is its status as the largest oil producer in Africa and the world's fifth-largest exporter of liquefied natural gas (LNG) as of 2018.[7] Oil and natural gas revenue is the country's main source of foreign exchange. The energy sector comprised approximately 86 percent of total exports in 2019.[8] These economic conditions are accompanied by the so-called resource curse endemic in countries where wealth derives from a single commodity.

Resource curse theory holds that the fluctuations of commodity prices for extractive industries inhibit national investments that would otherwise lead to a more stable economy, which would, in turn, promote human development. Furthermore, extractive industries tend to employ fewer people than sectors like agriculture, thus concentrating wealth in the hands of the political elite and leading to governance that is relatively more authoritarian, corrupt, and prone to conflict. It is therefore not surprising that the country ranks 144 out of 180 states in Trans-

Extremist Violence in Nigeria   113

parency International's Corruption Perception Index.[9] Meanwhile, economic inequality in Nigeria is extreme and getting worse; as of 2019, 94 million Nigerians live on less than $1.90 a day.[10]

Nigeria's economic security depends somewhat heavily on the agricultural sector, which accounts for more than 21 percent of GDP and roughly 70 percent of employment.[11] Only 40 percent of the available land is cultivated, leaving room for further expansion of this sector.[12] As a response to declining oil prices and the need to diversify the economy, the Nigerian government implemented the Agricultural Transformation Agenda (ATA), shifting investment "to create over 3.5 million jobs," especially among the youth and female populations. The ATA prioritizes cultivation of rice, sorghum, cassava, cotton, cocoa, and oil palm as well as animal husbandry and fishing.[13] Endemic violent conflicts raise the question of whether the Nigerian government has the political and economic focus and capacity to complete agricultural reforms such as the ATA that could reduce reliance on the oil and gas sector.

Meanwhile, an insurgency has long festered in southeastern Nigeria that pits separatists from the state of Biafra against the Nigerian government. After a protracted and bloody conflict, the separatists were able to form a republic between 1967 and 1970. The insurgency was based largely on the inequitable distribution of profits from the vast regional oil reserves, but it had strong ethnic, cultural, and religious components too. The Igbo people saw a degree of autonomy under the British mandate.

In the area, successive militant and separatist groups have seized oil primarily with the practice of "bunkering" the oil pipelines scattered across the region, where the pipelines are illegally tapped and the oil is loaded onto barges in the marshy Niger River delta. The process is environmentally destructive because oil is routinely leaked into the water. The degradation has spoiled arable land and devastated the fishing industry in some areas. Also, many residents have reported oil residue in their drinking water. In 2015, bunkering accounted for roughly 15 percent of Nigeria's production of 2.4 million barrels per day; these actions by separatists compound the existing ecological destruction caused by the extractive processes of the oil industry.

Conflict in Nigeria is diffuse, but the three major internal conflicts roughly correspond with distinct geographical areas: the arid north, the Middle Belt region, and the Niger River delta in the south. In the river delta, rebel groups have waged insurgency related to the distribution of oil wealth for decades. There, the Niger Delta People's Volunteer Force has reconstituted as the major actor.

114   *Weaponizing Water*

Concentrated in the north and northeast regions, the militant Islamist group Boko Haram has waged a violent insurgency since 2010 to establish an Islamic caliphate, although the group's attack footprint has been wider, encompassing major population centers across Nigeria. In 2015, Boko Haram attacks killed an estimated 11,000 people, nearly doubling the level of violence from the year before and making Boko Haram one of the deadliest militant groups in the world.[14] Boko Haram's history, mission, and tactics will be explored later in this chapter.

Finally, in a region widely referred to as the Middle Belt, sectarian conflicts pit members of the seminomadic Muslim Hausa-Fulani tribe against predominantly Christian farmers. The primary issue is access to arable land in an area that has been ravaged by climate change and drought. The resulting violence has left thousands dead over the last decade. Since January 2018, more than 1,300 people have been killed, more Nigerians than were killed by Boko Haram in the same period.[15] Water stress plays a variable but significant role in each of these three cases.

Water Stress in Nigeria

Water stress is prominent among the factors contributing to the conflicts in the Middle Belt and the northern regions of the country. The third one, the low-intensity rebellion festering in the delta region of Nigeria, also has significant connections to water stress, but it lies outside the scope of this book because it does not involve Islamic extremist organizations. Therefore, this chapter focuses on two of the three conflict areas and the subnational groups involved. The terrorist organization Boko Haram is based in the north, and militant Muslim Fulani herdsmen stage belligerent actions in Nigeria's Middle Belt region.

The amount and quality of water resources varies greatly in Nigeria because of the vast diversity of the environment. Water supply is sufficient in some regions, but in other areas it poses significant concerns. The country spans six vegetation zones, from mangrove saltwater swamps to grasslands and desert. Weather and precipitation patterns vary widely, and altitudes range from 10 to 3,000 feet above sea level.[16] Three distinct natural water systems are also present, including ground aquifers, rivers, and wetlands, and provide services for irrigation, human consumption, hydroelectric power generation, and navigation.

Despite sometimes-copious water resources, Nigeria faces nationally pervasive challenges with both availability and quality of water.

Extremist Violence in Nigeria · 115

Water for human consumption is at a premium, with about 67 percent of the population having access to improved water supply—meaning water that is likely to be unpolluted and free from fecal contamination.[17] Poor access to improved water and sanitation in Nigeria is a major contributing factor to high morbidity and mortality rates among children under five. Consumption of contaminated water leads to the death of more than 70,000 children under the age of five annually.[18] As in other nations, poor water quality affects women and girls first and worst. Across Africa, in addition to other domestic chores, finding safe drinking water normally falls on young girls, which leads to low school attendance and higher potential to be raped or kidnapped by insurgents. This potential has been too often realized in Nigeria.

Water distribution networks in Nigeria are poor. Only 8 percent of homes nationwide have improved water delivered through pipes.[19] Whereas some regions suffer from physical water scarcity, economic water scarcity is a greater overall trend. Economic water scarcity occurs when private individuals and governments lack the relevant technical and financial capacity to access available water supplies.[20] The level of water conservation is also insufficient to meet the scarcity: the United Nations Food and Agriculture Organization rates Nigeria's practices poor by all international and African standards.

Water and energy poverty are interrelated and reinforcing factors in Nigeria. Despite the existence of hydropower dams on the upper reaches of the Niger River, evaporation and abstraction of water for irrigation are factors that conspire to diminish overall national generation capacity. The unpredictability of water flows in times of drought and of unusually heavy rainfall associated with climate change–induced extreme weather changes are also contributory variables. These conditions commonly lead to power failures, forcing citizens to rely on privately owned generators.

Insufficient water for sanitation and hygiene affects approximately one-third of Nigeria's people.[21] Nationally, sanitation infrastructure such as piped sewerage is scarce, and installation rates are declining, according to reports by the World Health Organization. The Nigerian government struggles to provide adequate water for drinking and hygiene in the face of rising demand with burgeoning populations in urban areas.[22] Diseases are also a concern. Poor sanitation and hygiene have led to high rates of diarrhea and pneumonia as well as other diseases, such as trachoma and worm-related illnesses.[23] Diarrhea is the second-largest direct cause of child mortality in Nigeria.[24]

Climate Change Impacts

Nigeria is experiencing the full range of climate change impacts, including greater heat waves, erratic rainfall, and more droughts, floods, and storms. Climate change manifests in different ways across the country's ecozones. Relatively few climate models cover the territory of Nigeria exclusively, so a full understanding of climate conditions relies heavily on global models or those focused on West Africa in general.[25] Overall conditions in Nigeria are expected to align with predictions of the Intergovernmental Panel on Climate Change (IPCC) that climate change will amplify existing water stress across all of Africa.[26]

There is strong evidence that climate change is having a significant impact on water resources in Nigeria. Water-related conditions—in the form of storm surges, flooding, and droughts, for example—are often the leading indicator or the most visceral manifestation of climate change because of their impacts on human security. The southern coastal area is increasingly affected by rising sea levels, while higher temperatures and shifting rainfall patterns are most acutely felt in the northern regions. The effects of rainfall variation will be felt sooner and more acutely in northeastern areas, although sea level rise in the delta is a longer-term threat to populations.

In Nigeria, climate models indicate that rising average temperatures across the country increase the demands put on scarce water supply in some regions. Parts of the country, especially the arid north, are facing more heat accompanied by less precipitation. The historical climate record for Africa shows 0.7°C warming over most of the continent during the twentieth century. The IPCC Data Distribution Center, which uses results from several global general circulation models, predicts future warming throughout the continent, ranging from a low scenario of 0.2°C per decade to a high scenario of over 0.5°C per decade.

Increases in temperature are generally consistent with IPCC predictions that all of West Africa will see 10 percent less rainfall by 2100. Rainfall is also expected to decline over much of the Sahel—the transition area between the Sahara Desert in the north and the savannah regions to the south. Parts of Nigeria's northern Sahelian region now receive only 10 inches of rain annually, a full 25 percent less than thirty years ago.[27]

Like many parts of the world, weather in Nigeria is expected to be less predictable and more severe as a result of climate change.[28] Government figures show torrential rains and windstorms becoming more frequent and intense across the country: over the past forty years, recorded volumes of torrential rains increased 20 percent in various southern states, some of which already see up to 160 inches of rainfall a year.[29] Finally, sea levels could rise from 1.5 to 3 feet by century's end. These effects will not be exclusive to the Niger River delta region. Along Nigeria's southern coastline, rising seas and tidal surges will cause saltwater to destroy local crops and intrude into the public potable water supplies, among other effects.

The significant impacts of climate change in Nigeria are accompanied by poor national resilience: the ability of the nation to recover from and respond to climate shocks. The Notre Dame Global Adaptation Index (ND-GAIN) is a data-driven tool used to assess a country's exposure, sensitivity, and ability to adapt to the negative impacts of climate change. When assessing vulnerability, the index factors in the strength of six life-supporting sectors: food, water, health, ecosystem services, human habitat, and infrastructure. In addition to its rank as the fifty-fifth most vulnerable country in the world, Nigeria's resilience score is in the lowest 20 percent of countries. Volatility in crop yields, political instability, and weak governance in regions that require investments for climate change adaptation programs and projects are but some of the factors at play.[30]

Likewise, Nigeria needs water governance if conditions are going to improve. The water sector's vulnerability is affected by such factors as declining inflows into dams resulting from lengthening dry seasons and increases in flooding incidents, especially along the Niger and Benue Rivers. The country's rural water distribution infrastructure is also limited. Furthermore, Nigerian water policy focuses on engineering physical infrastructure as solutions and excludes indigenous perspectives on how water should be allocated. The country has adopted a command-and-control approach to water governance that is hampering efficient community-level access to water resources for irrigation.[31]

According to the US Agency for International Development (USAID), Nigeria ranks in the highest category of what is characterized as compound climate fragility risks. Compound fragility risks occur when a country's ability to combat the climate risks it faces is compromised, as it attempts to juggle several often cascading climate risk factors. According to USAID, Nigeria's drought situation presents emergency conditions and famine risks that are not caused by climate factors alone but also by long-standing environmental stress coupled with poor national management of the security, economic, and social conditions.[32]

118   *Weaponizing Water*

Droughts: 2011 Through 2019

Higher temperatures and a reduction in rainfall are the obvious manifestations of drought in Nigeria.[33] These factors came together frequently between 2011 and 2019, the focal time period of this book. Chronic aridity short of actual drought was also perennial. Because of the country's diverse environments, which include temperate forests, the drought has been largely contained to specific vulnerable regions.

Drought and aridity conflate to the greatest extent in the northeastern states of Borno and Yobe, followed by Kano, Jigawa, Katsina, Zamfara, and Sokoto States. Many locales in Yobe State experienced mild to moderate droughts between 2011 and 2019.[34] However, in settlements such as Maiduguri, Nguru, and Potiskum, extreme localized drought has occurred, affecting the agricultural sector and food availability and livestock production.[35]

Classifying droughts can be a nuanced endeavor. Scholars conclude that there are four types of drought, namely, meteorological drought, agricultural drought, hydrological drought, and socioeconomic drought. These distinctions add complexity to understanding the exact scope and nature of droughts in Nigeria. It was generally agreed that Nigeria had not experienced any so-called devastating droughts since about the year 2000.[36] However, in 2012, a drought swept across the Sahel, which encompasses the very northern region of Nigeria, sparking a humanitarian crisis of enormous magnitude in the Lake Chad region.

The impacts of droughts are especially troubling when considering government data that show rural households harvest rain for more than half their total water consumption, and groundwater tables in northern Nigeria have dropped sharply over the last half century, partly due to less precipitation.[37] In many areas, wells have already run dry because of unsustainable withdrawals; even deeper wells will still be exhausted without adequate hydrological replenishment.

Desertification is taking a heavy toll. The arid Sahel is expanding southward into Nigeria, with roughly 3,500 square kilometers of land turning to desert each year and significantly reducing the land area available for grazing and farming, which has contributed to the abandonment of as many as 200 villages.[38] The use of fuel wood as a main energy source in the Sahel has led to further desertification. The trees that are cut down for wood and charcoal production are needed to protect topsoil and replenish aquifers.

Fluctuating precipitation means that the chronically arid northern region of the country has also been ravaged by torrential rains and floods.

Especially severe flooding in 2010 tested the government's ability to build shelter and relocate populations.[39] The prevailing ecological conditions imperil livelihoods and create increased strain on institutions and communities that are already resource challenged.

In 2021, severe floods impacted Lagos, Africa's most populous city. By some estimates, the city, home to more than 24 million people and located on the low-lying Atlantic coast, may become uninhabitable by the end of this century as sea levels rise.[40]

The Lake Chad Crisis

Lake Chad sustains some 40 million people living in the lake's basin. Never have so many people relied on one lake for survival. The lake waters are essential for farming and animal husbandry, fishing, and trading. As the lake recedes, where fishing once served as the predominant form of livelihood, entire communities have been forced to switch from fishing to farming and livestock rearing on land that was once covered in water that is now inadequate to agricultural purposes.[41]

In October 2017, what has been characterized as the world's most extensive and complex humanitarian crisis since 1945 brought widespread attention to the Lake Chad region. The situation has roots in environmental change. The lake, which originally straddled Nigeria, Niger, Chad, and Cameroon, has since the 1970s receded at an unprecedented pace, with surface area shrinking to 10 percent of its previous span. What has resulted is a nearly complete recession from the territory of Nigeria, with the lake moving toward Cameroon and Chad.[42] Not all factors at play are natural. The desiccation of the lake has been accelerated by climate change, but damming of river systems has also contributed.[43]

There is some debate over whether the lake is constantly shrinking or whether more complex factors are involved. Janani Vivekananda, a lead researcher in this area, posits that increased variability and fluctuation in rainfall rather than aridity alone poses the greatest risk for existing populations. Erratic rainfall makes farming challenging, impacting harvest yields and preventing local residents from knowing the optimal time to switch seasonally from farming to fishing as their main source of sustenance.[44]

This food security crisis, coupled with increased violence and population growth, has caused people to flee the region in epic numbers. As of January 2019, the humanitarian catastrophe reached a crescendo with approximately 2.5 million people uprooted or displaced.[45] As of October 2019, 6.9 million people were in need of urgent food assistance, and

120   *Weaponizing Water*

more than half a million children were severely malnourished in Nigeria alone.[46] Vulnerable women and girls were subject to forced marriage and rape, increasing popular frustration with the Nigerian government. Feckless handling of the crisis has only lent credence to the jihadist narrative propagated by Boko Haram that the national authorities are incapable of providing security and sustenance.

The Lake Chad area, because of the porous nature of national boundaries, has long provided a suitable base for non-state armed groups to use to challenge state authorities. Boko Haram and its newer rival, Wilayat al Islamiyya Gharb Afriqiyyah (Islamic State in West Africa, or ISWA), have exploited the instability created by the severe drought to advance their causes and reach.

The government of Nigeria has struggled to respond effectively to the challenge of the depletion of water in the Lake Chad basin, and pressures have mounted. Governmental response has been tempered by the fact that the international community and involved national governments initially downplayed and underestimated the crisis. Further, the crisis began with the impacts of water scarcity alone but has been compounded by water mismanagement and pollution. The pumping of the lake's waters for the water-intensive mining of uranium in Niger is just one example of a destructive practice. Wasteful national irrigation projects conducted by the riparian states have all accelerated the recession of the lake.[47]

There is currently a proposal to divert water from the Congo River to the River Chari, which flows into Lake Chad, to revitalize the lake.[48] However, little progress has been made and, in any case, recharging the lake will not provide a permanent solution to changing weather patterns. The turmoil caused in large measure by regional environmental change remains a key challenge for the Nigerian government even as it provides a window of opportunity for extremists.

Demographic Challenges

Environmental degradation plays into concerning demographic trends, chief among which are high birth rates. By 2050, the population is expected to grow from 186 million in 2016 to 392 million, making Nigeria the fourth most populous country in the world.[49] Nearly half of Nigeria's people live in cities and the urban population is expected to grow by 3.75 percent annually.[50]

Migration is another concerning demographic trend. Rural-to-urban migration has increased economic inequality in large cities like Lagos and, in equal measure, has increased pressure on water service delivery. While the greatest number of refugees entering Nigeria come from neighboring Cameroon (44,524 in 2019), the majority of people actually migrate internally. As of 2019, there were more than 2 million internally displaced people (IDPs) in Nigeria, mostly resulting from insecurity caused by Boko Haram attacks, communal and ethnic conflict, and environmental degradation. External migration is still an important dynamic, albeit one that does not contribute to internal instability. Significant numbers of Nigerians continue to flee to European nations in search of economic, political, and educational opportunities.[51] Nigerians comprise the largest sub-Saharan African population of migrants to the United States and Europe, which, on balance, have not welcomed them with open arms.[52]

The age distribution of the Nigerian population, which favors younger people, is also problematic. The median age in Nigeria is nineteen years, and 62 percent of the population are under the age of twenty-five.[53] Social scientists concur that countries with a disproportionately large idle youth population, especially military-aged males, have a higher propensity for violence of all types and for instability, as the youths act as destabilizing agents, especially in states where the government and economy are incapable of incorporating them into the formal employment sector. Under such conditions, young people become susceptible to recruitment into violent extremist organizations.[54]

Demographic divisions based on class, religion, and tribal affiliation also contribute to tensions. Nigeria is home to 250 ethnic groups. Muslims make up slightly more than 50 percent of Nigeria's population (53.5 percent), Christians account for 35.3 percent, while Roman Catholics constitute 10.6 percent of the population.[55] Religious tensions are especially acute between the Muslim communities in the north/northeast and the predominantly Christian communities in the south.[56] Nigeria's political elite hail from the Hausa-Fulani Muslim community in the north. The community has produced recent national leaders, including President Buhari. These communal and often tribal splits in populations could impede governance even in the most stable and democratic nations. In Nigeria, they represent a near-fatal flaw.[57]

Water Governance Challenges

Although water supplies are theoretically sufficient for human use in absolute terms in many districts, Nigerians often experience economic

122 *Weaponizing Water*

water scarcity. As the population continues to expand, Nigerian policy-makers fail to properly manage, use, and protect water resources. The state water governance apparatus suffers from a lack of capacity and coordination among several layers of government.

The Federal Ministry of Water Resources has overarching responsibility for management and control of water resources in Nigeria. It is charged with ensuring the supply of underground and surface water resources for all domestic and agricultural uses. In addition, the ministry is charged with sustaining national water security by developing and supporting irrigation and other methods to reduce agricultural vulnerability to irregular rainfall.[58] The federal government also administers 12 river basin development authorities.[59] Water governance is further devolved to 37 state water agencies and 774 local government authorities responsible for maintaining rural water and sanitation facilities in conjunction with beneficiary communities. However, despite these wide-ranging responsibilities, only a few agencies have the resources and skilled workforce to carry them out.[60]

Equitable water allocation is also problematic. Diffuse government responsibility is again a contributing factor. The country's byzantine land-use systems and institutional governance of land are based on complicated allocation schemes at several levels. Water infrastructure is decrepit after years of improper operation and maintenance that have resulted from poor planning and public investment that has not been sustained.[61]

Overall, current water management practices in Nigeria are assessed to be insufficient in the areas of water supply reliability, flood risk, health, agriculture, energy, and aquatic ecosystems.[62] Good policy decisions have also been hampered by the lack of robust environmental and social impact assessments.[63] The failure of the Nigerian state to adequately provide basic water needs to its population through its water policy, when it ostensibly should have little difficulty in doing so, contributes to the idea that the state is corrupt and only interested in serving particular segments of the elite.

Northeastern Nigeria

Droughts are constraining resources in northeast Nigeria and exacerbating the risk of conflict. The Social Conflict Analysis Database (SCAD), maintained by the Climate Change and African Political Stability Program at the University of Texas, compiles data on protests, riots, strikes, intercommunal conflict, and violence perpetrated against civilians by governments. Some of these forms of conflict short of war are not regularly monitored in other conflict data sets.[64] The SCAD indicates that across Africa conflicts are more prevalent in extremely wet or dry years and that the coincidence of weather variations and war is dramatically higher in countries with interethnic tensions such as those found in Nigeria.[65]

Consistent with these findings, a study found a stronger correlation between conflict and weather extremes in Africa than with poverty, income inequality, or even past propensity for conflict—all conditions that are present to a lesser or greater extent in Nigeria.[66] A study that broke ground in the often-contentious literature surrounding climate change and conflict examined sixty examples of human conflict. These conflicts, which ran the full gamut from unrest involving a small number of people to full-blown wars at the national level, were situated relative to climate-related events. The study found that with warmer average temperatures and more extreme rainfall fluctuations such as those found in Nigeria, the estimate of the frequency of intergroup conflict—that is, civil war—rose by 14 percent.[67]

The Emergence of Boko Haram

Islamic fundamentalism in one form or another has been influential in northeastern Nigeria since the precolonial era. In 2002, a young Mohammed Yusuf founded the sect that became known as Boko Haram in Maiduguri, the capital of the northeastern state of Borno. He established Boko Haram under the formal name "The Congregation of the People of Tradition for Proselytism and Jihad." In the Hausa language, *Boko Haram* translates to "Western Education Is Sinful," though the group's members now prefer the name Ahlus Sunna liddawa'ati wal Jihad, or Brethren of Sunni United in Pursuit of Holy War.[68] Yusuf reportedly became a Salafist after studying the teachings of Ibn Taymiyyah, an austere thirteenth-century Sunni scholar, and he assumed the title of *Ustaz*, or "Islamic scholar." At first Yusuf's aims seemed peaceful enough. He established a religious complex and Madrassa (school) that attracted unemployed youth and poor Muslim families from across Nigeria and even neighboring countries.

Yusuf's preaching reflected his goal of establishing a pure Islamic state ruled by Sharia law. In addition to the achievement of spiritual objectives of purity, Boko Haram is based on the belief that the creation of an Islamic state with Sharia law as the legal and ideological guiding

124   *Weaponizing Water*

principle would end the poverty and corruption that has become endemic in Nigeria.[69]

Boko Haram has spread its wings but conducts its most extensive operations in the majority Muslim Adamawa, Borno, and Yobe States, close to Maiduguri, where it was born. It also maintains an international presence. Since early in its existence, Boko Haram militants have made frequent incursions into Chad, Cameroon, Niger, and Mali, often to flee Nigerian governmental forces, and it has subsequently established some roots in these countries. In January 2013, Boko Haram was pushed out of Mali as a result of a French military operation.[70] But later that year Boko Haram gunmen attacked civilians in several areas of northern Cameroon.

Boko Haram has repeatedly targeted Western-influenced schools. Its aversion to Western education can be seen, in part, as a reaction to endemic government corruption. In Nigeria, a civil service job cannot be held without a diploma from the heavily Westernized school system, and all levels of the civil service suffer from corruption. According to Boko Haram's thinking, this is proof that a Western education will lead one to be corrupt rather than nurture any sort of ethical framework or develop desirable professional skills.[71]

Yusuf's leadership lasted approximately seven years. The predominant narrative is that in July 2009 he was killed by Nigerian police after a firefight, although many eyewitness accounts indicate that he was executed extrajudicially while in government custody.[72] Abubakar Shekau, who had served as Yusuf's deputy and who seemed to be the natural successor, assumed control of Boko Haram in 2009. The bookish Shekau shared a name with his home village in Yobe State and was first introduced to Yusuf through a mutual friend in the city of Maiduguri.

Boko Haram's attacks, having subsided following the death of Mohammed Yusuf, were vigorously renewed under Shekau's leadership. Shekau was an erratic leader and Boko Haram fighters lost discipline under his tutelage and became more abusive toward civilians. He was bloodthirsty even by the standards set by Boko Haram and many global jihadists, saying at one point, "I enjoy killing anyone that God commands me to kill—the way I enjoy killing chickens and rams."[73]

The bombing of the UN headquarters in Abuja in 2011, when the people stationed there presented no direct threat to Boko Haram, epitomized the group's brutality under Shekau's leadership. The car bomb gutted a lower floor of the headquarters, smashed almost all of the building's windows, and wounded seventy-six people. The driver was also killed in what may have been Nigeria's first vehicular suicide bomb attack. This incident set off a wave of attacks, including planting bombs in public places and churches. These actions were in sharp contrast to the conduct of traditional guerilla warfare against the Nigerian military as part of the insurgency.[74]

One action was especially prominent and drew both widespread attention and universal condemnation around the world. This was the kidnapping of over 200 schoolgirls in the town of Chibok in Borno State in 2014.[75] Despite the attention that this act attracted from many observers, including Michelle Obama, the First Lady of the United States, these Chibok girls represent only a small percentage of the total number of people abducted by Boko Haram.[76]

In the course of renewed attacks, Nigerian Security Forces wounded Shekau multiple times and he was mistakenly reported dead in both 2009 and 2013. His luck finally ran out in 2021. Shekau committed suicide on May 18 when confronted by Islamic State West African Province (ISWAP) fighters following a battle between the rival groups. ISWAP had broken off from Boko Haram five years earlier, pledging allegiance to the Islamic State (IS). Interestingly, the one issue that caused the split was ISWAP's aversion to Boko Haram's indiscriminate slaughter of civilians. According to their reports, ISWAP fighters gave Shekau a chance to "repent" for his actions, but instead Shekau chose to end his life by detonating an explosive.[77] In the last two years, ISWAP has emerged as a dominant force in the region, capable of mounting large-scale attacks against the Nigerian military.

Boko Haram has widely targeted government officials, security agents, and religious leaders who speak out against the group.[78] However, there is long-standing speculation that Boko Haram sympathizers exist in the Nigerian parliamentary and military ranks.[79] Surprisingly, despite their notoriety, the US Department of State did not declare Boko Haram a terrorist organization until November 2013. It is unclear whether the presence of influential supporters played a role in the US hesitancy to do so.

Boko Haram employs a range of traditional guerilla tactics typical of jihadist organizations. The group's primary weapons are AK-47 rifles and RPG-7 rocket launchers. Attacks are normally staged using light motorcycles and a few pickup trucks, with some of the trucks modified to include mounted machine guns. Smaller cars have also been acquired or stolen to be used in suicide bombing attacks. On occasion, attacks have used captured Nigerian military vehicles and high-quality weapons, while others have been conducted with implements as crude as machetes and bows and arrows.[80]

Boko Haram employs tactics that are possibly second only to the Islamic State's in brutality. To amplify their actions, Boko Haram has

126 Weaponizing Water

taken advantage of social media to feature gruesome punishments such as the beheading of opponents who refuse to convert to Islam.[81] The group has targeted Christian churches, communities, and establishments specifically on holidays.[82] They have also kidnapped foreign nationals to gain wider attention. Moreover, they have kidnapped young Nigerian girls, forcing them into servitude. The organization is also known to kidnap and recruit gang members from border areas of Niger to turn them into fighters. These youths are not necessarily adherents to Boko Haram's ideological views but are attracted to steady meals and, to some extent, adventure.

The central government's response to the emergence of Boko Haram was brutal and, at times, indiscriminate against civilians. The Nigerian government imposed mass detentions and extended emergency declarations in several northeastern states. These measures were viewed as draconian by local populations and amplified existing grievances, some of which were based on the government's inability to provide services such as adequate water.[83]

Boko Haram's motivations are not one-dimensionally focused on establishing a Sharia state and opposing Western influence, although this message resonates with many people in northeastern Nigeria. Boko Haram also harbors long-standing grievances with the federal government over unequal wealth distribution.

John Campbell, a former US ambassador to Nigeria, writes, "Boko Haram 'writ large' is a movement of grassroots anger among northern people at the continuing deprivation and poverty in the north."[84] Ironically, Boko Haram's insurgency—driven in part by environmental degradation—has damaged the economy, diverting national funding and resources toward combating terrorist activity. The national government's economic and political capacity to initiate and maintain new water infrastructure projects that could improve conditions in a region dependent on agriculture has been diminished. The environmental conditions that in part gave rise to insurgency thus can prolong the violence by compromising the population's capacity to resist. As Boko Haram becomes more violent, it undermines the credibility of its declared goal of improving the living standards of Nigerian people.

Environmental changes in the Lake Chad basin are by no means solely responsible for regional insecurity. These changes, however, have increased conflicts over limited land and water resources that, in turn, have led to extremely vulnerable populations and provide Boko Haram with a powerful rhetorical tool that attracts disenchanted individuals. As Boko Haram gained control over more lands near the Lake Chad basin, they were able to monopolize access to the waters of Lake Chad, and so the group leveraged water insecurity rather than ideology to recruit members of vulnerable populations.[85, 86]

Clearly, heightened food and regional water insecurity offered recruitment opportunities to Boko Haram, which proposed pathways toward alternative livelihoods. A survey of civic leaders conducted for the United Nations University revealed how people affected by poverty and climate shifts have joined Boko Haram as well as its adversaries. The survey found that leaders in Borno State overwhelmingly acknowledged that members of their communities were adversely affected by climatic shifts. In the survey, 41 percent of respondents knew people who had joined Boko Haram as a result of climate-related difficulties with farming, fishing, or herding. Similarly, 64 percent of the respondents knew people who had joined the Civilian Joint Task Force (CJTF), Yan-Gora, or other self-defense forces that oppose Boko Haram as a response to loss of livelihood in farming, herding, or fishing more than because of inherent opposition to the group.[87]

The next section examines how environmental conditions, including lack of water, have bolstered Boko Haram recruitment. Boko Haram has been able to weaponize water in alignment with its objectives and structure all the more easily because of existing stresses on this resource.

Boko Haram and the Water Weapon

Boko Haram has deliberately incorporated water weaponization into its ongoing insurgency against the Nigerian state in many of the same ways described in the previous chapter on Syria and Iraq. However, Boko Haram's use of the water weapon is less frequent, strategic, and systematic than that of their Islamic State counterparts. This is due in large part to Boko Haram's tendency to characterize weaponizing water resources as ad hoc opportunities rather than as integrated part of a deliberate warfighting strategy. Nevertheless, distinct patterns and trends are visible in the group's actions, and the impacts on human security are no less damaging than those in other regions where violent extremist groups proliferate.

Boko Haram employed the water weapon most frequently from 2014 to 2016. This outcome is predictable because, like IS, the time frame coincides with Boko Haram's control of its greatest territorial extent. Geographically, the majority of incidents of water weaponization perpetrated by Boko Haram were in the arid reaches of northeast Nigeria, particularly in the states of Borno, Yobe, and Adamawa that border the troubled Lake Chad region.

128   *Weaponizing Water*

Boko Haram employed the water weapon on fewer occasions than IS in Syria and Iraq. Evidence can be drawn from several sources. The Social Conflict Analysis Database is a tool that tracks terrorist attacks across the African continent. These data indicate that in Nigeria seventeen incidents can be classified as water terrorism by Boko Haram in 2014–2015, the time frame covered by the data. The researchers found that Boko Haram directed more than half of the attacks at rural residents. The remainder of the attacks directly targeted military personnel and water infrastructure.[88]

Another authoritative study finds that Boko Haram's use of the water weapon was not as prevalent as IS's. In a review of the University of Maryland's Global Terror Database (GTD), two scholars, Veilleux and Dinar, found that only 1 percent of all global terrorism incidents during the study period of 1970–2016 were related to water.

In the GTD data, these events accounted for a total of 675 incidents in seventy-one countries, involving 124 perpetrator organizations. It is notable that although these attacks were infrequent, they resulted in a clearly nontrivial number of casualties, at 3,391. According to these data, Boko Haram was found to be responsible for only five water-related incidences of terrorism.[89]

But these findings must be viewed in the context of Veilleux and Dinar's definition of water terrorism, which is less inclusive than the overall definition of water weaponization used in this volume. In their work, *water terrorism* is defined largely as how terrorist organizations use water resources either directly or indirectly to challenge standing governments and achieve various objectives. These findings are analogous to the aspects of coercive water weaponization and psychological water terrorism offered in this volume. Veilleux and Dinar do not broach the questions of whether water can be weaponized as a tactical tool on the battlefield or whether states can employ the water weapon.[90]

Veilleux and Dinar found that, generally, a low number of water-related terrorism incidents occurred on the African continent. However, a considerable number of the incidents perpetrated by Boko Haram were notable for their lethality. Boko Haram was responsible for 227 of the 1,243 (18.26 percent) casualties in water weaponization incidents. Overall, Boko Haram was ranked as the fourth-deadliest water weaponizer among a comprehensive list of terrorist organizations in the study. Boko Haram ranked only behind IS and "Christian extremists," presumably including the farmers from Nigeria's Middle Belt who are engaged in violence against Muslim Hausa-Fulani herders.[91]

Extremist Violence in Nigeria **129**

In general, studies tracking water-related terrorist incidents in Nigeria face several limitations common to all zones of violent conflict that may lead researchers to undercount incidents. Some of these data problems include poor reporting in isolated regions, imprecise death counts, and varying accounts of the same incidents across information platforms and sources. There is also a strong potential that government-controlled or -influenced media sources mitigate the severity of terrorist attacks. My research, on the other hand, which synthesizes data on water weaponization incidents across information platforms, is based on a wider set of sources and utilizes a more expansive definition of water weaponization that includes hostile actions beyond those included in the more narrow definition of water terrorism.

Nonetheless, the overall number of times that Boko Haram used the water weapon is very significant if not numerous. Boko Haram was responsible for incidents that fall into every category of water weaponization and meet every goal of weaponization proposed in this volume. The group's actions ranged from poisoning wells with human remains and animal carcasses at the tactical level to coercion of subjugated populations (terrorism) and the strategic destruction or vandalism of larger water infrastructure such as pumps and reservoirs.[92]

Strategic weaponization. A look at Boko Haram's use of the water weapon in Nigeria reveals classic strategic intentions even as the group first emerged. In October 2015, the Nigerian authorities learned of a large conspiracy to poison a variety of water sources across a vast expanse of northeast Nigeria. In a press release, the Nigerian military warned that Boko Haram terrorists planned to buy large quantities of rat poison and other substances and use them to contaminate water sources and storage systems.[93] The reports of these actions turned out to be exaggerated. The attacks were never brought to fruition for whatever reason, but it is credible that Boko Haram nonetheless contemplated these actions as part of a wider insurgent strategy. Creating a fear of attacks may have been the insurgents' sole and original intention.

However, actual strategic use of the water weapon faces challenges in Nigeria. Northeastern Nigeria's physical environment and topography offer a possible explanation for the paucity of weaponization incidents. Much of the population subjugated by Boko Haram lives in the Lake Chad region and relies on the lake as a water source. The Chinese revolutionary Mao Zedong famously observed that a guerrilla swims among the people like a fish swims in the sea. This proximal relationship is borne out by the fact that Boko Haram itself draws its water from the lake and is as dependent on maintaining the viability of this source as is the nearby population.

In the arid northern region, water boreholes are scattered and rivers are largely nonexistent. Not only do Boko Haram and the local population share water sources, but also, as an expert on security in the region pointed out to me based on her observations, large bodies of water such as Lake Chad do not lend themselves to sabotage because they are so extensive. Poison, for example, would only dissipate. It is clear that the quantity of poison necessary to affect a water source of over 500 square miles such as Lake Chad renders this option impractical. In other areas farther from the lake where boreholes are prevalent, Boko Haram and their potential victims share overlapping territories. Because Boko Haram is not clearing and holding territory where the water sites are located, the group must return to these mutual sources constantly. Destroying or poisoning shared water is an option that is largely off the table.

The man-made infrastructure, such as dams and municipal water supplies, that is the most attractive target for strategic weaponization or so-called spectacular terrorist attacks is also absent from northeastern Nigeria. Spectacular attacks, today probably most closely associated with al-Qaeda, are the type of terror strike such as the attack on the World Trade Center that can awe the enemy and create as much disruption to society as possible.

In Iraq, the Tigris and Euphrates river system presented a battlespace ripe for spectacular attacks. There, the Islamic State took advantage of the populations' reliance on an extensive series of dams and used the infrastructure to its strategic advantage. In Syria, major water supply pipelines were severed and water treatment plants were destroyed. But in northeastern Nigeria, these types of targets are few and far between. The river system that includes the Niger River and its delta lay to the south.

Although Boko Haram has not targeted dams, those that do exist are a great security liability. Hydropower generation currently accounts for a nonnegligible 32 percent of total installed commercial electric capacity. Nigeria plans to further exploit hydropower.

The concentrated nature of water infrastructure is a concern. Sixty-five percent of Nigeria's existing dam infrastructure is located in a region where a handful of rivers originate in the wet highlands and meander before reaching Lake Chad. This is concerning given that this is where Boko Haram maintains a strong presence on the ground and has concentrated its greatest number of attacks.

Understanding the risk, experts conducted a study that assessed the consequences of the destruction of existing dams as well as planned hydropower development on four major rivers that together impound over 90 percent of the hydropower resources in northern Nigeria. The study found that dams within the Hadeja-Jama'are and Kamadugu Yobe river basins have the highest potential for exploitation by terrorists. This study took into account such risk factors as geographic location, vulnerability and socioeconomic status of the local populace, and proximity to porous international borders that allow insurgents to smuggle small arms.

The authors found that despite these identified risks, as of 2013 no federal funds had been allocated to the protection of dams in Nigeria.[94] A scan of available sources finds no indication that the Nigerian government has made any subsequent investments to address these security vulnerabilities. Protecting the dams has been hampered by administrative and financial factors among which are the diverse nature of dam ownership which is distributed between the public and private sectors and the overall scarcity of financial resources for further investment in these projects after sunk costs of construction are accounted for.

The study makes the convincing case that it is imperative for the Nigerian government to finance security upgrades for these facilities.[95] The government of Nigeria is planning more dam projects, and continued inaction affords Boko Haram the opportunity to strategically expand its footprint of territorial control by seizing or destroying dams, as IS was able to do at Mosul Dam and other locations during the height of its power in Iraq and Syria.

Tactical weaponization. Boko Haram uses the water weapon in a tactical capacity more frequently, a fact borne out on the battlefield. In early 2015, the Nigerian military reported that in confrontations, Boko Haram routinely poisoned water sources, including wells and streams. In Gwoza, a city of 300,000 in Nigeria's extreme northeastern corner, Boko Haram used wells and streams as dumping sites for corpses.[96] These actions were taken in areas where the Nigerian troops had dislodged insurgents and occupied those positions. Boko Haram also poisoned cattle water ponds in Kangallam village in Borno State, killing a large number of cattle. Boko Haram engineered these attacks to stymie the Nigerian Army's advance and to take revenge on the general population in the area for supporting the government troops.[97]

The placement of mines at water sources is another form of water weaponization more common in Nigeria than in other areas of conflict.

132   *Weaponizing Water*

Boko Haram deployed mines at water sources and in the surrounding fields, a deadly calling card, especially in Borno State.[98] There, in 2016, large numbers of internally displaced people began to return to their homes after fleeing an intense period of warfare. They found that water had been weaponized in three ways: homes and water infrastructure were devastated, water sources were polluted with human and animal bodies, and mines and unexploded ordnance were scattered near the wells.[99]

A contemporary aspect of water weaponization is especially troubling. In 2021, a Nigerian barrister, Pamela Okoroigwe, surfaced a report on the impact of conflict in northeast Nigeria on the sexual and reproductive rights of women and girls. The report reveals a history of how access to water in this region has been used to extort individuals in the most inhumane ways. Boko Haram infiltrated IDP camps and raped girls and women who were seeking access to food and water. The victims who were surveyed revealed that these incidents occurred while IDPs in Borno, Adamawa, and Yobe States and even in the distant capital of Abuja were confined to camps. These acts were just one aspect of Boko Haram's systematic exploitation of vulnerable groups. Gender inequality is endemic to Nigeria but amplified by environmental scarcity. Women and girls across Nigeria remain vulnerable to all forms of gender-based violence, including rape, sex trafficking, forced marriages, and the consequences of unplanned pregnancies.[100]

Incentivization and coercive weaponization. As recently as the summer of 2021, Boko Haram has taken advantage of the lack of effective governance in Borno State, a region extremely stressed by climate change, to wield access to water as a coercive tool on a much greater scale than it did in locations such as the IDP camps.

In the areas of Borno adjacent to the Lake Chad basin, Boko Haram has realized the revenue generation capacity of controlling agriculturalists' access to water. The group imposed taxes on irrigated land and sales of crops. Some who could not pay were wholly susceptible to recruitment.

Climate change and the accompanying scarcity of water are now permanent parts of the microlevel conflict dynamic. As climate impacts intensify, in this relatively ungoverned space Boko Haram must contend with regional strongmen and other criminal groups who are wielding authority over populations whose resilience has been weakened by environmental factors. This situation will prevail for the foreseeable future

Extremist Violence in Nigeria   133

given the state of climate dynamics that undermine national institutional reach and governance.

On the other side of the coin, rather than withholding water, to build popular support Boko Haram has sometimes used water as an incentive by digging boreholes for small communities. These localized actions were undertaken with an explicit goal of recruiting local fighters, but there is no evidence that they have been employed on a widespread basis. Incentivizing the population in this way might have been just as fruitful as taxation had it been pursued with the same conviction.

Given their inherent brutality and lack of imagination, Boko Haram's failure to monopolize water to build support should not be a surprise. In 2016, it was reported that in Borno State, Boko Haram repeated a typical pattern of pillaging food, stealing cattle, and poisoning water sources rather than wooing neglected villagers with promises of resources.[101] Sometimes Boko Haram's need to quench its own fighters' thirst caused outbreaks of violence with local populations that also relied on scant water resources. Throughout modern history, most guerilla and terrorist groups have been poor administrators of territory. Accordingly, Boko Haram was distinctly inept at administrating the territory under its control, an area that had at least theoretically grown to nearly the size of Belgium in 2015.

As of 2018, the Lake Chad region had become a stronghold for the emergent Islamic State in West Africa (ISWA). ISWA split from Boko Haram in 2016, and the two groups have become bitter rivals, actively engaging in combat. By 2018, the ranks of ISWA had grown to as high as 5,000 fighters. Islamic State in West Africa has been more creative than its rival in attempts to win over locals. The organization has done so by digging wells, distributing seeds and fertilizer, and providing protection for herders' pastures in exchange for set fees. ISWA's strategy centers on the idea that it is best to build up a local economy, rather than destroy it, so that there is a sufficient revenue base to tax. For these reasons, ISWA is seen by some locals as more moderate than its Boko Haram counterpart and certainly more so than its sister organization in Syria and Iraq, which used water as a weapon ruthlessly and without hesitation. There may be another explanation for ISWA's hesitation to use the water weapon locally. The vast majority of ISWA fighters are drawn from the indigenous populations in Nigeria. Foreign fighters, who made up a larger percentage of the IS army in Syria and Iraq, may very well be less restrained in destroying lands that are not tied to by ancestry.[102]

134   *Weaponizing Water*

It is logistically difficult to sustain any army in the field and this is especially true of guerilla forces. As this type of force, Boko Haram lacks reliable supply lines, and fighters are compelled to live off of the land and pilfer resources. The need for food and water, while providing impetus for attacks against the population, runs counter to the need to recruit new members. Fighters have undermined the organization's ability to recruit when they targeted vulnerable communities for supplies, especially in areas where they had little regard for whether the citizens were in sympathy with jihad against the state.

Psychological Terrorism. Poisoning water supplies to instill popular fear in urban settings is a classic and efficient approach to water weaponization as terrorism. Boko Haram generally did not employ the water weapon on such a large scale. However, one incident that took place in Maiduguri, the capital and largest city in Borno State, stands as a stark exception.

In August 2013, eleven girls who were victims of human trafficking fell under the control of Boko Haram. The actions that followed were most likely motivated by so-called Stockholm syndrome, where victims held for long periods of time and subject to intensive indoctrination begin to sympathize with their captors. Thus, Boko Haram convinced children, especially girls, to hide explosive devices in their traditional loose-fitting clothing and carry out attacks that were invariably fatal to them. This practice has become so frighteningly common that military officials in the areas where Boko Haram operates warn citizens to be constantly vigilant for girl suicide bombers.

In 2013, a group of such girls armed with a poisonous powder snuck into Maiduguri's Ajelari Ward. Their objective was to poison the underground water reservoirs of residents in the adjacent Bulunkutu and Gomari Wards, but they were intercepted before the damage was done. Local authorities observed that this sort of action by girls under the control of Boko Haram draws less suspicion, especially when girls also carry infants on their backs.[103] However repugnant they are, the use of these tactics demonstrates that Boko Haram became more innovative and more ruthless in its terror attacks.

Unintentional weaponization. As the principal belligerent against the government of Nigeria, Boko Haram is responsible for widespread and arguably unintentional destruction of municipal water infrastructure. Nigerian military forces also bear some of the blame for destruction of water infrastructure because of their massive, violent, and sometimes imprecise responses to Boko Haram's provocations in heavily populated areas.

In 2016, the growing conflict resulted in widespread and often intentional damage to water and sanitation infrastructure, particularly in the states of Borno, Yobe, and Adamawa. The fighting also destroyed community and institutional facilities such as schools and health centers. Damage was done in Borno State (75 percent), Adamawa (17 percent), and Yobe (9 percent).[104] The scope of the destruction cannot be overstated. A 2017 report by UNICEF indicated that Boko Haram had destroyed an astonishing 75 percent of the water infrastructure in northeast Nigeria during the group's relatively brief and nominal control of the region.[105]

This chapter illustrates that Boko Haram has made comprehensive use of the water weapon across northern Nigeria and the Middle Belt regions. Table 3.1 lists weaponization incidents in northern Nigeria that have involved Boko Haram.

Climate conditions, including drought, were a backdrop to the events that unfolded in northeast Nigeria. A changing climate has resulted in fluctuating rain patterns and increased aridity, which exacerbate existing drought and make the onset of new droughts all the more likely. The resulting food insecurity created desperate conditions that have diminished Nigeria's societal resilience and ability to resist Boko Haram. There is every reason to expect that this trend will continue as long as Boko Haram maintains capacity to operate across the region. The equation is simple: as water becomes scarcer, for whatever reason, the remaining supply becomes easier to weaponize.

Cycle of Water Stress and Conflict in Northeastern Nigeria

In Nigeria, as in Syria and Iraq, there is a cycle of water stress and conflict. The cycle features a feedback loop where climate change–induced water stress drives conflict, and the conflict limits options for climate adaptation. Drought and related factors such as the desiccation of Lake Chad led to a collapse of the agricultural system. The resulting famine sparked migration. Those who remained had little capacity to resist attacks by Boko Haram. The Nigerian government lost effective control of vast areas of the north, which prevented the implementation of effective water policies or at least the effective distribution of food and water aid. Figure 3.2 illustrates this cycle in detail.

Climate change is a continuing risk. Rising temperatures and more variable rainfall patterns will continue to decrease water availability. The risk of more frequent and prolonged droughts in Nigeria is growing. Boko Haram's relation to water and conflict in Nigeria can be seen through four lenses:

136   *Weaponizing Water*

Table 3.1   Summary of Water Weaponization Incidents in Nigeria

Weaponization Type	Location/Event	Perpetrators	Date
Strategic	Northeastern Nigerian states: widespread threats to poison water sources and markets	Boko Haram	2015
Tactical	Borno State and small villages: placement of mines at water sources and in the surrounding fields	Boko Haram	2015–2016
Tactical	Gwoza, a town of 300,000: using wells and streams as dumping sites for corpses	Boko Haram	September 2018
Psychological terror	City of Maiduguri: girls armed with poisonous powder and ammunition to poison underground water reservoirs	Boko Haram	August 2013
Psychological terror	Borno State: pillaged food, stolen cattle, and poisoned water	Boko Haram	2016
Unintentional	States of Borno Yobe, and Adamawa: serious damage to water and sanitation infrastructure	Boko Haram	2016
Unintentional	Northeastern Nigeria: 75 percent of water infrastructure destroyed	Boko Haram and Nigerian forces	2017
Incentivization	Lake Chad regions: digging wells, giving out seeds and fertilizer, and providing protection for herders' pastures in exchange for set fees	Islamic State in West Africa (ISWA)	2016
Trigger for conflict	Middle Belt: farmers retaliate against pastoralists with physical attacks or by poisoning the water or grass, contributing to conflict	Militant Fulani herdsmen and farmers	2015–present

1. Boko Haram weaponized water in the conduct of its struggle.
2. Water scarcity and the Nigerian government's inability to provide relief lent credence to the jihadist narrative and contributed to Boko Haram's popular support.
3. Despite rising popular support, Boko Haram occasionally attacked the population for access to water.
4. Boko Haram preys upon a population that has been weakened and displaced by water scarcity.

Figure 3.2 Water Stress and Conflict Cycle in Northern Nigeria (Boko Haram)

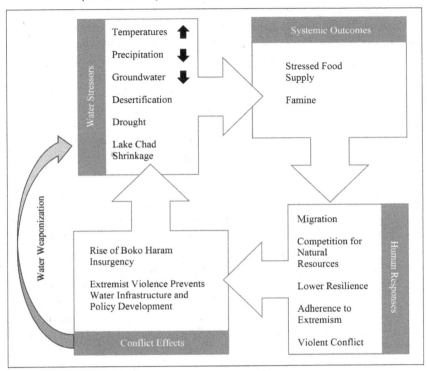

The Middle Belt

The region colloquially known as Nigeria's Middle Belt forms the transition space between the extremes of the temperate Niger River delta in the south and the country's dry northeast. It is an area of great natural diversity. The Middle Belt's ecoregions are predominantly tropical and subtropical and include savanna, grasslands, shrubland, and some forest.[106] The impacts of climate change vary but are uniformly negative across the region and include drought, less-predictable precipitation patterns, and desertification.[107] The Middle Belt area is adjacent to the northeast and suffers from some of the same environmental stressors, such as drought-diminished crop yields.

Droughts have caused shifts in pastoralist migratory patterns, pushing herders into areas traditionally dominated by farming communities. The competition for arable land amid a long-running drought has had

138   *Weaponizing Water*

severe effects on food security. Crop yields have declined in areas where most of the population relies on agriculture or animal husbandry as the sole source of sustenance and income.[108]

The arable land is cultivated mostly by Christian tribes. The Middle Belt lies on the traditional migration route of herdsmen who originate in northern Nigeria and beyond. Herdsmen belong to the Hausa-Fulani, a large Muslim ethnic group spread across a number of countries, including Niger, Cameroon, Chad, Nigeria, Senegal, and Mali.[109] The Hausa and Fulani were formerly two distinct ethnic groups that are now intermixed to the extent that they are regarded as one inseparable ethnicity.

Their annual migratory search for grazing land with sufficient water resources to support cattle is known as transhumance. As the region becomes more arid, the overall quantity of water available for grazing declines and their migration has begun to encroach on farming communities. Due to changing weather patterns, Hausa-Fulani herders are also staying longer in the Middle Belt, where the rainy season lasts longer than it does in their traditional ranges to the north of the Middle Belt.

Hausa-Fulani herders are attempting to settle in the Middle Belt in increasing numbers. The farmers generally believe they have the right to the land, citing inheritance rights and Nigerian land tenure laws, which give special recognition and provide social services to generational landowners, also known as indigenes.[110] Both state and local governments privilege the rights of indigenes, which has become a contributing factor to the conflict.[111]

When cattle consume or trample their crops, the farmers retaliate against the pastoralists by destroying their livestock with physical attacks or by poisoning the water or grass. These actions, combined with dissatisfaction with sparse economic opportunities, have created a conflict spiral that has led to thousands of deaths with no signs of abatement.

Although the nomadic Hausa-Fulani do not meet all of the characteristics of a traditional terrorist group, according to data compiled in the 2015 Global Terrorism Index, Nigeria's Hausa-Fulani militants were the fourth most deadly terrorist group in the world.[112] In 2014 alone, Hausa-Fulani militants were responsible for the deaths of 1,229 people. Violence has resulted in the deaths of more than 25,000 people since 2009. Since 2019, clashes involving Hausa-Fulani militants have caused more casualties than conflict caused by Boko Haram.[113]

Moreover, evidence links Boko Haram's insurgency in the north with the herdsman–farmer conflict in the Middle Belt. As of 2016, sources within the Nigerian military allege that Boko Haram members have infiltrated Hausa-Fulani communities in an attempt to flee the Niger-

Extremist Violence in Nigeria   139

ian military's advances.[114] The idea that Boko Haram may have joined forces with the Hausa-Fulani is disturbing in that this development could precipitate a new, more destructive chapter in Nigeria's internal wars.

In fact, many Nigerians no longer distinguish between Hausa-Fulani herders and Boko Haram extremists, seeing both as a singular terrorist front whose sole aim is to Islamize Nigeria, although this view is not always well supported by the facts on the ground. It is true that Christians' homes have been specifically targeted by both groups, but Hausa-Fulani herders and Boko Haram have separate ideologies and interests. Cooperation between Hausa-Fulani herders and Boko Haram militants has been limited, though not entirely negligible. Jihadist groups such as Boko Haram, ISWA, and al-Qaeda in the Islamic Maghreb (AQIM) all take advantage of any grievances leveled at Christians for their full propaganda value and use them to build their recruitment base.[115]

Insurgency in northeast Nigeria and the Middle Belt has intensified and new actors such as AQIM have entered the fray. Nigerian authorities' attempts to mitigate and manage the conflict have been largely ineffective. Local authorities expelled pastoralists from a number of northeastern states in an attempt to lessen retaliatory killings. By expelling only one of the groups, local governments have depicted pastoralists as the aggressors, whereas farmers have also perpetrated violence, while creating the perception of taking sides rather than remaining neutral.[116] In the Middle Belt, as in the northern region, ongoing conflict absorbs the attention of authorities and hampers the implementation of more effective water and land management policies that could ease the competition for arable land.

Farmer-Herder Violence and Water Weaponization

The weaponization of water is sporadic in the Middle Belt, so it is not a defining element of the conflict but is undoubtedly a conflict driver. It is harder to identify individual cases of water weaponization in this area and understand their larger significance. Reporting tends to focus on the role of water in the broader conflict as casus belli as opposed to pinpointing specific clashes. There are, however, numerous reports of sabotage, such as farmers poisoning wells to kill Hausa-Fulani cattle as revenge for encroachment.

Lack of specific information on water weaponization, especially that which is classified as terrorism, may stem from the fact that researchers do not categorize the belligerents in this ongoing conflict as terror groups and thus they do not show up in databases that track so-called water

140   *Weaponizing Water*

terrorism.[117] One possible exception is Veilleux and Dinar's study, which found that Christian extremists (not necessarily coded to Nigeria in the database) were responsible for 300 water weaponization–related casualties.

This lack of notoriety may also reduce the newsworthy appeal of these clashes, hence so little information about water weaponization in Nigerian media coverage. News of clashes over individual water sources spreads by word of mouth, but these individual incidents go largely unrecorded. However, taken as a whole, they are more than enough to cause the widespread resentment needed to motivate an escalation to violent and often deadly clashes. The water stress and conflict cycle in the case of farmer–herder violence in the Middle Belt is illustrated in Figure 3.3.

Conclusion

As this chapter has demonstrated, the characteristics of water weaponization in Nigeria are quite different from those in Iraq and Syria and Somalia, the subject of the next chapter. Although the water and conflict cycle is recognizable in each context during the time covered by this volume, Boko Haram's use of the water weapon cannot be considered intensive as measured by number of attacks. But the attacks that did occur were no less lethal. It is notable, however, that Boko Haram employed the water weapon at all levels and for every purpose described in this volume.

The evidence of Boko Haram pursuing a deliberate strategy of water weaponization is inconclusive. As noted, Boko Haram's hesitancy to deploy the weapon at a strategic scale may be explained by limited access to major built and natural water infrastructure. The group also relies on some of the same water sources as their victims, such as Lake Chad. Although water may not have been weaponized in a wholly strategic manner, it is clear that Boko Haram took advantage of diminished societal resilience resulting from an existing lack of access to water to enable mass killings, kidnappings, and rape.

Looking forward, the government of Nigeria and concerned outside parties must remain vigilant. Boko Haram has not used the water weapon to its full advantage, but its use could easily find its way into the group's strategic planning if, for example, fighters started targeting dams. Failure to appreciate this potential and intervene accordingly could not only bring additional misery to the Nigerian people but also inspire other extremist actors such as AQIM and ISWA to incorporate

Figure 3.3 Water Stress and Conflict Cycle in Nigeria's Middle Belt

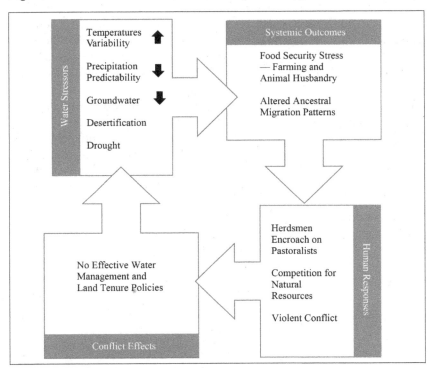

water weaponization into their operations. It is clear that food and water security must be taken into greater consideration in battling Islamic extremism. A failure to do so could see regional governments fueling the very grievances that cause people to support insurgency.

This chapter illustrates how water stress and associated responses have created cycles of conflict in two distinct ecoregions in Nigeria. It characterizes the extent of water weaponization methods employed by Boko Haram and militant Hausa-Fulanis and emerging extremists such as ISWA and AQIM. There is a need for more effective water governance and land tenure policy in the face of growing environmental scarcity in these regions. However, the goal of improved governance seems unobtainable when Nigerian policymakers are hamstrung by constraints of their own making, such as corruption, which causes a very real drain on resources and deflects attention from intensifying conflicts across the nation.

142 *Weaponizing Water*

The situation in Nigeria presents an opportunity for thoughtful interventions by international actors, including national governments and multilateral development institutions. It is therefore advisable that a comprehensive US policy designed to assist the government of Nigeria in addressing water challenges and stymieing use of the water weapon start with mitigating existing conflict and preventing future conflict. An integrated approach that foregrounds development strategies as well as direct military assistance, if requested, will go furthest toward this goal. It can also jump-start new development and technical-assistance initiatives that will provide the government of Nigeria the ability to uphold the social contract in a way that counters the spread of extremism. Chapter 5 provides a more specific framework for how to craft such an approach. While the overall outlook for continued conflict in Nigeria is murky at best, given the array of influencing factors, it is in the interest of the United States and other actors to double down on efforts to stabilize one of the most economically and geostrategically important nations in the world.

Notes

1. "Fragile States Index 2019," US Fund for Peace, 2016, https://fundforpeace .org/2019/04/10/fragile-states-index-2019/.

2. US Central Intelligence Agency (CIA), "Nigeria," *World Factbook*, 2019, updated August 31, 2022, https://www.cia.gov/the-world-factbook/countries/nigeria/.

3. UN Department of Economic and Social Affairs, *World Population Prospects 2019: Highlights* (New York: United Nations, 2019), https://population.un .org/wpp/Publications/Files/WPP2019_Highlights.pdf.

4. CIA, "Nigeria," *World Factbook*, 2019.

5. "Nigeria Economic Outlook," African Development Bank Group, https:// www.afdb.org/en/countries/west-africa/nigeria/nigeria-economic-outlook.

6. Simon Chukasi Ononihu and Mike Chidebe Oddih, "Nigeria's Quest for a Permanent Seat at the United Nations Security Council: An Appraisal," *IOSR Journal of Humanities and Social Science* 22, no. 4 (April 2017).

7. International Gas Union, *2019 World LNG Report* (Barcelona: International Gas Union, 2019), https://www.igu.org/sites/default/files/node-news_item-field_file /IGU%20Annual%20Report%202019_23%20loresfinal.pdf.

8. "Nigeria Facts and Figures," Organization of the Petroleum Exporting Countries, 2019, updated 2022, https://www.opec.org/opec_web/en/about_us/167.htm. Accessed July 15, 2020.

9. "Our Work in Nigeria," Transparency International, https://www.transparency .org/country/NGA.

10. "Nigerians Got Poorer in Muhammadu Buhari's First Term," *The Economist*, May 30, 2019, https://www.economist.com/middle-east-and-africa/2019/05/30/nigerians -got-poorer-in-muhammadu-buharis-first-term.

11. Chinedum Nwajiuba, "Nigeria's Agriculture and Food Security Challenges" (Green Deal Nigeria Study paper, Heinrich-Böll-Stiftung, 2013), https://ng.boell.org /sites/default/files/uploads/2013/10/agriculture_-_green_deal_nigeria_study.pdf.

12. CIA, "Nigeria," *World Factbook.*

13. Nigerian Federal Ministry of Agriculture and Rural Development (FMARD), *Agricultural Transformation Agenda Support Program—Phase 1 (Atasp-1): Strategic Environmental and Social Assessment* (African Development Bank Group, July 2013).

14. Alexander Smith, "ISIS Owns Headlines, but Nigeria's Boko Haram Kills More Than Ever," NBC News, January 1, 2016, http://www.nbcnews.com/storyline /2015-year-in-review/isis-owns-headlines-nigeria-s-boko-haram-kills-more-ever-n 480986.

15. "Stopping Nigeria's Spiraling Farmer-Herder Violence," International Crisis Group, July 25, 2018, https://www.crisisgroup.org/africa/west-africa/nigeria/262 -stopping-nigerias-spiralling-farmer-herder-violence.

16. Aaron Sayne, "Climate Change Adaptation and Conflict in Nigeria" (special report no. 274, United States Institute of Peace, Washington, DC, June 7, 2011), 3, http://www.usip.org/publications/climate-change-adaptation-and-conflict-in-nigeria.

17. World Health Organization, "GLAAS Nigeria 2018/2019 country highlights," September 12, 2018, https://www.who.int/publications/i/item/9789241516297.

18. "Water, Sanitation and Hygiene," UNICEF, https://www.unicef.org/nigeria /water-sanitation-and-hygiene.

19. Sayne, "Climate Change Adaptation and Conflict," 4.

20. Claudia Ringler, "What's Really Causing Water Scarcity in Africa South of the Sahara?" International Food Policy Research Institute, August 29, 2013, http://www.ifpri.org/blog/what%e2%80%99s-really-causing-water-scarcity-africa -south-sahara.

21. "Nigeria," WaterAid, http://www.wateraid.org/ng.

22. O. B. Akpor and M. Muchie, "Challenges in Meeting the MDGs: The Nigerian Drinking Water Supply and Distribution Sector," *Journal of Environmental Science and Technology* 4, no. 5 (2011): 480–489, https://doi.org/103923/jest.2011.480.489.

23. UNICEF, *Progress for Children: A Report Card on Water and Sanitation* (UNICEF, September 2006), 4, https://www.unicef.org/reports/progress-children -no-5.

24. A. K. Peter and U. Umar, "Combating Diarrhoea in Nigeria: The Way Forward," *Journal of Microbiology and Experimentation* 6, no. 4 (2018): 191–197.

25. Sayne, "Climate Change Adaptation and Conflict," 2.

26. I. Niang et al., "Executive Summary, Chapter 22 Africa," in *IPCC 5th Assessment Report*, ed. Core Writing Team, R. K. Pachauri, and L. A. Meyer (Geneva: Intergovernmental Panel on Climate Change, 2014), 1202, https://archive .ipcc.ch/pdf/assessment-report/ar5/wg2/WGIIAR5-Chap22_FINAL.pdf.

27. Ibid.

28. Sayne, "Climate Change Adaptation and Conflict," 3.

29. P. Odjugo, "An Analysis of Rainfall Pattern in Nigeria," *Global Journal of Environmental Science* 4, no. 2 (2005): 139–145.

30. "Nigeria," Notre Dame Global Adaptation Index, updated 2020, https://gain -new.crc.nd.edu/country/nigeria.

31. "How Nigeria Is Wasting Its Rich Water Resources," The Conversation, September 5, 2017, https://theconversation.com/how-nigeria-is-wasting-its-rich -water-resources-83110.

32. Ashley Moran et al., *Country Brief: Fragility and Climate Risks: Nigeria* (USAID, 2019), https://reliefweb.int/sites/reliefweb.int/files/resources/PA00TKRT.pdf.

33. Mohammed Sanusi Shiru et al., "Trend Analysis of Droughts During Crop Growing Seasons of Nigeria," *Sustainability* 10 (March 2018): 871, https://www .mdpi.com/2071-1050/10/3/871/pdf.

34. Ibid.

144 Weaponizing Water

35. Jude Nwafor Eze, "Drought Occurrences and Its Implications on Households in Yobe State, Nigeria," *Geoenvironmental Disasters* 5, no. 18 (2018), https://doi.org/10.1186/s40677-018-0111-7.

36. Sanusi Shiru et al., "Trend Analysis of Droughts."

37. Sayne, "Climate Change Adaptation and Conflict," 4.

38. Michael Werz and Laura Conley, "Climate Change, Migration and Conflict in Northwest Africa: Rising Dangers and Policy Options Across the Arc of Tension," Center for American Progress, April 18, 2012, 15.

39. Ibid., 24.

40. Nimi Princewill, "Africa's Most Populous City Is Battling Floods and Rising Seas. It May Soon Be Unlivable, Experts Warn," CNN, August 1, 2021, https://www.cnn.com/2021/08/01/africa/lagos-sinking-floods-climate-change-intl-cmd/index.html.

41. Cody Pope, "Vanishing Lake Chad—a Water Crisis in Central Africa," Circle of Blue, June 24, 2008, https://www.circleofblue.org/2008/world/vanishing-lake-chad-a-water-crisis-in-central-africa/.

42. "How to Stop the Decline of Lake Chad?" UN Development Programme, November 21, 2017, https://stories.undp.org/how-to-stop-the-decline-of-lake-chad.

43. Will Ross, "Lake Chad: Can the Vanishing Lake Be Saved?" BBC News, March 31, 2018, https://www.bbc.com/news/world-africa-43500314.

44. Natalie Sauer, "Lake Chad Not Shrinking, but Climate Is Fuelling Terror Groups: Report," Climate Home News, May 16, 2019, https://www.climatechangenews.com/2019/05/16/lake-chad-not-shrinking-climate-fuelling-terror-groups-report/.

45. UN Office for the Coordination of Humanitarian Affairs, "Lake Chad Basin: Crisis Overview—Nigeria" (infographic), ReliefWeb, January 23, 2019, https://reliefweb.int/report/nigeria/lake-chad-basin-crisis-overview-23-january-2019.

46. Food and Agriculture Organization of the United Nations, *Lake Chad Basin Crisis—Response Strategy (2017–2019)—Short Version* (FAO, March 2017), https://www.fao.org/resilience/resources/resources-detail/en/c/471497/.

47. Oxfam, *Lake Chad's Unseen Crisis: Voices of Refugees and Internally Displaced People from Niger and Nigeria* (Oxford: Oxfam, 2016), https://www.oxfam.org/sites/www.oxfam.org/files/file_attachments/bn-lake-chad-refugees-idps-190816-en.pdf.

48. P. Obaji Jr., "Recharging Lake Chad Key to Ending the Conflict Between Nigeria's Farmers and Herders," IPI Global Observatory, September 5, 2018, https://theglobalobservatory.org/2018/09/recharging-lake-chad-end-conflict-farmers-herders/.

49. CIA, "Nigeria," *World Factbook*.

50. "Nigeria," Notre Dame Global Adaptation Index.

51. CIA, "Nigeria," *World Factbook*.

52. "At Least a Million Sub-Saharan Africans Moved to Europe Since 2010," Pew Research Center, March 22, 2018, https://www.pewresearch.org/global/2018/03/22/at-least-a-million-sub-saharan-africans-moved-to-europe-since-2010/.

53. Ibid.

54. Lionel Beehner, "The Effects of 'Youth Bulge' on Civil Conflicts," Council on Foreign Relations, April 13, 2007, https://www.cfr.org/backgrounder/effects-youth-bulge-civil-conflicts.

55. CIA, "Nigeria," *World Factbook*.

56. Moses Ochonu, "The Roots of Nigeria's Religious and Ethnic Conflict," GlobalPost, The World, March 10, 2014, http://www.pri.org/stories/2014-03-10/roots-nigerias-religious-and-ethnic-conflict.

Extremist Violence in Nigeria 145

57. Jeffrey Haynes, "Conflict, Conflict Resolution and Peace-Building: The Role of Religion in Mozambique, Nigeria and Cambodia," *Commonwealth & Comparative Politics* 47, no. 1 (2009): 52–75, http://dx.doi.org/10.1080/14662040802659033.

58. Federal Ministry of Water Resources, Federal Republic of Nigeria, http://www.waterresources.gov.ng.

59. Berta Macheve et al., "Water Sector Institutions and Governance," in *State Water Agencies in Nigeria: A Performance Assessment*, Directions in Development—Infrastructure (World Bank, September 2015), 17–30, https://doi.org/10.1596/978-1-4648-0657-5_ch2.

60. Ibid.

61. Akpor and Muchie, "Challenges in Meeting the MDGs," 480–489.

62. Senator Ireogbu, "Expert Proffers Solution to Fulani Herdsmen, Farmers Clashes," *This Day Live*, July 9, 2016, http://www.thisdaylive.com/index.php/2016/07/09/expert-proffers-solution-to-fulani-herdsmen-farmers-clashes-2/.

63. Yunana Magaji Bature, Abubakar Aliyu Sanni, and Francis Ojo Adebayo, "Analysis of Impact of National Fadama Development Projects on Beneficiaries Income and Wealth in FCT, Nigeria," *Journal of Economics and Sustainable Development* 4, no. 17 (2013): 11–23.

64. "Social Conflict Analysis Database," Climate Change and African Political Stability, Robert Strauss Center, University of Texas at Austin, accessed 2016, https://www.strausscenter.org/scad.html.

65. Idean Salehyan et al., "Social Conflict in Africa: A New Database," *International Interactions* 38, no. 4 (2012): 503–511.

66. Carl-Friedrich Schleussner et al., "Armed-Conflict Risks Enhanced by Climate-Related Disasters in Ethnically Fractionalized Countries," *Proceedings of the National Academy of Sciences of the United States* 113, no. 33 (May 20, 2016): 9216–9221, http://www.pnas.org/content/113/33/9216.

67. Solomon M. Hsiang, Marshall Burke, and Edward Miguel, "Quantifying the Influence of Climate on Human Conflict," *Science* 13 (September 2013): 341, https://doi.or/10.1126/science.1235367.

68. Haruna Umar, "Violence Surges from Islamic Uprising in Nigeria," *News Tribune* (Jefferson City, MO), April 16, 2014, https://www.newstribune.com/news/2014/apr/16/violence-surges-islamic-uprising-nigeria/.

69. Associated Press, "A Look at the Nigerian Extremist Group Boko Haram," AP News, April 14, 2014, https://apnews.com/5a70eba16ff14934a16e4b63672cce59.

70. Derek Henry Flood, "A Review of the French-Led Military Campaign in Northern Mali," *CTC Sentinel* 6, no. 5 (May 2013), https://ctc.westpoint.edu/a-review-of-the-french-led-military-campaign-in-northern-mali/.

71. Sarah Chayes, "Nigeria's Boko Haram Isn't Just About Western Education," *Washington Post*, May 16, 2014, http://www.washingtonpost.com/opinions/nigerias-boko-haram-isnt-just-about-western-education/2014/05/16/d9bb5824-d9de-11e3-bda1-9b46b2066796_story.html.

72. Associated Press, "A Look at the Nigerian Extremist Group Boko Haram."

73. "Nigeria's Boko Haram Leader Abubakar Shekau in Profile," BBC, May 9, 2014, http://www.bbc.com/news/world-africa-18020349.

74. Andrew Walker, *What Is Boko Haram?* (special report no. 308, United States Institute for Peace, 2012), 1, http://www.usip.org/publications/what-boko-haram.

75. Terrence McCoy, "The Man behind the kidnappings of the Nigerian schoolgirls,"*Washington Post*, May 6, 2014.

76. "Nigeria Chibok Abductions: What We Know," BBC News, May 8, 2017, https://www.bbc.com/news/world-africa-32299943.

146   *Weaponizing Water*

77. "Boko Haram Leader Is Dead, Rival Daesh in West Africa Province Confirms," Arab News, June 6, 2021, https://www.arabnews.com/node/1871636/world.

78. Associated Press, "A Look at the Nigerian Extremist Group Boko Haram."

79. Ringler, "What's Really Causing Water Scarcity."

80. "Boko Haram Timeline: From Preachers to Slave Raiders," BBC News, May 15, 2013, http://www.bbc.com/news/world-africa-22538888.

81. Timothy Ola, "How Boko Haram Leader Beheaded 3 Pastors for Refusing to Accept Islam—Violent Crimes—Nairaland," Nairaland Forum, http://www.nairaland.com/307020/how-boko-haram-leader-beheaded.

82. Will Ross, "Nigerians' Fear of Northern Atrocities," BBC News, November 1, 2012, http://www.bbc.com/news/world-africa-20166065.

83. CNA, *The Role of Water Stress in Instability and Conflict* (CRM-2017-U-016532. Final, CNA, 2017), https://www.cna.org/CNA_files/pdf/CRM-2017-U-016532-Final.pdf.

84. Walker, "What Is Boko Haram?" 9.

85. Mervyn Piesse, "Boko Haram: Exacerbating and Benefitting from Food and Water Insecurity in the Lake Chad Basin," Future Directions International, September 19, 2017, https://reliefweb.int/report/nigeria/boko-haram-exacerbating-and-benefiting-food-and-water-insecurity-lake-chad-basin.

86. Buddhika Jayamaha et al., "Changing Weather Patterns, Climate Change and Civil War Dynamics: Institutions and Conflicts in the Sahel," *Seton Hall Journal of Diplomacy and International Relations* 20, no. 1 (Fall/Winter 2018): 70–87, https://search.proquest.com/docview/2212819139?accountid=11243&rfr_id=info%3Axri%2Fsid%3Aprimo.

87. Jessica Caus, *Climate-Driven Recruitment into Armed Groups in Nigeria* (MEAC Findings Report 1, United Nations University, 2021), file:///C:/Users/cmpal/Desktop/MEACFindings1.pdf.

88. Idean Salehyan et al., "Social Conflict in Africa: A New Database," *International Interactions* 38, no. 4 (2012): 503–511, https://www.strausscenter.org/ccaps/social-conflict-presentation/.

89. Global Terrorism Database, National Consortium for the Study of Terrorism and Responses to Terrorism (START), accessed 2020, https://www.start.umd.edu/gtd/.

90. Jennifer Veilleux and Shlomi Dinar, "A Global Analysis of Water-Related Terrorism, 1970–2016," *Terrorism and Political Violence* 33, no. 6 (2021): 1191–1216, https://doi.org/10.1080/09546553.2019.1599863. Citations refer to the advance online publication in 2019.

91. Ibid.

92. John S. Olanrewaju, "Terrorism and Its Socio-Economic Impacts on Nigeria: A Study of Boko-Haram in the North East" (PhD thesis, Kwara State University, Malete, Nigeria, January 2019), 187, https://search.proquest.com/docview/2217883483/?pq-origsite=primo.

93. Michael Kaplan, "Nigeria's Boko Haram to Poison Water? Army Urges Northeast to Stock Up Amid Fears of Terrorist Plot," *International Business Times*, October 26, 2015, https://www.ibtimes.com/nigerias-boko-haram-poison-water-army-urges-northeast-stock-amid-fears-terrorist-plot-2155999.

94. Mohammed A. Al Amin, "Hydropower Resources as Target of Terrorism: Case Study of Selected Water Bodies in Northern Nigeria," *International Journal of Engineering and Science* 2, no. 11 (2013): 52–61, http://theijes.com/papers/v2-i11/Part.2/H021102052061.pdf.

95. Ibid.

Extremist Violence in Nigeria 147

96. Chika Oduah, "Lost Childhood: Boko Haram Victims Gripped by Thoughts of Revenge," Al Jazeera, September 5, 2018, https://www.aljazeera.com/features /2018/9/5/lost-childhood-boko-haram-victims-gripped-by-thoughts-of-revenge.

97. World Bank, *North-East Nigeria—Volume II Component Report* (Washington, DC: World Bank, 2016), http://documents.worldbank.org/curated/en/318981479876 741883/pdf/110424-v2-WP-NorthEastNigeriaRecoveryandPeaceBuildingAssessment VolumeIIweb-PUBLIC-Volume-2.pdf.

98. Ibid.

99. Ibid.

100. Levinus Nwabughiogu, "Boko Haram: Women and Girls Randomly Raped in IDP Camps in Exchange for Food and Water," Vanguard Nigeria, March 30, 2021, https://www.vanguardngr.com/2021/03/boko-haram-women-girls-randomly -raped-in-idps-camps-in-exchange-for-food-water-ledap/.

101. "Nigeria's Food Crisis: Hunger Games," *The Economist*, https://www .economist.com/middle-east-and-africa/2016/09/01/hunger-games.

102. Paul Carsten and Ahmed Kingimi, "Islamic State Ally Stakes Out Territory Around Lake Chad," Reuters, April 29, 2018, https://www.reuters.com/article/us -nigeria-security/islamic-state-ally-stakes-out-territory-around-lake-chad-idUSKB N1I0063.

103. Ndahi Marama, "JTF, Vigilante Arrest Female Boko Haram Suspects," Vanguard Media, August 17, 2013, https://www.vanguardngr.com/2013/08/jtf-vigilante -arrest-female-boko-haram-suspects/.

104. World Bank, *North-East Nigeria—Component Report*.

105. NAN, "Boko Haram Destroyed 75% Water, Sanitation Infrastructure in Northeast—UNICEF," *The Guardian*, August 30, 2017, https://guardian.ng/news /boko-haram-destroyed-75-water-sanitation-infrastructure-in-northeast-unicef/.

106. "Ecoregions," World Wildlife Fund, https://www.worldwildlife.org/biomes.

107. Peter Akpodiogaga-a Ovuyovwiroye Odjugo, "General Overview of Climate Change Impacts in Nigeria," *Journal of Human Ecology* 29, no. 1 (January 2010): 47–55, https://doi.org/ 10.1080/09709274.2010.11906248.

108. E. Akinwotu, "Drought Worsens Deadly Battle Between Fulani Herdsmen and Farmers in Nigeria," *The Guardian*, January 3, 2017, https://www.theguardian .com/global-development/2017/jan/03/drought-worsens-deadly-conflict-between -fulani-herdsmen-nigeria-farmers.

109. IRIN News, "Bandit Attacks Displace Nigeria Herders," New Humanitarian, June 19, 2013, http://www.irinnews.org/news/2013/06/19/bandit-attacks-displace -northern-nigeria-herders.

110. Al Chukwuma Okoli and Atelhe George Atelhe, "Nomads Against Natives: A Political Ecology of Herder/Farmer Conflicts in Nasarawa State, Nigeria," *American International Journal of Contemporary Research* 4, no. 2, (2014): 76–88, aijcrnet .com/journals/Vol_4_No_2_February_2014/11.pdf.

111. Aaron Sayne, *Rethinking Nigeria's Indigene-Settler Conflicts* (Special Report no. 311, United States Institute of Peace, 2012), 2, http://www.usip.org/publications /rethinking-nigeria-s-indigene-settler-conflicts.

112. "Nigeria: Investigate Massacre, Step Up Patrols: Hundreds Killed by Mobs in Villages in Central Nigeria," Human Rights Watch, March 8, 2010, https://www .hrw.org/news/2010/03/08/nigeria-investigate-massacre-step-patrols.

113. "Nigeria: Scramble for Land, Water Deadlier Than Boko Haram," APA News, June 18, 2019, http://apanews.net/en/news/nigeria-scramble-for-land-water-deadlier -than-boko-haram/.

148   *Weaponizing Water*

114. Chika Oduah, "Nigeria: Deadly Nomad-Versus-Farmer Conflict Escalates," Al Jazeera, July 6, 2016, http://www.aljazeera.com/news/2016/07/nigeria-deadly-nomad-farmer-conflict-escalates-160704043119561.html.

115. Michael Nwankpa, "The North-South Divide: Nigerian Discourses on Boko Haram, the Fulani, and Islamization," Hudson Institute, October 26, 2021, https://www.hudson.org/research/17072-the-north-south-divide-nigerian-discourses-on-boko-haram-the-fulani-and-islamization.

116. Lourdes Eliacin Mars, Alyssa Gomes, and Maya Jacobs, interview by Nate Haken, Fund for Peace, for "Environmental Peacebuilding: Nigeria," *Elliott School of International Affairs Report*, March 13, 2015.

117. Veilleux and Dinar, "A Global Analysis of Water-Related Terrorism."

4

Al-Shabaab in Somalia

THE SOMALI PEOPLE ARE A RELATIVELY HOMOGENEOUS GROUP, unlike peoples in neighboring states in the Horn of Africa. The populations of Somalia largely identify as Somali, speak dialects of Somali, and are practicing Sunni Muslims. This is the same with the population in the independent yet internationally unrecognized Republic of Somaliland in the northwestern part of the country. Geographically, Somalia occupies the Horn of Africa between the Gulf of Aden and the Indian Ocean. Figure 4.1 shows a map of Somalia that includes its major water bodies.

Characteristics of Somalian Society

Clan Structure

It is impossible to understand Somalia without taking the deep influence of the clan system into account. The system is complicated, but generally it includes four or five predominant clans: Darood, Dir, Hawiye, and Raxanweyne. The fifth is the Isaaq, which experts debate as being inside or outside of the Dir group. Clan lineage is traced through male ancestors, who are understood to ultimately link back to Arabia and the prophet Mohammad. Because of their nomadic heritage, the clans are not necessarily associated with a fixed territory, although they often have de facto control of specific lands, outside of the jurisdiction of the state. Clans are frequently condemned as divisive and hampering unification of the state.[1]

149

Figure 4.1 Political Map of Greater Somalia

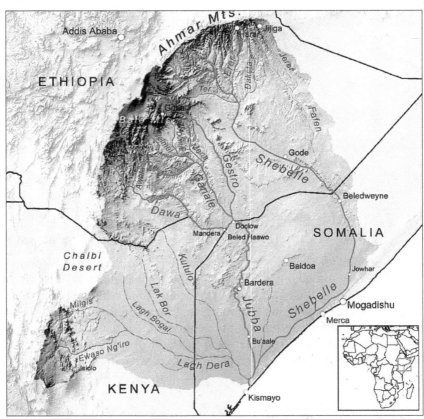

Source: US Central Intelligence Agency, "Somalia," World Factbook, https://www.cia.gov/the-world-factbook/countries/somalia/.

Adherence to clan rule is solidified in Somali legal and political structures. First, the clans are responsible for the establishment of Somali customary law, which continues to function in south and central Somalia in the absence of state control. Second, the Somali federal government has institutionalized the clans in the developing federal structure under what is known as the 4.5 rule, which prescribes clan representation in the Somali Parliament. Under the law, each of the four main clans receives an equal share of representatives and the remaining half share goes to minority groups that sit outside the clan system.

Competition among clans is often violent, and the different pastoral groups have a long history of confrontation. This is partially attributable to clan members' history as nomadic herders in one of the driest places on earth. Access to water and grazing is often a matter of life and death.[2]

Therefore, a challenge of identifying types of violence in Somalia is the need to separate clan violence from insurgency and state violence. These forms of violence differ in context, scale, and intensity and should not be considered the same, even though there is a pervading influence of the clan structure.

Weak Central Government and Economy

In 1960, British-controlled Somaliland and Italian-controlled Somalia both gained independence and combined to form the United Republic of Somalia.[3] Resulting border disputes with neighboring Kenya and Ethiopia erupted in conflict. Elected in 1967, Abdirashid Ali Sharmarke served as the first president of Somalia until he was assassinated in 1969, whereupon Mohamed Siad Barre assumed power in a coup d'état. In 1991, Barre was ousted, precipitating a bloody struggle for control among competing clans.[4]

That same year, Somaliland also declared independence as the Somaliland Republic, though it remains officially unrecognized by any government. Somaliland continues to enjoy stability. This is at least partially attributable to the remaining economic infrastructure in place after Russian, British, and American military assistance.[5] In 1998, the Puntland region of Somalia also declared its autonomy, but unlike Somaliland, which sought full independence, Puntland aspired to self-governance but as a federal state of Somalia.[6]

The Transitional National Government (TNG) was formed in 2000 in an aspirational attempt to restore federal control. The TNG was subsequently unable to reunify the rump Somalia with Somaliland and Puntland.[7] The TNG continued to struggle, owing to a myriad of factors, including insurgency and famine. In 2012, after fourteen attempts, the TNG established the first formal parliament in two decades, concluding eight years of governmental transition.[8] Since that time, the TNG has held tentative control of the country. Given this history of unstable governance, lack of monopoly force within its borders, and inability to provide reasonable public services, it is not surprising that in 2021 Somalia ranked as second highest on the Fund for Peace's Fragile State Index. It has consistently ranked as one of the two most fragile states included in this index since 2007.[9]

152 *Weaponizing Water*

Though the international recognition of Somalia's new government is an important step toward greater stability, governance inefficiencies are borne out in the country's economic performance. The government is unable to collect external debt or domestic revenue, which amounts to a loss estimated to have been 93 percent of gross domestic product (GDP) in 2014. Somalia also has a significant trade deficit given its high dependence on imports and low export market. In 2016, Somalia's GDP was $6.2 billion, two-thirds of which came from imports, whereas exports made up only 14 percent of GDP.[10] Although many international organizations have been supporting economic growth in the country with some success, 73 percent of Somalis lived below the poverty line in 2015.[11, 12] Additional obstacles to improving the economy include a limited tax base, sparse regulatory and legal frameworks, and the government's inability to completely control its territory.[13]

Challenging Demographics

Despite mortality from conflict and famine and the exodus of over 2 million Somalis,[14, 15] Somalia has witnessed an explosion in population, and it suffers from other structural demographic disadvantages. Since its independence in 1960, the population has increased from almost 3 million to a little over 14 million in 2016.[16] The country has one of the highest fertility rates in the world at about six children per woman, and over 60 percent of the country's population is below the age of twenty-five.[17] Unlike other sub-Saharan African nations, annual population growth from 1950 to 2000 in Somalia was a staggering 7 percent, which then slowed to today's rate of 3 percent, which is still very high among the most fragile states in the world.[18] Somalia also has one of the world's lowest primary school enrollment rates and one of the world's highest youth unemployment rates. The lack of educational and professional opportunities for youths makes them more vulnerable to recruitment into gangs or as pirates or extremists.[19]

The Advent of al-Shabaab

The aforementioned conditions, including poor governance and political pressure from disaffected and jobless youths, enabled one extremist group that was more determined and organized than its rivals to emerge: the Harakat al-Shabaab al-Mujahideen, which can be translated as the

"Mujahideen Youth Movement." The group is better known by its short form, simply, al-Shabaab, translated as "the Youth." Al-Shabaab traces its roots to al-Itihad al-Islami, an Islamic fundamentalist organization born in the 1990s with the objectives of opposing General Barre's military regime and establishing Sharia law. Al-Shabaab later evolved into the youth wing of a group of the Islamic Courts Union (ICU), a political alliance established to administer territory seized from the military Barre regime. By 2006, the ICU had taken control of the capital Mogadishu and most of the territory of southern Somalia. The group splintered later in 2006 when countervailing forces of the Transitional Federal Government (TFG) and Ethiopian allies expelled the ICU from the capital. Al-Shabaab zealots were considered the most hardline faction within the greater ICU movement, but they were very popular, nonetheless. Over the next two years, membership in al-Shabaab grew from hundreds to thousands.

At this point, the West could no longer ignore the situation. The existence of an extremist threat growing in the ungovernable space of the Horn of Africa was inimical to regional and now global stability. The US State Department formally declared the group a foreign terrorist organization in 2008, and the act was soon followed by the EU and the UN. At that time, the logic for designation rested in part on an understanding that several individuals in the group were affiliated with al-Qaeda. Many of al-Shabaab's senior leaders were believed to have trained and fought with al-Qaeda in Afghanistan.[20] These claims were most likely exaggerated. In any case, the point proved moot as al-Shabaab leader Ahmed Abdi Godane formally pledged allegiance to al-Qaeda in February 2012.

Within two years, the situation changed considerably, and internally al-Shabaab debated whether to ally with the Islamic State (IS), which was extending its reach on the African continent. This alliance did not come to fruition, but IS subsequently maintained a small presence in Somalia, acting as a fairly insignificant rival to the much larger and powerful al-Shabaab.

By 2008, al-Shabaab had gained sufficient strength to go on the offensive. By exploiting the country's weak central government, al-Shabaab took control over large parts of Somalia. At the peak of its expansion in 2011, the group had retaken parts of Mogadishu, the national government's stronghold, and held substantial territory across the country, including the strategic port city of Kismayo. It was at this time that al-Shabaab also launched attacks in neighboring countries, most notably Kenya, to deter outside involvement in Somalia's affairs.[21]

154   *Weaponizing Water*

The attempt to deter foreign intervention was unsuccessful and counterattacks by the TFG and African Union Mission to Somalia (AMISOM), composed of forces from Uganda, Burundi, Kenya, Ethiopia, and Djibouti, greatly weakened the organization.[22] Al-Shabaab was pushed out of Mogadishu and Kismayo. Since 2011, al-Shabaab's freedom of movement and territorial control has diminished, but the group has been able to continue terrorist attacks on city centers and to exert control over rural communities (see Table 4.1). AMISOM's mandate ended on 31 March 2022, before the mission achieved its full objectives and it was replaced by the African Union Transition Mission in Somalia.[23]

In Somalia's northern Puntland region, IS eventually coalesced into a more lethal and organized group led by former al-Shabaab commander Abdulqadir Mumin. Despite a humble start, IS grabbed international headlines when it seized the Puntland port city of Qandala in 2016.[24] Since that time, IS has grown not only in Puntland but across Somalia and has been extorting citizens in areas that it controls. IS and al-Shabaab formally declared war on each other in 2018, and there have been continual clashes between the two groups, yet all indications are that al-Shabaab will remain the dominant jihadi actor in Somalia for the foreseeable future. Aside from IS, there have been numerous reports that al-Shabaab has linked with other militant groups in Africa, including Boko Haram in Nigeria and al-Qaeda in the Islamic Maghreb (AQIM), but these relationships remain largely opaque.

Table 4.1   Selected Mass Casualty Attacks by al-Shabaab

Year	Location	Number Killed
2010	Restaurant in Kampala, Uganda, against those watching a World Cup match	74 dead
2013	Westgate Shopping Center in Nairobi, Kenya	67 dead
2015	Garissa University in Kenya	148 dead
2016	Kenyan Military Base	Approximately 180 dead
2017	Truck bombing in Mogadishu (al-Shabaab does not claim responsibility)	At least 500 dead

Doctrine and Organizational Structure

Al-Shabaab is a Salafist group with an ideology inspired by Wahhabism. This conservative Islamic reform movement, upon which the kingdom of Saudi Arabia was founded, has influenced Islamic extremist movements worldwide, including IS and Boko Haram.[25] Al-Shabaab is also a Takfiri group, meaning that it declares Muslims who do not adhere to its doctrine as apostates who must be punished with death. This is true to the group's aim of creating a pure fundamentalist Islamic state that would include not only Somalia but also the neighboring states of Djibouti, Kenya, and Ethiopia.[26]

Al-Shabaab exists in parallel with the complex Somali clan system. Although al-Shabaab has not moved to abolish the traditional system, it has manipulated it by consistently trying to channel Somalis' popular frustrations with the hierarchy that it imposed. The group has touted the potential for religious militancy to prevail over clan interests and other seemingly intractable political divides. Although al-Shabaab's propaganda emphasizes impartiality in relations between the clans, it frequently acts as an arbitrator of local disputes and has been able to manipulate interclan conflict to its advantage.[27]

Al-Shabaab's organizational structure is strictly hierarchical. Ahmed Umar Abu Ubaidah (formerly Ahmed Diriye) is the emir, a title that translates to "prince" or "commander." Abu Ubaidah rose through the ranks of the organization to the post that was the rough equivalent of interior minister before he became emir. Al-Shabaab's first two emirs, Aden Hashi Ayro and Ahmed Abdi Godane, were both killed by US airstrikes, one in May 2008 and the latter in September 2014.[28]

Unlike other global jihadist groups, al-Shabaab has few academics in its leadership. Formal education has never been a status symbol among the ranks of al-Shabaab and very few current high-ranking officials have received one. The exception was Godane, who had an MBA in economics and experience working in nongovernmental organizations. His successor, Abu Ubaidah, has no higher education.[29]

Members of the organization are drawn from the Islamic Institutes system, a branch of the group's educational system, where dependable and ideologically pure fighters are trained and where attendance is mandatory. This system is regimented, self-financed, and run by al-Shabaab, which banned all other forms of Islamic schools. Each clan is required to annually enroll a certain number of children and finance their education. Children are indoctrinated with a jihadist worldview and are taught about the illegitimacy of the Somali government and the

156   *Weaponizing Water*

obligatory nature of joining al-Shabaab's jihad. Graduates are then sent to camps at the age of fifteen for military training.

The conventional military wing of al-Shabaab, as distinct from the militarized religious police, is known as the Jabahaat, which translates as "the fronts." At its peak, the Jabahaat's ranks exceeded 8,000. Most of the soldiers are child recruits who have gone through the al-Shabaab educational system. As of 2018, the Jabahaat membership stood at approximately 5,000 men.[30] In 2016, projections placed the number of fighters between 6,000 and 12,000 and between 7,000 and 9,000 in 2017.[31] The recent reduction in forces is due partially to a shift in tactics. The group increased deployment of guerilla tactics in place of conventional military operations, which require larger militant formations. Al-Shabaab continues to manage the Jabahaat and training camps with limited disruption from the outside.[32]

In comparison to other theaters of war, such as Iraq and Syria, foreign fighters are a modest presence in Somalia, with numbers estimated at 200–300.[33] The American contingent of fighters is drawn from the Somali diaspora in Minneapolis, Minnesota—home to the largest concentration of recent Somali immigrants, many of whom have found the transition to American life difficult. Between October 2007 and October 2009, more than twenty young men were known to have left the Minneapolis area with aims of taking up jihad.[34] According to a 2015 Federal Bureau of Investigation report, al-Shabaab's recruitment of Somali immigrants rose to the level of a top domestic terrorist threat.[35]

Financing

In Somalia, a large share of jihadist fundraising takes place in the form of Zakat collection. Zakat is a mandatory pillar of Islam, wherein each Muslim gives a proportion of their wealth to charity. The calculation for giving is 2.5 percent of an individual's annual wealth or income.[36] Contrary to Islamic law, which prohibits fundraising by militants, in the areas that it controls, al-Shabaab requires each business to provide, in cash, 2.5 percent of its monetary value before profit, as assessed by the organization.[37]

The collection of Zakat does not vary across regions of south and central Somalia, or even in areas that are not under al-Shabaab's direct control. While the religious purpose of Zakat is to donate to the less fortunate, much of what is collected in Somalia is sent directly to the al-Shabaab Finance Office for operational purposes.[38]

Other forms of taxation have also become a large source of income for al-Shabaab. Militants inspect each shop, and their accountants inspect inventory and demand payment. Additionally, large cargo trucks, notably water carriers, are often taxed significantly each time they use roads controlled by al-Shabaab. As a result of hefty road collections, al-Shabaab is estimated to bring in approximately $15 million annually from its regional checkpoints.[39]

Alongside taxing cargo trucks and inventory, al-Shabaab has been able to fund and sustain its insurgency through illegal charcoal smuggling in southern Somalia. In the Arabian Gulf nations, charcoal from Somalia's acacia tree is particularly desired because it burns longer than its counterparts and brings a high price. With approximately 3 million bags of charcoal smuggled out of Somalia in 2017, the charcoal trade brought in $150 million in revenue, by some estimates. Although the Port of Kismayo, the main international port of embarkation, was liberated by Kenyan forces in 2012, images emerged in 2018 showing continued smuggling when truckloads of illicit charcoal were loaded onto boats that set sail for the Middle East.[40]

Recruitment

Al-Shabaab's recruitment patterns reflect the realities on the ground. In the early years, the group recruited heavily from urban areas under its control. However, as it has lost urban territory, most recruits are drawn from rural areas, specifically the Bay and Bakol regions.[41]

Al-Shabaab draws on younger recruits to replace aging fighters. The group seeks out adolescents and kidnaps some directly from schools, a tactic that forces others to flee areas of control to avoid conscription. Al-Shabaab has drawn many young recruits from marginalized clans and those outside the clan system such as the Jareer (or Bantu) populations. The Jareer are an ethnically distinct group descended from slaves brought in from southeast Africa as part of the Arab slave trade.

The use of child soldiers is prevalent. In January 2017, UN Secretary-General Antonio Guterres observed that more than half of al-Shabaab's fighters may be children. A United Nations Security Council report recorded the recruitment of a staggering 4,213 children into al-Shabaab between April 1, 2010, and July 31, 2016. Almost all of them were male.[42] An adolescent's attraction to al-Shabaab is not surprising because incentives for impoverished youth are generous by the standards of the region. In addition to basic housing, clothing, and food, youths are

158   *Weaponizing Water*

offered cell phones and salaries of up to $700 a month. They are promised additional payments if they bring a wife and children.

While al-Shabaab recruits males for combat roles, it has also kidnapped and enslaved both Muslim and Christian women and girls in Somalia and Kenya. The group forces some hostages to work in brothels while forcing others into marriages with al-Shabaab fighters. Al-Shabaab has regularly killed women and girls who refuse to be forced into marriage. Children are among the most vulnerable of the thousands of internally displaced people.[43]

Ecological Context

It is hard to paint an accurate picture of Somalia's historical ecological condition because of a lack of data, understandably absent given the country's perpetual instability. However, some aging records exist. In the 1970s, Somali dictator Barre founded the National Range Agency to spearhead the country's conservation efforts. In support of this agency through the 1980s, the famed British ecologist Murray Watson led a team of scientists to conduct the most comprehensive natural resources and land survey ever completed in the country.

These efforts were largely futile. Many records were destroyed during the coup that overthrew Barre in 1991. Property belonging to the National Range Agency was destroyed, though some data smuggled out of the country by Watson has recently been uncovered and efforts have been made to piece together the available scientific records.[44] While international organizations such as the United Nations Intergovernmental Panel on Climate Change (IPCC) offer climate data on the regional level, more national data such as that collected by Watson is needed to develop statistical downscaling models to better assess climate conditions in Somalia.

To address this issue, the UN's Food and Agriculture Organization established the Somalia Water and Land Information Management Project (SWALIM) in 2003. SWALIM is a joint effort of several donors, including Italy, the European Union, the US Agency for International Development (USAID), and the United Nations International Children's Emergency Fund (UNICEF), that collects data for better assessment of rainfall, river flows, and available groundwater resources as well as land use, soil characteristics, and land use suitability. The goal is to establish a hydrometeorology monitoring network to improve Somalia's flood and early warning systems. Project members have gathered as

Al-Shabaab in Somalia   159

much environmental data as possible during the early phases. The current phase is funded at a modest $19 million, so more support for this organization seems like a good step forward.[45]

Water Resources and Management

Somalia's two permanent rivers, the Jubba and the Shabelle, are of great importance to the country. A few seasonal rivers such as the Kutulo, Lak Bor, and Lagh Bogal carry water from the Ethiopian highlands that bisect the country before they join the Jubba and Shabelle and drain into the Indian Ocean near Kismayo.

The Jubba and Shabelle river systems also originate in the Ethiopian highlands and run through major Somali population centers. Civilization in Somalia has long relied on the rivers. As far back as the Middle Ages, plantations supporting the Ajuran Empire were established. The Ajuran was Africa's only hydraulic empire, meaning it drew power from its exclusive control over and access to water resources. Innovations such as flood control and irrigation call for a centralized bureaucracy.[46]

Today, these rivers provide critical irrigation to maintain the country's agricultural sector. Fertile floodplains are cultivated and nourish crops for domestic and international markets. The Jubba River basin is primarily savanna, and it is the most fertile part of the country. The savanna supports a wide range of native wildlife not seen in other parts of the African continent.

The Somali government, however, continues to face many challenges to proper development, cultivation, and management of these valuable river systems. The irrigation infrastructure has been allowed to deteriorate, and it is in poor condition, which has major impacts on national agricultural production. Furthermore, al-Shabaab's presence in southern Somalia prevents the national government and development agencies from accessing these areas to make improvements.

Deforestation is a ubiquitous problem in the major watersheds. Somalia has limited forest cover; the forests that do exist are mostly in the south of the country. Massive deforestation for charcoal production and from climate change has led to drought, desertification, increased soil erosion, and land degradation.[47] Meanwhile, poor water management practices contribute to shortages. Somalia faces acute water stress and scarcity.

The baseline water stress in Somalia is medium-high—between 20 percent and 40 percent—and the country's overall water risk is listed as extremely high, according to the authoritative Aqueduct Water Risk Atlas,

160   *Weaponizing Water*

a project of the World Resources Institute (WRI). To determine scarcity, the WRI tool measures baseline water depletion by analyzing the ratio of total water consumption to existing available renewable water. Here, total water consumption includes surface and groundwater, as well as water used domestically, industrially, for irrigation, and for livestock. Overall water risk is the totality of all water-related risks that accounts for physical quantity, quality, and regulatory and reputational risks.[48]

In addition to access issues brought about by the violence that has beset the country, including the war against al-Shabaab, the complex governance system in Somalia challenges the management of the country's riverways. One major challenge is flood control. Regular flooding of the Jubba and Shabelle Rivers is a dangerous characteristic of the hydrological system. After the collapse of the Somali government in 1992, flood and irrigation water control and management suffered accordingly. Furthermore, owing to political fractures, the three separate ministries charged with water governance fail to communicate with one another. The Ministry of Water and Energy is the government authority mandated to manage river networks. However, water management in Puntland, given its state of quasi-independence, is conducted by the Puntland State Agency for Water, Energy and Natural Resources (PSAWEN). Likewise, the Ministry of Water Resources (MoWR) is responsible for water management in Somaliland.

Although efforts such as the SWALIM project are building capacity to better manage the rivers, all ministries remain poorly equipped to do so.[49] From the perspective of the Somali national government, there are two main limiting factors. Essentially, Somalia does not have the funding it needs to support an integrated water resources management system. This challenge is reflected in the country's modest groundwater monitoring network.[50] Additionally, there is a lack of necessary technical skills in the population needed for managing resources. Humanitarian crises coupled with perennial conflict further hamper limited administrative capacity.[51]

Boreholes, springs, and shallow wells are the primary sources of groundwater for the country. Compromised groundwater quality and quantity also present unique challenges. Groundwater is the only water source for most Somalis, save for those who reside along the Jubba and Shabelle Rivers. As such, groundwater provides 95 percent of the country's drinking water. Despite its importance, the hydrogeology, quantity, and quality of groundwater resources remain poorly understood. Systematic data collection on well capacity, exploitation, and groundwater level fluctuations is lacking. Unregulated water exploration and drilling is a partial result. Weak water governance institutions fail to regulate these practices.

Lack of access to the potable water that exists is an ongoing hardship for the Somali people. The situation is exacerbated by the fact that most groundwater sources in Somalia have high salinity, with electrical conductivity measures that exceed 2,000 μS/cm (low conductivity indicates fresh, clean water; conductivity levels over 1,000 μS/cm indicate saline conditions), making much of this water unsuitable for drinking. Also, many shallow wells are exposed, creating vulnerabilities to microbiological and other contamination.[52] Access to improved water sources remains poor throughout the country, but there is also a discrepancy between urban and rural access. During the onset of the 2011 drought (discussed below), these figures were 69.6 percent and 8.8 percent, respectively.[53] By 2015, when the drought conditions had subsided somewhat, 70 percent of the population still lacked access to safe drinking water.[54, 55]

Drought Conditions

Drought is a cyclical phenomenon in Somalia. Moderate drought takes place every three to four years, with severe drought occurring every seven to nine years.[56]

The term *drought* is often used, particularly in the context of describing conditions that require humanitarian responses. But in a country that is perpetually arid, the term lacks a common definition and clarity.[57] Given this prevalent lack of clarity, the UN Food and Agriculture Organization (FAO) has developed a robust definition of drought and an index that can be applied to countries like Somalia. The index defines drought in Somalia as an extended period during which freshwater availability and accessibility in a given ecosystem at a given time and place are below normal as a result of unfavorable spatial and temporal distribution of rainfall, temperature, soil moisture, and wind characteristics.[58] Using this definition, Somalia is under nearly continuous drought conditions.

Forecasting the timing of onset and severity of droughts in Somalia is complicated by normally high interannual variations in rainfall. The country has two rainy seasons: the *gu* from April to June, which brings the most rains; and the shorter *deyr*, from October to November. During the rest of the year, precipitation is negligible. Whether a drought is formally declared, some common observable characteristics of drought are long, below-average periods of rainfall; high temperatures and prolonged, above-average hot periods; low soil moisture content;

162 *Weaponizing Water*

and high-velocity winds with extended duration.[59] In recent times, severe droughts in Somalia occurred on several occasions in 1964, 1969, 1974, 1987, 1988, 2000, 2001, 2004, 2008, 2011, and 2017.[60] Scientists have found that the accelerated frequency of drought, which occurred during the 2000s, was likely caused by anthropogenic climate change.

Consistent with regional climate trends that affected both Syria and Nigeria, the summer months of 2011 brought one of the worst droughts in over six decades to the Horn of Africa. Neighboring countries, including Kenya, Somalia, Ethiopia, Eritrea, and Djibouti, all suffered.[61]

Key factors can explain the relative severity of the drought in Somalia: several preceding seasons with very low rainfall, a total failure of the October–November 2010 *deyr* rains, and meager April–June 2011 *gu* rainfall. These conditions amplified regional aridity, which was particularly severe and led to "the worst annual crop production in 17 years, excess animal mortality, and very high food prices."[62] The food security situation was austere and at a breaking point. In this case, the UN famine declaration came in late July 2011 when the drought was reaching its peak. Over 3.7 million people eventually faced a humanitarian crisis, which was felt throughout the country but manifested predominantly in the southern part of Somalia.[63]

Again coincident with regional trends in Africa and the Middle East, a severe drought struck in 2017. Some areas of Somalia experienced the driest conditions in a century.[64] Similar to 2011, this drought resulted from poor performance of the *gu* rains, which led to a third consecutive below-normal rainy season. The results were depletion of pasturelands and water resources for pastoralists in central Somalia and devastation in the farmlands of southern Somalia.[65] The droughts of 2011 and 2017 stand out as major inflection points because of their environmental impacts. They also drove the rapid disintegration of the country's social fabric that has resulted in a perpetual cycle of internal violence that continues to this day.

Climate Change

Because of its geographical location and other societal factors that limit its resilience, Somalia cannot withstand many climate change impacts. The scientific consensus is that rising temperatures, greater frequency and intensity of droughts, and extreme weather events will affect the entire Horn of Africa in the next decades. On balance, these changes will register negative impacts on both environmental and human systems that will be felt very deeply in Somalia.

Droughts are the most immediate and visceral impact of climate change in Somalia as compared to, say, sea level rise. The foremost indicators connecting the changing climate to the worsening of droughts are rising temperatures, scarce rainfall, and unpredictable rainfall patterns.[66]

In Somalia, the compounding impacts of climate change are especially dangerous. Consider the situation of sudden onset of cyclones or massive rain events that lead to flooding and dislocation of populations occurring in the midst of a longer period of drought emergency.

Temperature extremes are common. Evidence shows that human-induced climate change has led to increased warming across Africa. Regional climate models of East Africa indicate an average temperature increase in all four representative scenarios.[67] Likewise, land surface temperatures along southern Somalia's coast have been extremely high, far above the recent ten-year average temperatures.[68] In light of these indicators, scientists are confident that climate change will magnify current stress on water availability by increasing desertification and decreasing crop yields. Combined with nonclimate drivers, climate change impacts are also very likely to amplify existing agriculture system vulnerability in semiarid areas of the continent, including the Sahel.[69] These trends are accelerating. As of 2016, eastern Kenya and southern Somalia were dry for ten out of the past sixteen years compared to historical averages.[70]

Researchers at the University of Notre Dame's Global Adaptation Index (ND-GAIN) applied their analytic method to Somalia despite some deficiencies in the gathered data. They found that Somalia's vulnerability to climate change and its readiness to deal with the impacts—also referred to as resilience—placed Somalia in a much worse position than other arid countries, including, for example, Nigeria. In fact, Somalia's GAIN score placed it dead last out of more than 170 nations for which data is available.[71] As in other nations, the connection between climate change and societal impacts and poor security outcomes in Somalia is complicated yet meaningful.

A 2012 report on global water security issued by the US intelligence community judged that in the coming decades countries with weak political institutions and climate-induced threats to food security will experience an increased risk of social disruption, migration, or large-scale political instability.[72] Nearly ten years later, the events that continue to unfold in Somalia demonstrate all three of these outcomes. The US intelligence community's forecast was prescient for the Somali people; the results are devastating.

Systemic Impacts of Water Stress

Weakened Rural Livelihoods

Rural agriculture is the cornerstone of the Somali economy. Animal husbandry accounts for over 50 percent of export earnings and around 40 percent of GDP.[73] Severe drought in Somalia has led to food shortages, and the dramatic decreases in water availability have crippled agricultural production and hampered livestock rearing across the country.

More than 60 percent of the population depend on the livestock sector for food and income.[74] The majority of livestock raised for export are sheep and goats. Generally, the agricultural sector makes up 15 to 20 percent of GDP even though only 35 percent of Somali land is arable, which places monumental strain on water resources.[75] In 2014, an astonishing 99.48 percent of the total freshwater withdrawal for the country was destined for agricultural uses compared to only 0.45 percent for domestic uses.[76] Despite agriculture's reliance on water, unlike in most other arid countries, irrigation is not widespread in Somalia. Here about 90 percent of all cultivated land is directly rain-fed, and the rest is under irrigation.[77]

Given these factors, the impacts of lack of rainfall associated with the droughts of 2011 and 2017 are hard to overstate. The two droughts caused upheaval throughout the economy with dramatic spikes in agricultural prices. The 2011 drought resulted in the worst annual crop production in seventeen years and excessive animal mortality.[78]

As of September 2017, the major crop-producing region of southern Somalia saw 37 percent lower cereal production than the long-term (1995–2016) average. A more dramatic change took place in the country's northwest, where the harvest was 87 percent lower than the 2010–2016 average. Higher-than-average local prices for cereals persisted in the years after the 2017 drought along with significant livestock losses.

Somalia is home to large communities of pastoralists whose livelihoods depend on herding livestock, and they are found in all regions of the country. Goat and sheep herders are most common in the north. The southern regions, on the other hand, are home to people who pursue agro-pastoral livelihoods, where they cultivate the land to support higher densities of cattle and camel herds.[79]

Pastoralists in both areas account for roughly 60 percent of Somalia's population. Profits from this sector make up almost 40 percent of Somalia's GDP and more than half of the country's exports.[80, 81] Drought impacts pastoralists directly, leading to poor grazing, lack of drinking water, and massive livestock casualties. During the drought in 2016–2017, pastoralists commonly lost up to 90 percent of their herds. These herders were then pushed into internally displaced peoples (IDPs) camps where they lived in substandard shelters built of rocks and sticks or tarpaulin tents. When this drought-sensitive sector is hit hard in Somalia, people have no formal coping mechanisms to fall back on because a functional central government is lacking. In Somalia, any semblance of a public safety net is absent, so coping measures used in other places, such as drought-based credit and insurance, are mostly out of reach to Somali agriculturalists.[82]

Therefore, herders' most common response in times of drought is to reduce their herds, also called destocking. This practice can lead to sharply declining livestock prices, as large numbers of households sell their animals on already strained local markets. The depression of livestock prices reduces herders' income and purchasing power, which is in turn already diminished by drought-induced spikes in staple food prices.[83] In turn, lower livestock exports resulting from drought have contributed to a fall in foreign exchange earnings. The subsequent problems of declining herd sizes combined with low birth rates, low conception rates, and low milk production in many pastoralist zones are projected to continue.[84] Regional trade barriers, including frequent import bans by Arab gulf countries based on communicable disease concerns, compound these pressures.[85]

Water-Related Illness

Poor water conditions are also inimical to human health. Factors such as severe flooding in Somalia magnify the threat of waterborne illness. In January 2017, acute watery diarrhea (AWD) and cholera outbreaks took place in thirteen of the country's eighteen regions owing to a lack of safe drinking water.[86] The death toll has since increased as lack of clean water has led to Somalia's largest cholera outbreak in five years.[87]

Cholera is an acute diarrheal disease caused by drinking water contaminated with *Vibrio cholerae* bacteria. Susceptibility to waterborne disease is further intensified in times of reduced access to clean water because those suffering from malnutrition have less resilience, making them more susceptible to other diseases as well.[88] Women and children are the most vulnerable to poor water quality in Somalia. In the last three years, most people who have died from cholera have been under the age of five.[89] Alongside the ravages of this infectious disease, the worst measles outbreak took place in Somalia, with 14,800 cases reported between January and July 2017.[90]

166   *Weaponizing Water*

Physical vulnerability associated with poor water conditions also increases with the onerous task of fetching water from long distances. This is often a gender-based problem. As traditional caretakers of the household in Somali culture, women and girls are responsible for traveling long distances to fetch water, putting them at risk of physical and sexual assault.

Flooding

Flood damage is a near constant factor in Somalia. For example, in 2015 heavy rains hit south-central Somalia, an area already vulnerable to environmental stress from civil war. At this time, the Shabelle River flooded its banks. That year, El Niño was one of the strongest on record and is thought to have augmented the amount of rain that fell in the Horn of Africa.[91] Damages to roads, bridges, and airstrips disrupted humanitarian aid delivery to those in need. Without aid reaching markets, local food prices rose. As the waters rose, creating unsanitary conditions, the cases of waterborne diseases like AWD and cholera soared in over two-thirds of the regions in south-central Somalia. At the end of November, the flooding had internally displaced around 60,000 people.[92]

May 2016 was another instance when heavy precipitation in the Ethiopian highlands caused the River Shabelle to flood. In Beledweyne, the damage was extensive. Small businesses, on which much of the community depended, were submerged, homes and crops were destroyed, and access to fields was blocked for extended periods.[93] Around June, cereal costs doubled from US $0.70 to $1.50, and destroyed infrastructure at the local hospital worsened conditions.[94] Between May and June, thousands of people were displaced, the majority of whom moved to Beledweyne to escape conflict in neighboring districts. After the flood, an estimated 30,000 people lacked food and drinking water.[95]

Extreme changes in weather are showing no signs of abatement. The country was hit by a double climate disaster in summer 2021. Drought had been declared in April and then torrential rains hit Somalia and the Ethiopian highlands. From the highlands, water streamed into Somalia, displacing at least 166,000 people. Drought followed by heavy rains that cause flooding raise concerns for humanitarian organizations working to provide aid.[96]

Famine

In 2011, famine occurred in Somalia in part as a result of conflict in the southern and central regions of the country. The conflict intensified the famine by hindering traditional coping mechanisms for drought and limiting access for humanitarian agencies providing aid. The neighboring countries of Ethiopia and Kenya had benefited from superior early warning and early response systems, which allowed them to better respond to the drought.[97] In Somalia, although experts issued drought warnings in 2010, international action did not occur until famine was formally declared in 2011.

That year the United Nations did not declare a famine until three criteria were met: the occurrence of extreme food shortages that affected at least 20 percent of households with a limited ability to cope; acute malnutrition rates among children above 30 percent; and more than two people per 10,000 dying per day.[98]

In southern Somalia, however, the death rate had already reached three times this level.[99] Even with the UN reporting that food security outcomes in Somalia were the worst globally, partly because of delayed international responses, 260,000 Somalis perished, representing approximately 4.6 percent of the total population.[100] Some aspects of the disaster were man-made. A 2010 United Nations Security Council report obtained by the *New York Times* indicated that up to half of the food aid sent to Somalia was pilfered away from those in need primarily by al-Shabaab, but local UN staff and corrupt government officials were also accused.[101]

Humanitarian agencies continued to warn about a changing environment and a failed harvest in 2011. By June of that year, an exodus was well underway, with Somalis crossing into Ethiopia and northern Kenya to escape the famine. A late relief campaign was finally initiated, prompted by reports of children abandoned by the side of the road as a result of the mass movement across the border. The UN declared a famine over six regions and a humanitarian emergency in others. However, workers from the nongovernmental organization (NGO) CARE and the UN World Food Programme faced pushback in the region, where al-Shabaab accused them of being spies and working with the Somali government. Aid efforts were thwarted that included the distribution of water, which al-Shabaab banned these agencies from carrying out.[102]

In 2017, conditions had deteriorated to the point where international aid officials described the state of Somalia as one of the greatest humanitarian disasters since World War II. A tangle of political, economic, social, and environmental conditions had intersected and combined to create a tragic situation. Moreover, a weak central government, informal economy, and complex demographic conditions resulted in poor water management, limited economic capital, and

168   *Weaponizing Water*

additional stresses on available water resources. The high levels of instability in the country, coupled with abnormally high temperatures and increased frequency of drought, were a lethal combination. As of February 2017, more than 4 percent of the total population had perished.[103] As of August 2017, 6.2 million people needed aid, 388,000 children were acutely malnourished, and over 87,000 children were severely malnourished.[104]

It is remarkable that a regional drought led to famine only in Somalia even as a wider region of Africa was subjected to the same conditions. Indigenous factors that compounded the impacts of the drought include poor governance, interclan and extremist violence, inflated food and water prices, and inadequate foreign aid reaching the most remote places.

Human Responses

Somalia's droughts continue to decimate rural livelihoods, which causes affected populations to turn to other pursuits that are destructive to the natural environment, such as charcoal manufacturing, banditry, and livestock raiding.[105] The charcoal trade contributes to deforestation and environmental degradation, and the revenue from this activity has sparked conflict among the clans. As noted, al-Shabaab ultimately controls most of the charcoal trade in Somalia, and the revenue supports its terrorist activities.[106]

The Charcoal Trade

The environmental impact of the charcoal trade is dramatic. Whereas forests represented about 13 percent of Somalia's land area in 1990, they covered only about 10.7 percent in 2010, with signs of deforestation rates accelerating in recent years.[107] Furthermore, it has been estimated that al-Shabaab reaps between $38 million and $56 million annually from charcoal exports and $8 million to $18 million annually mainly from taxing charcoal traders at roadblocks and checkpoints. This makes charcoal one of the group's main sources of income but also an issue of conflict with clan members who also ply the trade. Aside from supporting extremism, charcoal production has become an important source of income for many in the rural populations affected by environmental hardship, displacement, and conflict. Left with few alternatives, more and more pastoralists turn to charcoal trading to survive.

Charcoal trading is also at the heart of a vicious cycle of environmental degradation, depleted livelihoods, and further cutting of trees, accelerated by and exacerbating the local impacts of climate change. In order to tackle these issues, the federal government and international organizations are trying to not only restrict charcoal exports from Somalia but also implement programs to reduce local charcoal consumption and promote alternative livelihoods.

A 2011 spike in maritime piracy along the Somalian coast also connects to environmental degradation. That year, the European Union Naval Force Somalia (EUNAVFOR) reported 176 attacks and twenty-five vessels pirated. Somali pirates held dozens of merchant ships and hundreds of hostages.[108] General Thomas Waldhauser, the Marine officer leading the US Africa Command at that time, and other analysts cited the destructive economic consequences of widespread drought and famine in the region as a reason for the uptick in piracy.[109] Others attribute the uptick at least in part to declining fish stocks, another environmental problem.

Illegal fishing by foreign fleets in Somali coastal waters was the final aggravating factor that caused the pirates to begin to refer to themselves as the Somali Coast Guard. US Africa Command's coordination with navies of other countries that were effected by piracy successfully reduced the initial wave of piracy in 2011. However, after a few years of calm, the year 2017, a time coincident with the second severe drought, saw a slight resurgence in piracy. In May and April 2017, there were five or six attacks.[110]

The desperation of those times is reflected by the fact that only sporadic incidents of piracy off the Somalia coast have occurred since 2017. In more recent years, attacks were few and far between compared to the height of Somali piracy. Today the numbers have dropped to nearly zero thanks in part to the international naval forces patrolling the area and the use of armed guards on merchant vessels but also coincident with some improvement in the Somali people's environmental conditions since the drought.[111]

Migration and Displacement

In 2011, the number of Somali refugees and internally displaced persons grew sharply with the exodus across borders.[112] As of 2016, Somalia had 1.1 million IDPs.[113] Over 879,000 registered Somali refugees have crossed borders, the majority residing in neighboring countries. More than 250,000 Somali refugees are in Kenya, Yemen, and Ethiopia.[114]

170   *Weaponizing Water*

Somali refugees in Yemen are one factor eroding the security situation in that country, which already faces extreme scarcity based on environmental conditions and a severe ongoing civil war. Other regional countries are facing their own challenges with resource allocation, governance, and sometimes insurgency. Cross-border migration was a key reason that Kenya sent troops to Somalia, which became deeply embroiled in the country's conflict, in an attempt to close the border to Somalis trying to leave their country.[115]

Water Weaponization

A large body of research has found that droughts in Somalia have both direct and indirect impacts on the number of local conflicts, especially those involving rival clans. As is the case in Nigeria, and indeed across the Sahel, the scarcity of water has compelled nomadic herders to venture farther south in Somalia with their herds, where clashes often ensue over use of the land occupied by established farming communities.[116]

Because of many factors, not the least of which is accelerating environmental degradation, clashes between clans have escalated in Somalia in recent years, although this belligerence is by no means a new development. An estimated 95 percent of southern Somalia's network of wells were filled in with rocks or otherwise destroyed during the interclan violence of the 1990s.[117]

Clan hostilities around water were renewed in 2013, when heavy fighting erupted in the central part of the country. The rival Dir and Hawadle clans advanced competing claims on irrigable land near the village of Deefow.[118] The ensuing interclan conflict resulted in the death of more than 100 people and the displacement of 9,000 others.[119] By limiting the availability of essential resources, water scarcity drives local communities such as the Sa'ad and Suleiman of the Habar Gidir clans into fierce competition for access to wells and grazing land.[120] There is little doubt, therefore, that the clans weaponize water on a local level, though these local instances of water weaponization are disparate and hard to track.

Al-Shabaab's weaponization of water in Somalia remains a distinct issue given the historical role of water as a root of conflict among pastoralists and farmers and clans at the local level. Water stress is a catalyst for conflict in Somalia on several levels, and its role as a driver for extremist violence, including water weaponization, is examined in depth here.

Al-Shabaab and the Water Weapon

As with the other case studies in this volume, the insurgent group's attacks on water infrastructure and manipulation of water resources became routine strategies employed in the larger war in Somalia from roughly 2011 to 2017 but led to human suffering on a scale not matched elsewhere. In the following pages, I intend to chronicle water weaponization by al-Shabaab in detail. I have separated this narrative from that of the parallel and constant clashes between clans over water resources, which have also led to significant casualties and deaths across the country. However, in the violent and chaotic milieu of the conflict in Somalia, usage of the water weapon may overlap between al-Shabaab and clans. The cycle of water stress and conflict that originates as the physical impacts of climate change and drought wreaked havoc on social structures and human security, which set the stage for violence that was itself characterized by the use of the water weapon.

First, it is important to consider that the areas around the two main rivers in Somalia, the Shabelle and the Jubba, have long been strongholds of al-Shabaab, providing the group with easy access to water. These rivers factor prominently in the group's strategic use of water. Baardheere, a city that sits on the Jubba River, served as a main stronghold of al-Shabaab from 2009 to 2015, allowing the group to control major trading routes in and out of northern Kenya. In addition to the virtual capture of these trade routes, the militants occupied the city itself for a considerable amount of time. In doing so, they were able to deny people from adjacent government-controlled areas the ability to fetch water from the main supply, which lay in the city itself.

Strategic Weaponization

On the strategic level, al-Shabaab used the water weapon on a grander scale and to a more deadly effect on civilian populations than did the Islamic State (IS) or Boko Haram. The group established virtual control over large geographies and, accordingly, al-Shabaab's manipulation of natural resources and humanitarian assistance provides the most vivid and largest-scale example of strategic water weaponization in comparison to IS and Boko Haram. The group's actions center around the droughts of 2011 and 2017 and the ensuing famines. Although the al-Shabaab insurgent campaign and the famines were generally well documented, water weaponization is lesser known.

As stated earlier, the 2011 drought encompassed much of the Middle East and North Africa region, but famine was not widespread. The severity and duration of the famine in Somalia was in some ways due to al-Shabaab's deliberate actions. In November 2011, the group officially banned international organizations and nongovernmental organizations from providing famine relief in its zones of control.

In addition to being a transparent and blatant attempt to subjugate the Somali people, these restrictions also arose in part from the group's ideology, which viewed international organizations as puppets of the West, a view shared almost universally by jihadist groups. Al-Shabaab accused these organizations of misappropriating funds, promoting secularism and democratic values, and conspiring to convert Muslim children to Christianity. This type of thinking provided the impetus for al-Shabaab's campaign to assassinate humanitarian workers.

Al-Shabaab's embargo, while aimed at foodstuffs, was intrinsically damaging to the provision of water too, which is distributed through the same networks. In fact, these actions against foodstuffs were directly related to water in several ways. First, food aid in the form of grains, for example, are very water-intensive to cultivate. Also, high-energy biscuits and grains, the standard items distributed by many relief organizations, must be mixed with water to be palatable and edible. It is also significant that direct food provision and safe access to water, sanitation, and hygiene (WASH) are generally bundled together by aid programs such as those administered by the US Agency for International Development (USAID). If access to an area is denied, then neither element of the relief program can be provided. Finally, the comprehensive ban on international agencies prevented aid workers from entering al-Shabaab territory to dig boreholes near the camps for internally displaced people, where misery had spread because of lack of access to potable water sources.

Al-Shabaab's long-time neglect and lack of strategy or policies for allocating water resources under its control played a role in the tragedy. For over five years, al-Shabaab failed to regulate the use of wells, maintain water infrastructure including canal systems, or fix wells damaged in the civil war in lands it controlled.[121] This neglect contributed greatly to the group's inability to provide water in local communities and eroded its status. The group's reputation was further sullied by the fact that it violated traditional pastoral customs. Al-Shabaab seized and incorporated areas where nomadic herders would traditionally move on to, away from unproductive land, a centuries-old coping mechanism against the effects of droughts, that the extremist organization ended.

Finally, al-Shabaab contributed directly to desertification. Its felling of sparse forests to produce charcoal for trade were especially destructive at a time when the demand for potable water was increasing. In 2011, this was among a series of miscalculations and deliberate harmful interventions that alienated the general population upon which the group would otherwise rely for sympathy and recruits. These missteps exacerbated a political split that was emerging within al-Shabaab itself.

The drought that struck Somalia in 2017 was a crescendo in the complex emergency that had been evident in the country perhaps as far back as 1991. The Somalia situation easily met the UN's definition of a complex emergency: a situation of disrupted life produced by warfare and large-scale movements of people and where emergency response must be carried out in a difficult political and security environment.

In response, the next year marked the beginning of Operation Restore Hope, a US-led UN-sanctioned operation that created a military task force charged with carrying out United Nations Security Council Resolution 794. The resolution aimed to protect humanitarian famine relief operations in the southern part of the country. In addition to the threat posed by al-Shabaab, food shipments had to be transported across territory that was controlled by dozens of rival factions with various clan affiliations. Troops on the ground were targets along with aid ships and even cargo aircraft. Aid workers were targeted for assassination.

For Western aid workers, the renewed assassinations undoubtedly brought back bitter memories of the events that unfolded in 1991. On September 25, 1991, a US Black Hawk helicopter was shot down by Somali forces, leading to a battle that eventually claimed the lives of eighteen US soldiers. In response, President Bill Clinton ordered troops to withdraw from Somalia to prevent any more casualties. However, this withdrawal had dire implications for humanitarian response in Somalia because the ensuing conflict destroyed basic infrastructure and made it dangerous for aid groups to provide necessary resources.

Understandably, the events of 1991 may have informed the international community's hesitation in use of force to protect aid shipments for successful intervention. In any case, such military force might not have been necessary because al-Shabaab seemed to have learned its lesson from its 2011 debacle. Instead, the group wielded the water weapon strategically as a tool of incentivization to placate the population rather than to cause widespread misery. Rather than obstructing aid, the militants moved quickly to establish drought committees and distribute aid in several

174   *Weaponizing Water*

regions under their control, including Bay, Bakol, Mudug, Hiraan, and Galguduug. On at least one occasion, the group made a media spectacle of digging canals to help farmers gain access to water for irrigation.[122]

According to the group's pronouncements, al-Shabaab also spent about $2 million to dig new canals in Bulo Mareer, a town in Somalia's Lower Shabelle Province, along with others like it in that region of south and central Somalia.[123] The militants established twelve water distribution centers in March and April 2017 alone.

The organization's leadership appreciated the fact that the group's limited actions to improve human conditions would have a disproportionate impact compared to that of the Federal Government of Somalia and outside humanitarian organizations. Al-Shabaab was acutely aware that, as an insurgent group, it did not need to meet all the basic requirements for sustaining the population in order to gain large propaganda benefits from its charitable actions, whereas the Somali federal government's inability to provide comprehensive services to its people further undermined its shaky authority.[124]

The 2017 situation was exacerbated by the fact that relief organizations were, once again, slow to respond to the disaster. The international community's slow humanitarian response also created an opportunity that al-Shabaab was more than happy to exploit. The delay in outside aid gave al-Shabaab's leadership time to rethink its actions in 2011. A regional expert at the Atlantic Council, an American think tank, observed of al-Shabaab: "This is a resilient group. They do learn their lessons" and "the militants learned that part of their [previous] military defeat was due to the improved training of the peacekeeping force that opposed them, but also their own handling of the 2011 famine."[125]

A change in the organization's leadership structure was another factor that may have contributed to al-Shabaab's shift in strategies. Ahmed Abdi Godane, the emir who oversaw the organization in 2011, was killed in a US airstrike in 2014 and Ahmed Omar took over. Godane hailed from northern Somalia, whereas most al-Shabaab fighters are southerners, with clan and family links to areas where the 2017 drought hit hardest. Ahmed Omar and his deputy Mukhtar Robow were from Kismayo and the Bay regions, respectively—both in the south of the country. They were undoubtedly sensitive to the drought's effects on their kin.

The results of al-Shabaab's new strategy of benevolence were a mixed bag. On the one hand, it is possible that al-Shabaab gained more adherents either through the gratitude or desperation of impacted populations, who had limited choices. On the other hand, it can be said that the benefit of these gains in new adherents paled against the overall humanitarian losses created by the epic misery of the situation. More than 250,000 people perished, and waves of people migrated away from al-Shabaab-controlled regions.

Also, it must be emphasized that whatever funds al-Shabaab possessed to buy food supplies had been raised largely through the Zakat at a time when people could least afford the payment. Some sources also suggested, unsurprisingly, that al-Shabaab was directly pilfering the aid agencies' food supplies and equipment.[126] Collection of the Zakat was then a double-edged sword because, though it was lucrative, it also led to more human suffering. The UN reported that by February 2017, thousands of women and children had fled to the Bay and Bakol regions and into Ethiopia to avoid the Zakat, the payment of which required money, which many were unable to provide, or the seizure of food, animals, and land.[127]

Al-Shabaab's provision of humanitarian assistance, although significant, was not on a scale necessary to change the realities on the ground for the vast majority of displaced and starving people. The scope of the group's aid to perhaps a few hundred families at a time was paltry in the face of the needs of an estimated 6 million people, according to UN data, but this was hardly the point.

It is tempting to view the militants' distribution of food and water assistance as a simple propaganda stunt, but a wider view is that the gesture was critical and indeed strategic. Militarily, al-Shabaab was on the defensive and scattered across rural areas where they had sought refuge. Their distribution of aid allowed them to return to the cities and reestablish influence.

Al-Shabaab's actions during the 2011 and 2017 famines can be categorized as strategic water weaponization, the intentions and results of which were diametrically opposed in each case. In both cases the water weapon was imperfect in that it caused a lot of collateral damage and was difficult to control. But, in the end, it was a powerful asset at a time when the organization needed to recover from setbacks on the battlefield.

Tactical Water Weaponization

Herein, tactical weaponization is generally defined as the use of water against targets of strictly military value in the battlespace. Instances of al-Shabaab's use of the water weapon on the tactical level were less numerous than, for example, those of ISIS in Syria. Water weaponization can't be considered a normal part of the extremists' battlefield doctrine, per se, but there are several significant examples of its use.

176   *Weaponizing Water*

Destroying water sources was a tactic favored by al-Shabaab fighters. Al-Shabaab used weaponization of water in attempts to halt the advances of enemy troops on at least three instances. As early as 2012, residents reported that al-Shabaab had worked to hamper the movements of Somali national army troops and Kenyan forces by attacking water trucks traveling by convoy through the areas that the group controlled. Al-Shabaab also destroyed levees along the Shebelle River in Somalia to make roads unusable by opposing military forces. The group regularly attempted to cut off water supply to enemy forces by various methods, including burying bore wells, destroying infrastructure, and generally restricting access to the Jubba River.[128]

The areas around the two transboundary rivers, Jubba and Shabelle, have been traditional strongholds of al-Shabaab. The group has also used the rivers to its advantage on the tactical as well as strategic level. The opportunity to do so came during an engagement with US forces. In June 2018, an American Special Forces unit was conducting a multiday operation to liberate villages in Lower Jubba from al-Shabaab control and establish what they characterized as "a permanent combat outpost designed to increase the span of Federal Government of Somalia (FGS) security and governance."[129]

In response to these maneuvers, al-Shabaab diverted water from the Jubba River to flood the area under surveillance, forcing the US military to move the site of the planned outpost by two kilometers. As the opposing forces relocated, al-Shabaab gunmen set an ambush that killed an American soldier. This was an extremely rare US battlefield death in Africa, the first since another US Special Forces soldier had been killed by Islamic extremists in an ambush in Niger in October 2017, and it raised a good amount of consternation in US military planning circles.[130] The Jubba corridor action was especially significant because it forced AMISOM to change its operational plans to an extent that was unprecedented by other attempts to weaponize water.

Al-Shabaab's actions before the attack were environmentally and economically destructive to the surrounding region. Two weeks earlier, al-Shabaab militants had taken measures to protect their access to the river by bringing in reinforcements from surrounding villages. They swapped their military uniforms for civilian clothing and dug out the banks to create a pseudo-dam.[131] As a result, water from the river flooded the surrounding area and farms became wetlands. Fruit and vegetable prices soared fivefold in the nearby city of Kismayo.

Water weaponization also became an inherent part of al-Shabaab's siege tactics. In June 2012, al-Shabaab staged an attack on the town El

Adde in the Gedoa region that was occupied by Kenyan and TFG forces and destroyed the town's sole water pump. According to reports, al-Shabaab either intended to affect the coalition forces directly and drive them from the area or to put pressure on the population to ask the forces to leave.[132]

Al-Shabaab's approach to tactical water weaponization is illustrated by its use against AMISOM forces. In 2012, al-Shabaab sabotaged water infrastructure in Jana Cabdalla, an area approximately 40 kilometers outside Kismayo, to halt the advance of Kenyan soldiers under AMISOM command who were marching toward the city. Al-Shabaab insurgents dropped poison in one well and vandalized pipes from another with the purpose of denying water supply to the troops. This time, their attempts were not successful: AMISON dispatched air support and vehicles to supply water to the Kenyan troops on the front line.[133]

In another incident in August 2018, al-Shabaab used canal locks to divert the flow of the River Shabelle and flooded the area in the Qoryooley district to stop the advance of AMISOM forces.[134] While this action was immediately successful against AMISOM, the diverted river displaced hundreds of families. Like previous weaponization actions, the diverted river also inundated surrounding farmland during planting season.

Al-Shabaab's tactical use of the water weapon against water supplies also backfired in much the same way that strategic use had during the drought of 2011. Both caused what can be framed as unintended collateral damage to vulnerable populations. In February 2017, almost three dozen people were killed and more than twenty other Somalis, mostly women and children, were in critical condition after drinking from well water poisoned by al-Shabaab in the southwestern city of Baidoa. The poisoning of the well was a suspected attempt to stop government soldiers from drinking the water. Nonetheless, civilian casualties were inflicted because it was the only source of potable water in the area.[135]

Although al-Shabaab was the main perpetrator of water weaponization and IS also employed the tactic, water weaponization was not exclusive to jihadist organizations. Other organizations occasionally employed the water weapon, especially for tactical gains. The Ethiopian army was complicit on at least two occasions. The first example predates the drought of 2011 by half of a decade. In 2006, al-Shabaab and the Ethiopian army had their largest battle to date near the town of Idale. It lasted over three days and each side made the denial of the other's access to water reservoirs its top priority.[136] Another example of state-sanctioned

178   Weaponizing Water

use of the water weapon came during the 2017 drought. Ethiopian forces initiated an attack on a key water source used by al-Shabaab, leading to further fighting in the Bulo Burto District of Hiiraan.[137]

The ascendant Islamic State in Africa also employed the water weapon on a tactical basis. In 2017, the group cut off the water supply for the Bari community in Somalia during a violent confrontation with Puntland security forces.[138] The conflict that erupted between IS and al-Shabaab in 2018 featured a clash over water. Then, on February 1, 2019, al-Shabaab seized control of El-Miraale, a critical water source in the northeastern Somali region of Bari where IS has established its regional base. The water point had been the focus of clashes between al-Shabaab and pro-IS forces in Puntland.[139] Al-Shabaab has fought IS not only for territory but also for the ability to collect extortion money from Somali business owners.[140]

Water Terrorism

Al-Shabaab's use of the water weapon in sieges was a blunt tool of terror against the general population. The first use followed a string of territorial losses in 2014, when al-Shabaab began to cut off water supplies to cities liberated by opposing forces. Garbaherey, a city in the southern part of the country, was a victim. Somali government forces had already retaken control of Garbaherey when al-Shabaab snuck into the town at night and buried the main borehole that provided water to the city.

Al-Shabaab had a virtual grip on the territory because it also controlled the nearby city of Badheere along the Jubba River, the closest alternative water source. The liberated city of Hudur in southwest Somalia was also in a crisis. Like in Garbaherey, al-Shabaab controlled access to the water supplies outside the city. Al-Shabaab was once again able to exert influence by denying access to water in an area that was not under the group's immediate control.[141]

The deliberate targeting of water infrastructure is another form of water terrorism. As AMISOM troops began to liberate El Bur in 2014, al-Shabaab retaliated by stealing power generators and ransacking two power stations, including water pumps.[142] During its retreat, al-Shabaab managed to fill the local wells with rocks and thieve the generators that provided electricity. The Turkish Red Crescent, alongside the Somali government, stepped in to donate food aid and water pumps to the town, but they were unable to save many vulnerable elderly residents, who perished from thirst.[143]

Also in 2014, al-Shabaab played on popular fears about the safety and security of drinking water. The contaminated water extracted from a well in northern Mogadishu resulted in a mass casualty incident where 50 Somalis were killed and 150 were hospitalized. Officials implicated al-Shabaab in the attack, but the action was not necessarily attributable to the group.[144] Responsibility for an incident in 2017 was clearer. Al-Shabaab poisoned a water hole in Baidoa, killing 32 people, mostly women and children.[145] Likewise, in December 2017, al-Shabaab militants destroyed an important water well that had been drilled by the Kenyan army in the town of Lafey, Mandera County, leaving hundreds of residents without water.[146]

The Somali government has also been involved in the fighting. In November 2014, conflict erupted between local government militias and clans in Galguduud, killing fifteen and injuring at least twenty others. Once again, clan militias were heavily armed and clashed over historical and agricultural land disputes in the region.[147] Overall, there were approximately twenty-six reported incidents of water weaponization in Somalia between 2012 and 2019 that involved either al-Shabaab or clans (see Table 4.2).

Radicalization

The connections between drought conditions and increased violence, suffering, and radicalization in Somalia are relatively clear. On June 25, 2016, a bomb was detonated outside a hotel in the Somali capital of Mogadishu. Immediately following the detonation, gunmen stormed the building and killed at least fourteen people.[148] The targeted building was known to be frequented by government ministers, lawmakers, and Somali business leaders.

Among those killed was Buri Hamza, Somalia's top environmental official. Only a month earlier, Hamza had spoken with journalists on the issue of the connection between extremism and Somalia's environmental problems. Hamza stressed that climate change had made these problems worse, adding "The fact that many of our youth have lost jobs because of desertification, deforestation . . . It's not the only cause, of course, of radicalization, but this is one of the major causes of radicalization because of the linkages between violence and environmental degradation."[149]

Broadly speaking, drought-induced hardship is an important factor supporting successful al-Shabaab recruitment. As noted, this was

180 *Weaponizing Water*

Table 4.2 Summary of Water Weaponization Incidents in Somalia (2012–2019)

Weaponization Type	Location	Perpetrators	Date
Strategic	Widespread in southern Somalia	al-Shabaab	2011 and 2017
Tactical	Shabelle River	al-Shabaab	8/2018
	Jubba River	al-Shabaab	6/2018
	Baidoa	al-Shabaab	2/2017
	Bulo Burto/Hilran	al-Shabaab/ Ethiopia	2017
	Lafey	al-Shabaab	2017
	Bari	Islamic State in Africa/Puntland Forces	2017
	Shabelle River	al-Shabaab	2014
	El Adde Town	al-Shabaab	6/2012
		al-Shabaab	2012
	Idale	al-Shabaab/ Ethiopia	
Psychological Terror	Baidoa	al-Shabaab	2017
	Garbaherey	al-Shabaab	?
	Hudur	al-Shabaab	?
	El Bur	al-Shabaab	2014
	Mogadishu	al-Shabaab	2014
	Bay Region	al-Shabaab	2013
	Kismayo	al-Shabaab	2012
Incentivization	Lower Shabelle	al-Shabaab	2013
Unintentional			2011/2017 *see strategic*
Trigger for Conflict	El-Miraale, Bari	al-Shabaab/Islamic State in Africa	2019
	Garowe	Clans	2017
	Gaalkacyo	Clans	2017
	Hirran	Clans	2015
	Galgaduud	Clans	2014
	Lower Jubba	Clans	2012
Total Incidents		26	

frequently the case among al-Shabaab fighters who hailed from the south with clan and family links to areas where the drought hit hardest. However, drought is never the sole or even the primary reason for the proliferation of violent extremism at the subnational level. Drought interacts with other numerous structural drivers of violence.

Rather than rely on the opinions of government ministers, the best way to understand the motivations of the fighters is to listen to their narratives. Two security analysts, Botha and Abdil, conducted a study of radicalization based on a series of interviews of al-Shabaab members in 2014. Their study found that, not surprisingly, 39 percent of the interviewees cited economic reasons as their primary motivation for joining al-Shabaab.[150] Looking more deeply, economic hardship can be a second-order consequence of isolated environmental forcing factors specifically or factors that act in conjunction with non-economic circumstances.

Al-Shabaab bolsters its ranks by preying on individuals who are reeling from decimated pastoral livelihoods. Offering basic protection, food, and money to attract recruits has proved starkly effective. This story is illustrated by the words of this former al-Shabaab warfighter, who was interviewed for the study:

> I was working hard, but during the last days the farm wasn't producing well, and I consulted some of my friends, some family members, and I decided to join them. When I joined them there was no more taxation imposed against me. And I felt like now—how should I put?—I feel like I'm now a blessed person, because I have enough things to eat.[151]

Another poignant story comes from Halima, a disabled single mother from War Dararow, a town in central Somalia. She recounts how Somali government and AMISOM troops liberated the town. Al-Shabaab withdrew to neighboring rural areas but was still able to cut off War Dararow's water supply. It was because of these desperate conditions that Halima sent her oldest boy to fetch water from the closest well, which had fallen under the control of al-Shabaab. Halima recounted what happened next:

> I kept on waiting for him, but he did not come back. Twenty days later I learned that he was recruited by al-Shabaab. They have occupied all the routes to the city, and we cannot get water nor can we get food, and whenever we send out children to get us water . . . they don't come back.[152]

In Somalia, conditions of water stress that was man-made, in this case, played a greater role in enabling extremist recruitment than was the case with IS in Iraq and Syria. The relationship is more analogous to Boko Haram's successful recruitment among the beleaguered and non-resident populace of Nigeria.

Conclusion

In Somalia, the confluence of water stress and instability mutually reinforce each other to the detriment of effective governance and human security. The water and conflict cycle in Somalia is illustrated in Figure 4.2. When unchecked, these collectively amplifying forces kindle proverbial fires in ungoverned spaces, erect barriers to the consolidation of a state, and provide the opportunity for insurgency. Water governance becomes nearly impossible under these conditions. The resulting mismanagement of already-stressed water resources, as well as the weaponization of water, further exacerbate human insecurity, and accelerate conflict drivers that are based on historical ethnic, economic, and sectarian cleavages. It does not take a massive disaster to trigger such responses. Even marginal increases in water stress amplify instabilities that have plagued Somalia and the Horn of Africa for decades.

Figure 4.2 Water Stress and Conflict Cycle in Somalia

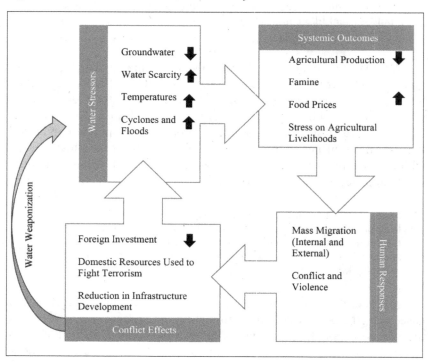

Water is a key ingredient in Somalia's stirring cauldron of violence. Against a backdrop of a complex emergency, a pathway of influence leads from the initial geophysical impacts of climate change–induced drought to the endgame of conflict and famine. Famine conditions created the opportunity for al-Shabaab to fully exploit the water weapon in 2011 and 2017, while also building popular support in the latter case.

Unlike the case with IS in Syria and Iraq, there is little evidence that al-Shabaab employed the water weapon as part of a sustained and concerted warfighting strategy. The group's callous attitude toward civilian causalities was similar to IS. Differences may be, in part, attributable to the divergent physical characteristics of the battlefields. Unlike in Iraq, the lack of large water infrastructure in Somalia, especially dams, prevented al-Shabaab's greater use of the water weapon, at least on the strategic level.

In Nigeria, Boko Haram had the opportunity and mentality to incorporate water weaponization into its warfighting planning and did so across a wider range of engagements than its al-Shabaab brethren. Likewise, Boko Haram also did not take full advantage of existing strategic water infrastructure targets. Overall, it can be said that the two African jihadist groups treated water more as a natural target of opportunity than as a deliberate strategic and tactical weapon in warfare. Certainly, they have drawn less attention from scholars and the media for any such use. It is possible that these African groups will be inspired by IS's successes with a deeper reliance on the water weapon and the notoriety associated with it.

It is also natural that al-Shabaab would be wary of the water weapon because it had backfired so violently on the group in 2011. Indeed, the strategic use of the water weapon during the drought and famine in 2011 was ultimately a blunder that not only squandered popular support but also may have precipitated the downfall of Godane, the group's leader. It was, in effect, a weapon of mass destruction rather than a convenient military option given the scope of the corresponding famine.

Al-Shabaab's tactical use of the water weapon was more frequent and successful. The success is best exemplified by the attack against AMISOM and US forces in 2018. Al-Shabaab's efforts to placate the population through such actions as the construction of canals and waterworks, in the hopes of incentivizing popular support, were modest gestures when measured against the scale of the need. However, these actions even at the low magnitude provided some much-needed popular legitimacy while the organization was on its heels militarily.

184   *Weaponizing Water*

Al-Shabaab may be the primary user of the water weapon in Somalia, but water as a flashpoint for conflict predates the group, perhaps by centuries. Water has been a prominent trigger for violence in Somalia at least since clans contended over water access during the wars of the 1990s. The key difference is that al-Shabaab was responsible for introducing the widespread use of water as a tool for conducting warfare rather than it being the subject of warfare. In Somalia, the Ethiopian army or clan-based forces used the water weapon, by comparison, only on the rarest of occasions.

Drought conditions in Somalia are relatively latent as of the writing of this chapter, certainly as compared to conditions during the twin humanitarian crises of 2011 and 2017. However, as an arid country with increasingly unpredictable weather, overall water conditions remain bleak in Somalia and are continuing to bolster al-Shabaab by diminishing societal resilience. The organization is persistent, and it appears stable for the foreseeable future because of a variety of factors, including the power vacuum in Mogadishu and a drawdown of US forces in the region. All indications are that this group will continue to use the promise of alleviating economic hardship stemming from drought-induced decimation of livelihoods as a major recruitment tool for their next generation of warfighters.

These outcomes naturally lead to the question of what the international community, including the United States, might do to improve water conditions and build a more resilient Somalia. Instability in Somalia reaches beyond its borders and plays a part in fomenting multiple geopolitical risks, including increased demand for humanitarian assistance, internationalization of conflict across borders into surrounding nations such as Kenya, and increasing displacement of populations. Somalia is positioned on the Bab-el-Mandeb Straits, a vulnerable touchpoint between the continent of Africa and the Middle East. Maritime traffic supports the trade of approximately 4.7 million barrels per day of crude oil and piracy remains a latent possibility. In this way, the impacts of water stress in Somalia have implications on regional and, ultimately, global security.

The US strategic goal is to stunt the growth of violent Islamic extremist organizations across the globe. Moreover, the United States seeks to maintain stability in the Horn of Africa and to prevent Somalia from becoming a refuge for al-Shabaab while other extremists such as IS gain footholds. The US military has been the main instrument for implementing a counterinsurgency strategy in pursuit of these goals. In 2017 alone, the United States conducted thirty airstrikes against al-Shabaab in Somalia and provided more than half a billion dollars to the African Union forces combating al-Shabaab on the ground. This was separate from direct aid to the Somali national government.

While this highly militarized approach has been somewhat successful in preventing the extremists' gains, other foreign policy instruments can and should be brought to bear. One avenue is to address Somalia's exploding birth rate. It is the expansion of the youth demographic that is putting strain on the economy and the environment, and by extension water resources. Family planning is the key that has the potential to alleviate some of the systemic demographic issues that challenge stability and put pressure on water resources in the country. The United States and other concerned nations can provide greater support to organizations like the United Nations Population Fund and other NGOs that have provided reproductive health services such as family planning to thousands of Somalis.

The UN and international partners should support the Federal Government of Somalia by strengthening its institutional capacity to integrate responses to climate-related security risks such as drought across all levels of government. SWALIM, the underfunded organization supported by the Food and Agriculture Organization of the United Nations, is an example of such a coordination mechanism. It is a good base to build upon. Contributors can provide additional financial resources to bolster SWALIM's efforts in Somalia, particularly those that advance its ecological data collection, monitoring networks, and flood and early warning systems.

All of this work should be done in coordination with regional institutions that have capacity to assist. The Intergovernmental Authority on Development (IGAD), Conflict Early Warning and Response Mechanism (CEWARN), and the IGAD Climate Prediction and Applications Centre (ICPAC), as well as the African Union (AU), are vital stakeholders. They can integrate regional resources to capitalize on the existing African capabilities.[153] The governments of the autonomous regions of Somaliland and Puntland are also important stakeholders.

Lastly, foreign assistance budgets of the United States and others can be directed to increasing strategic investment in Somalia's economic development, especially in the areas of agriculture and animal husbandry. A vital component of this assistance should be programs that provide pastoralist community members suffering from drought with alternative economic prospects beyond joining al-Shabaab, such as technical assistance to adapt herds to be more drought resilient. By investing to diversify the Somali economy, the global community

186   *Weaponizing Water*

can take power away from al-Shabaab in two primary ways: by limiting the group's ability to recruit members and to reap profits from illicit economic activity under its control.

The international community has the responsibility and should be motivated to prevent weaponization of water in Somalia. Development projects are probably the most important vehicle for addressing the societal factors that support extremism and ultimately enable the weaponization of water. Development approaches are important and are vital to a comprehensive and effective counterinsurgency strategy. Implementation of such a strategy also depends on better predictive capabilities that provide early indications of outbreaks of drought and other severe weather events. Such measures will enable the pre-positioning of resources such as foodstuffs before conditions become dire enough for al-Shabaab to thrive and make more effective use of the water weapon against a weakened population.

In the end, we should recognize that any of these remedies will be hard to implement in the prevailing political situation in Somalia, where the nation is politically bifurcated and the authority of the FGS is diffuse and in most cases does not extend very far beyond Mogadishu. Therefore, an effective strategy means that stakeholders must work with existing power structures, which includes gaining approval from and coordinating with the powerful Somali clans. Since the 1990s, many organizations have tried myriad approaches to improve conditions in Somalia. If there are any silver bullets, then no one has yet found them. One thing is certain: the risks of expending effort in futile attempts to try to fix Somalia are outweighed by the risks of doing nothing.

Notes

1. Peter Chonka, "What You Need to Know to Understand al-Shabaab," Tony Blair Institute for Global Change, September 21, 2016, https://institute.global/insight/co-existence/what-you-need-know-understand-al-shabaab.

2. James Fergusson, *The World's Most Dangerous Place* (New York: Da Capo Press, 2013), 50.

3. "Somalia Profile—Timeline," BBC News, January 4, 2018, http://www.bbc.com/news/world-africa-14094632.

4. Ibid.

5. "Somalia," One World Nations Online, 2015, http://www.nationsonline.org/oneworld/somalia.htm#Search2.

6. Ibid.

7. Ibid.

8. "Somalia Profile—Timeline," BBC News.

9. "Fragile States Index," Fund for Peace, 2021, https://fragilestatesindex.org/.

10. "The World Bank in Somalia: Overview," World Bank, accessed October 13, 2017, updated April 14, 2022, http://www.worldbank.org/en/country/somalia/overview.

11. Ibid.

12. UNICEF, "Somalia," in *Annual Report 2015* (UNICEF, 2016), https://www.unicef.org/reports/unicef-annual-report-2015.

13. "The World Bank in Somalia," World Bank.

14. Ibid.

15. Andrew Carlson, "Pirates of Puntland, Somalia*,*" *Origins: Current Events in Historical Perspective*, June 2009, https://origins.osu.edu/article/pirates-puntland-somalia?language_content_entity=en.

16. "Data: Somalia," World Bank, 2016, https://data.worldbank.org/country/somalia.

17. US Central Intelligence Agency (CIA), "Somalia," *World Factbook*, accessed 2017, updated September 7, 2022, https://www.cia.gov/the-world-factbook/countries/somalia/.

18. Carlson, "Pirates of Puntland."

19. CIA, "Somalia."

20. "Foreign Terrorist Organizations," US Department of State, https://www.state.gov/foreign-terrorist-organizations/.

21. Center for Preventive Action, "Conflict Al-Shabaab in Somalia," Global Conflict Tracker, accessed October 23, 2017, updated May 12, 2022, https://www.cfr.org/global-conflict-tracker/conflict/al-shabab-somalia.

22. Ibid.

23. "Somali: Uncertain future as AMISOM transitions to ATMIS," The Africa Report, April 1 2022 https://www.theafricareport.com/190409/somalia-uncertain-future-as-amisom-transition-to-atmis/.

24. Caleb Weis, "Analysis: Islamic State Expanded Operations in Somalia in 2018," FDD's Long War Journal, January 4, 2019, https://www.longwarjournal.org/archives/2019/01/analysis-islamic-state-expanded-operations-in-somalia-in-2018.php.

25. Martin C. Richard, ed., *Encyclopedia of Islam & the Muslim World*, vol. 2 (New York: Macmillan Reference USA, 2016).

26. Jonathan Masters and Mohammed Aly Sergie, "Background Briefing: What Is al-Shabaab?" Council on Foreign Relations, PBS News, September 23, 2013, https://www.pbs.org/newshour/world/what-is-al-shabaab.

27. Chonka, "What You Need to Know to Understand al-Shabaab."

28. "Al-Shabaab," Counter Extremism Project, accessed 2019, updated August 19, 2022, https://www.counterextremism.com/threat/al-shabaab.

29. Harun Maruf and Dan Joseph, *Inside Al-Shabaab: The Secret History of Al-Qaeda's Most Powerful Ally* (Bloomington: Indiana University Press, 2018), 83.

30. Ibid.

31. "Who Are Somalia's al-Shabaab?" BBC News, December 22, 2017, https://www.bbc.com/news/world-africa-15336689.

32. "Al-Shabaab's Military Machine," Hiraal Institute, December 2018, https://hiraalinstitute.org/al-shababs-military-machine/.

33. Fred Dews, "Al Shabaab: Background on the Somalia-Based Terrorist Group That Attacked a Nairobi Mall," Brookings Institute, September 23, 2013, https://www.brookings.edu/blog/brookings-now/2013/09/23/al-shabaab-background-on-the-somalia-based-terrorist-group-that-attacked-a-nairobi-mall/.

34. Maruf and Joseph, *Inside Al-Shabaab*, 83.

35. Masters and Sergie, "Background Briefing."

188 *Weaponizing Water*

36. "Zakat," BBC, August 9, 2009, https://www.bbc.co.uk/religion/religions/islam/practices/zakat.shtml.

37. "The AS Finance System," Hiraal Institute, July 2018, https://hiraalinstitute.org/the-as-finance-system/.

38. Ibid.

39. Ibid.

40. Aggrey Mutambo, "Kismayu on the Spot over Charcoal Trade," *Business Daily*, February 13, 2018, https://www.businessdailyafrica.com/economy/Kismayu-on-the-spot-over-charcoal-trade/3946234-4303554-b786icz/index.html.

41. "Al-Shabaab's Military Machine," Hiraal Institute.

42. Edith M. Lederer, "UN Alarm That Most of al-Shabaab's Force in Somalia Are Kids," AP News, January 19, 2017, https://apnews.com/85093315baa644a6bee802b13fc343e5/un-alarm-most-al-shabaabs-force-somalia-are-kids.

43. "No Place for Children," Human Rights Watch, February 20, 2012, https://www.hrw.org/report/2012/02/20/no-place-children/child-recruitment-forced-marriage-and-attacks-schools-somalia.

44. Chris Funk et al., "The Centennial Trends Greater Horn of Africa Precipitation Dataset," *Nature*, art. no. 150050, September 29, 2015, https://www.nature.com/articles/sdata201550.

45. FAO SWALIM: Somalia Water and Land Information Management, https://faoswalim.org/about-us/who-we-are.

46. Raphael Chijoke Njokum, *The History of Somalia* (Santa Barbara: CA: ABC-Clio, 2013).

47. "Somalia," Global Forest Watch, https://www.globalforestwatch.org/dashboards/country/SOM?category=forest-change.

48. "Aqueduct Water Risk Atlas," World Resources Institute, https://tinyurl.com/5n88du8t.

49. Hussein Gadain et al., "Africa Groundwater Atlas: Hydrogeology of Somalia," British Geological Survey, accessed 2016, updated August 25, 2022, http://earthwise.bgs.ac.uk/index.php/Hydrogeology_of_Somalia.

50. "The Jubba and Shabelle Rivers and Their Importance to Somalia," Somalia Water and Land Information Management, Food and Agriculture Organization of the United Nations, http://www.faoswalim.org/article/juba-and-shabelle-rivers-and-their-importance-somalia.

51. Gadain et al., "Africa Groundwater Atlas: Hydrogeology of Somalia."

52. Ibid.

53. "Improved Water Source, Rural (% of Rural Population with Access)," World Bank, 2011, https://data.worldbank.org/indicator/SH.H2O.BASW.ZS?locations=SO.

54. Ibid

55. UNICEF, "Somalia Water, Sanitation and Hygiene," https://www.unicef.org/somalia/water-sanitation-and-hygiene#:~:text=Only%2052%20percent%20of%20the,and%20from%20unsafe%20open%20wells. Accessed June 20, 2020.

56. "Country Profile: Somalia, 2005," AQUASTAT—FAO's Global Information System on Water and Agriculture, http://www.fao.org/nr/water/aquastat/countries_regions/SOM/.

57. Ibid.

58. Michele Bernardi, "Combined Drought Index," Food and Agriculture Organization of the United Nations, 5.

59. Ibid.

60. "Drought Monitoring," Somalia Water and Land Information Management, Food and Agriculture Organization of the United Nations, http://www.faoswalim.org/water-resources/drought/drought-monitoring.

61. Elizabeth Ferris and Daniel Petz, "The Year That Shook the Rich: A Review of Natural Disasters in 2011," Brookings Institute, March 1, 2012, https://www.brookings.edu/multi-chapter-report/the-year-that-shook-the-rich-a-review-of-natural-disasters-in-2011/.

62. Ibid., 103.

63. Ibid.

64. "UN Warns Millions of Somalis Are at Risk of Famine," *Financial Times*, Jan 17, 2017 https://www.ft.com/content/2b72c8dc-dca7-11e6-9d7c-be108f1c1dce.

65. Ibid.

66. Tracy Carty, "A Climate in Crisis: How Climate Change Is Making Drought and Humanitarian Disaster Worse in East Africa" (Oxfam Media Briefing, Oxfam, London, April 27, 2017), 2–4, https://www-cdn.oxfam.org/s3fs-public/mb-climate-crisis-east-africa-drought-270417-en.pdf.

67. Geert Jan Van Oldenborgh et al., "Annex I: Atlas of Global and Regional Climate Projections," in *Climate Change 2013: The Physical Science Basis* (New York: Cambridge University Press, January 2013), https://www.researchgate.net/publication/264862528_Annex_I_Atlas_of_Global_and_Regional_Climate_Projections.

68. "Drought Conditions Exacerbated by Above-Average Surface Temperatures over Eastern Horn," *FEWS Net*, January 31, 2017, http://www.fews.net/east-africa/seasonal-monitor/january-2017.

69. I. Niang et al., "Africa," in *AR5 Climate Change 2014: Impacts, Adaptation, and Vulnerability. Part B: Regional Aspects*, contribution of Working Group II to the Fifth Assessment Report of the Intergovernmental Panel on Climate Change (New York: Cambridge University Press, 2014), 1199–1265, http://www.ipcc.ch/report/ar5/wg2/.

70. Carty, "A Climate in Crisis."

71. "ND-GAIN Country Index," Notre Dame Global Adaptation Initiative, University of Notre Dame, https://gain.nd.edu/our-work/country-index/.

72. National Intelligence Council, *Implications for US National Security of Anticipated Climate Change* (memorandum NIC WP 2016-01, National Intelligence Council, September 21, 2016), https://www.dni.gov/files/documents/Newsroom/Reports%20and%20Pubs/Implications_for_US_National_Security_of_Anticipated_Climate_Change.pdf.

73. CIA, "Somalia."

74. "Somalia Livestock Price Bulletin," FEWS NET, June 2016, https://fews.net/east-africa/somalia/price-bulletin/june-2016-0.

75. "Livestock and Agriculture," Somali Development and Reconstruction Bank, https://sodevbank.so/livestock-and-agriculture/.

76. "Annual Freshwater Withdrawals, Domestic (% of Total Freshwater Withdrawal)—Somalia," World Bank, https://data.worldbank.org/indicator/ER.H2O.FWDM.ZS?display=default%25%2525252020&locations=SO.

77. "Livestock and Agriculture," Somali Development and Reconstruction Bank.

78. "Chapter 3: Somalia: Drought Conflict = Famine?" Brookings Institute, https://www.brookings.edu/wp-content/uploads/2016/06/03_nd_review_chapter3.pdf.

79. Jean-François Maystadt and Olivier Ecker, "Extreme Weather and Civil War: Does Drought Fuel Conflict in Somalia Through Livestock Price Shocks?" *American Journal of Agricultural Economics* 96, no. 4 (2014): 1160–1161, https://doi.org/10.1093/ajae/aau010.

80. Ibid., 1159.

81. "Droughts, Livestock Prices and Armed Conflict in Somalia," Climate Diplomacy, https://climate-diplomacy.org/case-studies/droughts-livestock-prices-and-armed-conflict-somalia.

190 *Weaponizing Water*

82. Ibid.

83. Ibid.

84. Food Security and Nutrition Analysis Unit—Somalia, "Special Brief—Focus on Post *Gu* 2017 Assessment Results," *Food Security & Nutrition*, September 28, 2017, https://www.ipcinfo.org/fileadmin/user_upload/ipcinfo/docs/FSNAU-Special -Brief-September-2017.pdf.

85. Ibid.

86. "Somalia: World Bank Approves US$50 Million in Support of Emergency Drought Response and Recovery," World Bank, May 30, 2017, http://www.world bank.org/en/news/press-release/2017/05/30/somalia-world-bank-approves-us50 -million-in-support-of-emergency-drought-response-and-recovery.

87. "WHO Calls for Immediate Action to Save Lives in Somalia," World Health Organization, May 11, 2017, https://www.who.int/news/item/11-05-2017-who-calls -for-immediate-action-to-save-lives-in-somalia.

88. Colin Dwyer, "Drought Threatens to Drive Famine in Somalia as Hunger Kills More Than 100," NPR, March 5, 2017, http://www.npr.org/sections/thetwo -way/2017/03/05/518624610/drought-threatens-to-drive-famine-in-somalia-as -hunger-kills-more-than-100.

89. "Water, Sanitation, and Hygiene," UNICEF Somalia, https://www.unicef.org /somalia/water-sanitation-and-hygiene.

90. "WHO Calls for Immediate Action," World Health Organization.

91. Steff Gaulter, "Flooding Affects Tens of Thousands in Somalia," News Al Jazeera, November 8, 2015, http://www.aljazeera.com/news/2015/11/flooding -affects-tens-thousands-somalia-151108095538079.html.

92. UN News Centre, "Recent Floods Damage Supply Routes, Vital Infrastructure in Somalia, UN Relief Wing Warns," Hiiraan Online, November 24, 2015, https://www.hiiraan.com/news4/2015/Nov/102713/recent_floods_damage_supply _routes_vital_infrastructure_in_somalia_un_relief_wing_warns.aspx.

93. "FloodList News Desk," FloodList, June 13, 2016, http://floodlist.com /africa/somalia-30000-need-food-drinking-water-flooding.

94. "Humanitarian Bulletin Somalia," *ReliefWeb*, June 23, 2016, https://relief web.int/sites/reliefweb.int/files/resources/Somalia%20Humanitarian%20Bulletin %20for%20June.pdf.

95. FloodList News Desk, "Somalia—30,000 in Need of Food and Drinking Water After Flooding," FloodList, June 13, 2016, http://floodlist.com/africa/somalia -30000-need-food-drinking-water-flooding.

96. "Somalia Floods," ReliefWeb, accessed February 2021, updated May 2021, https://reliefweb.int/disaster/fl-2021-000051-som.

97. "Chapter 3: Somalia: Drought Conflict = Famine?" Brookings Institute.

98. Ibid.

99. Ibid.

100. "Somalia Famine Killed Nearly 260,000 People, Half of Them Children— Reports UN," UN News Center, May 2, 2013, https://news.un.org/en/story/2013/05 /438682-somalia-famine-killed-nearly-260000-people-half-them-children-reports-un.

101. Jeffrey Gettleman and Neil MacFarquhar, "Food Aid Bypasses Somalia's Needy, U.N. Study Finds," *New York Times*, March 9, 2010, http://www.nytimes .com/2010/03/10/world/africa/10somalia.html.

102. Maruf and Joseph, *Inside Al-Shabaab*, 173.

103. "OCHA Somalia," Human Data Exchange, https://data.humdata.org/organization /ocha-somalia.

104. Ibid.

105. Ibid.

106. "Climate Change, Charcoal Trade and Armed Conflict in Somalia," Climate Diplomacy, https://climate-diplomacy.org/case-studies/climate-change-charcoal-trade-and-armed-conflict-somalia.

107. M. Bolognesi et al., "Rapid Mapping and Impact Estimation of Illegal Charcoal Production in Southern Somalia Based on Worldview-1 Imagery," *Energy for Sustainable Development* 25 (April 2015): 40–49.

108. "IMB Piracy & Armed Robbery," International Chamber of Commerce Commercial Crime Services, https://icc-ccs.org/piracy-reporting-centre/live-piracy-map.

109. Thomas Gibbons-Neff, "Piracy Back on the Rise Off Somalia, U.S. Military Says," *Washington Post*, April 23, 2017, https://www.washingtonpost.com/news/checkpoint/wp/2017/04/23/u-s-monitoring-spike-in-pirate-attacks-off-horn-of-africa-officials-say/?utm_term=.0f39082e2f6c.

110. Ibid.

111. "Somali Pirates Hijack Panama-Flagged Ship," DW, August 20, 2020, https://www.dw.com/en/somali-pirates-hijack-panama-flagged-ship/a-54637865.

112. "Number of Somali Refugees Grows Sharply in 2011," United Nations High Commission on Refugees, April 29, 2011, https://www.unhcr.org/news/briefing/2011/4/4dba949d9/number-somali-refugees-grows-sharply-2011.html.

113. "Somalia: Events of 2016," Human Rights Watch, January 12, 2017, https://www.hrw.org/world-report/2017/country-chapters/somalia.

114. UNHCR Operational Data Portal, "Horn of Africa Somalia Situation," https://data.unhcr.org/en/situations/horn, accessed June 15, 2020.

115. "Chapter 3: Somalia: Drought Conflict = Famine?" Brookings Institute.

116. "A Very Black Market," *The Economist* 426, no. 9085 (March 31, 2018): 52.

117. Nicholas S. Robbins and James Fergusson, "Groundwater Scarcity and Conflict—Managing Hotspots," *Earth Perspectives*, art. no. 6 (February 12, 2014), https://earth-perspectives.springeropen.com/articles/10.1186/2194-6434-1-6.

118. AFP, "At Least 23 Killed in Somalia Clan Violence," *Daily Nation* (Kenya), January 22, 2015, updated on July 3, 2020, http://www.nation.co.ke/news/africa/At-least-23-killed-in-Somalia-clan-violence/1066-2598404-wnk51rz/index.html.

119. "Inter-Agency Initial Investigation Report—Inter Clan Fighting in Deefow, Deefow, Hiraan Region," United Nations Office for the Coordination of Humanitarian Affairs, June 25, 2015, https://www.humanitarianresponse.info/sites/www.humanitarianresponse.info/files/assessments/150625_deefow_initial_investigation_inter_clan_conflict.pdf.

120. Maystadt and Ecker, "Extreme Weather and Civil War," 1157–1182.

121. Fergusson, *World's Most Dangerous Place*, 50, 134.

122. Fredrick Nzwili, "Terrorist Group al-Shabaab Delivers Food Relief to Drought-Stricken Somalia," *National Catholic Reporter*, April 4, 2017, https://www.ncronline.org/news/world/terrorist-group-al-shabab-delivers-food-relief-drought-stricken-somalia.

123. Hamza Mohamed, "Somali Farmers Benefit from al-Shabaab Reforms," Al Jazeera, March 11, 2014, https://www.aljazeera.com/features/2014/3/11/somali-farmers-benefit-from-al-shabab-reforms.

124. Sunguta West, "Al-Shabaab Plays on Aid Distribution Role to Win Over Desperate Somalis," Jamestown Foundation *Terrorism Monitor* 15, no. 7 (April 7, 2017), https://jamestown.org/program/al-shabaab-plays-aid-distribution-role-win-desperate-somalis/.

192   *Weaponizing Water*

125. Larisa Epatko, "Al-Shabaab Militants Try Food to Win Hearts and Minds in Somalia," PBS, April 20, 2017, https://www.pbs.org/newshour/world/al-shabab -militants-try-food-win-hearts-minds-somalia.

126. West, "Al-Shabaab Plays on Aid Distribution Role."

127. Moses Rono, "Somalia Food Crisis: Has al-Shabaab Adopted New Approach to Food Aid?" BBC News, March 22, 2017, http://www.bbc.com/news/world-africa -39296517.

128. Shabelle Media Network, "Somalia: Al-Shabaab Claims Bomb Attack in Lower Shabelle Region," All Africa, June 10, 2019, https://allafrica.com/stories /201906100503.html.

129. Tres Thomas, "3 Notes on the Al-Shabaab Attack on U.S. Allied Forces in Somalia," Somalia Newsroom, June 12, 2018, https://somalianewsroom.com/2018 /06/12/3-notes-on-the-al-shabaab-attack-on-u-s-allied-forces-in-somalia/.

130. Ibid.

131. Christina Goldbaum, "To Ambush and Kill American Green Berets, Al Shabaab Diverted a River," *Daily Beast*, June 10, 2018, https://www.thedaily beast.com/to-ambush-and-kill-an-american-green-beret-al-shabaab-diverted-a-river.

132. Tahir Adnan, "Shabaab Destroys Only Source of Water," Somalia Report, April 6, 2012, http://piracyreport.com/index.php/post/3418/Shabaab_Destroys_Only _Source_of_Water.

133. Dominic Wabala, "Kenya: KDF Airlifts Water to Troops as Wells Poisoned," All Africa, September 24, 2012, https://allafrica.com/stories/201209250173.html.

134. Adriane Ohanesian, "In Photos: Tracking al Shabaab in Somalia," France 24, May 16, 2014, https://www.france24.com/en/20140516-operation-eagle-somalia -fight-against-al-shabaab-african-union-al-qaeda.

135. "32 People Die in Somalia After Drinking from Well," *Gulf Times*, January 30, 2017, https://www.gulf-times.com/story/530976/32-die-in-Somalia-after-drinking -from-well.

136. Maruf and Joseph, *Inside Al-Shabaab*, 42.

137. C. Raleigh et al., Armed Conflict Location and Event Data (ACLED) Project, data last exported February 2, 2018, https://www.acleddata.com/data/.

138. Harun Maruf, "Somalia: Al-Shabaab Battles Islamic Militants in Northeastern Somalia," All Africa, February 1, 2019, https://allafrica.com/stories/201902010619.html.

139. Ibid.

140. Ibid.

141. America Abroad, "Al-Shabaab's 'Water Terrorism' Is Yielding Results and Tragedy in Somalia's Civil War," The World, Public Radio International, August 12, 2014, https://www.pri.org/stories/2014-08-08/how-al-shabaab-using-water-tool -terrorism.

142. Maruf and Joseph, *Inside Al-Shabaab*, 246.

143. "Finally Free of al-Shabaab, Daily Life Resumes in El Bur," Hiiraan Online, December 17, 2014, https://hiiraan.com/news4/2014/Dec/97372/finally_free_of_al _shabaab_daily_life_resumes_in_el_bur.aspx.

144. Omar Nor and Greg Botelho, "At Least 50 Dead in Somalia After Drinking from Contaminated Well," CNN, December 11, 2014, https://www.cnn.com /2014/12/11/world/africa/somalia-drinking-water-deaths/index.html.

145. "Water Conflict Chronology: Conflict Map," Pacific Institute, http://www .worldwater.org/conflict/map/.

146. Sunguta West, "Resurgence of Al-Shabaab," Jamestown Foundation *Terrorism Monitor* 16, no. 3 (February 8, 2017), https://jamestown.org/program/resurgence-al -shabaab/.

147. "Somalia: Local Admin Forces, Militia Clash in Deadly Battle in Galgaduud," Garowe Online, November 29, 2014, https://www.garoweonline.com/index.php/en/news/somalia/somalia-local-admin-forces-militia-clash-in-deadly-battle-in-galgaduud.

148. Shanifa Nasser, "Somali Politician with Canadian Citizenship Killed in al-Shabaab Hotel Attack," CBS, June 26, 2016, https://www.cbc.ca/news/canada/toronto/somali-politician-with-canadian-citizenship-killed-in-al-shabaab-hotel-attack-1.3653654.

149. Laura Heaton, "Somalia's Climate for Conflict: How Drought Brings War to Somalia," Groundtruth Project, 2017, http://thegroundtruthproject.org/somalia-conflict-climate-change/.

150. Anneli Botha and Mahdi Abdile, *Radicalisation and al-Shabaab Recruitment in Somalia* (ISS Paper no. 266, Institute for Security Studies, September 2014), https://issafrica.s3.amazonaws.com/site/uploads/Paper266.pdf.

151. Heaton, "How Drought Brings War to Somalia."

152. "Al-Shabaab's 'Water Terrorism' Is Yielding Results."

153. America Abroad, "Climate, Peace and Security Fact Sheet: Somalia," Norwegian Institute of International Affairs, February 3, 2021, https://www.nupi.no/nupi_eng/News/Climate-Peace-and-Security-Fact-Sheet-Somalia.

5

Stemming the Tide of Water Weaponization

IT IS CLEARLY IN THE GLOBAL INTEREST TO STOP THE PROLIFER-
ation of water weaponization for a host of legal, ethical, and realpolitik
reasons. This chapter highlights possible pathways to meet this objective. Although water stress across the Middle East and Africa creates
instability that provides opportunities for violent extremist organizations (VEOs) to wage internal wars, it is also a driver of conflict that
crosses national borders and ripples into the global geostrategic land-
scape. Water weaponization is an enormously effective form of propaganda by deed. VEOs have thrown down the gauntlet.

Starting with the Islamic State (IS), water weaponization has been
mainstreamed as a tactic of terrorism. The world should be aware that
hundreds of hardened IS fighters inculcated in the use of the water
weapon have returned from the Middle East to dozens of home countries. Lone wolf terror attacks that target domestic populations and critical water infrastructure are now potential actions of this diaspora.

The case studies in this volume center on Middle Eastern and North
African countries that were affected by drought from roughly 2011 to
2017 and where Salafist jihadi groups were the primary perpetrators of
water weaponization. Syria and Iraq, Nigeria, and Somalia are important to global stability for geostrategic reasons that transcend the sole
motivation of stopping the spread of violent extremism.

A relatively stable Syria and Iraq are important to the United States
and its allies for many reasons, not the least of which is Iraq's role as the
lynchpin in a wider US strategy seeking to balance national interests in
the region in the face of an increasingly hostile Iran. Peace and stability

196   *Weaponizing Water*

in Syria and Iraq are key to the dual goals of preventing a resurgence of IS or a similar organization and diminishing Iranian influence.

Compound challenges emerge from the war in Somalia, including the demand for large-scale commitments of humanitarian assistance, displacement of refugees across borders, and internationalization of internal conflict to neighboring states. Somalia sits on the Bab-el-Mandeb strait, the vital maritime link between Africa and the Middle East. Somali pirates, also motivated in part by environmental degradation such as depleted fisheries, have attacked ships on this sea lane that moves Persian Gulf oil and natural gas shipments to Europe and North America.

In the next section, I use Nigeria as an example of one approach to countering water weaponization.

Nigeria: A Model for Countering the Water Weapon?

The prevailing conditions in Nigeria, although different in several respects from those in Syria and Iraq and Somalia, are relatively ripe for stemming water weaponization in ways that can serve as examples for other countries with similar circumstances. Also, owing to its vast and restive population, importance to world energy markets, and regional military posture, preventing further destabilization of Nigeria is an urgent task for the global community.

Outward migration from Nigeria, driven in part by environmental degradation, is a geopolitical issue with widespread repercussions. With numbers reaching over 2 million, internally displaced persons (IDPs) are by far the largest demographic challenge. Transboundary migration has put pressure on important US allies in southern Europe. Italy, Spain, and France have reacted in a sometimes-negative fashion as migrants have sought passage across the Mediterranean through the chaotic disembarkation points of Libya and North Africa.

The United States and the UK are also major destinations for West African migrants.[1] Increased migration is politically, if not physically, unsustainable in both countries. In fact, migrants from all four nations examined in this volume are seeking refuge in Europe. Migration is straining social and political systems from Malta to Belarus; countries are experiencing a tide of anti-immigrant sentiment.

Instability in Nigeria also carries global economic repercussions. This was realized in 2016 when the Niger Delta Avengers, the latest manifestation of an insurgency based on economic grievances in that region, destroyed oil infrastructure. These actions created upward pressure on oil prices that sparked uncertainty in world energy markets.[2] Oil price volatility, in turn, has negative internal repercussions on the Nigerian economy, which, under the resource curse, is overreliant on this sector.

Countries such as Nigeria that are plagued by the resource curse face both economic opportunities and challenges. When used well, key resources can create greater prosperity for current and future generations; used poorly, or squandered, they can cause economic instability, social conflict, and lasting environmental damage. Paradoxically, many oil-, gas-, and mineral-rich countries have failed to reach their full potential precisely as a result of their natural resource wealth. In general, these countries are also more authoritarian, more prone to conflict, and less economically stable than countries without these resources.[3]

Finally, from a geostrategic standpoint, Nigeria is a bulwark against extremism on the African continent through its support of international peacekeeping missions. But as Nigeria struggles to manage multiple internal conflicts, al-Qaeda in the Islamic Maghreb (AQIM) and the emergent Islamic State West Africa Province (ISWAP) have gained a foothold in neighboring countries or established cells in the country.

The confluence of all these factors underscores the urgency of implementing policies to address water stress as a source of instability, but Nigeria is in many ways ill-prepared to do so. As in the other case study countries, structural factors, such as the organization of the Nigerian government, hamper policy implementation.

In this bureaucracy, ill-defined and often conflicting responsibilities for water governance at the state, local, and tribal levels and endemic corruption are key impediments. Ideally, solutions will be locally designed. To be effective, water policies in Nigeria must be site-specific, considering not just social conditions but also Nigeria's diversity of climate zones and ecological conditions. The ecological zones often cross political and jurisdictional boundaries, hampering effective administration.

Northern Nigeria is an area where conditions are deteriorating most rapidly, and proactive policies are needed to prevent the worsening water crisis. The overwhelming priority there is to resolve the humanitarian crisis of displacement around Lake Chad, which has festered for more than a decade, with the help of international organizations. Elsewhere in Nigeria, preemptive targeted national investment is necessary to better protect water infrastructure such as dams because the infrastructure presents security vulnerabilities and provides essential functions, such as drinking water and power generation.

Food security is of utmost importance to include in Nigerian water policy. Considering the increasing climate impacts, the Government of

198 *Weaponizing Water*

Nigeria should encourage ongoing research on and deployment of drought-tolerant seeds for food crops. Use of resilient seedstock could increase yields of maize in Nigeria's north and Middle Belt regions. Greater maize crop productivity would be a step toward addressing immediate food insecurity while reducing frequent contention between farmers and herders.

It is reassuring that progress has been made in this area. Scientists at the International Institute of Tropical Agriculture (IITA) in Ibadan have developed and released several high-yield and drought-tolerant varieties, and promising research continues.[4] The US Agency for International Development (USAID) is also working across eighteen Nigerian states to facilitate the use and marketing of drought-resistant seeds. These actions are a part of the Feed the Future program.[5]

Cowpea is a staple food and is widely traded across West Africa. It is a highly nutritious traditional food and is somewhat drought resistant, grown as a rain-fed crop in the far northern area where few crop alternatives are viable. Borno State was once the largest cowpea producer in Nigeria, but deteriorating climate conditions and displacement resulting from the insurgency have disrupted production. As of 2018, the implementation team from the Feed the Future program has expanded its focus to include improving yields of cowpea, maize, rice, and soybeans in dry areas. Related programs supporting aquaculture and goat husbandry have also made progress toward achieving food security in the country's northeast.[6]

Reformation of land governance policies is another important task. Such measures should include funding for communities affected by clashes over water and improving security at local conflict hotspots. Another step is to establish grazing reserves for livestock and delineated migration corridors for herders. This approach has been implemented sporadically and has brought some good results. To be more successful, regulation of these designated areas requires increased cooperation between the Nigerian federal and state governments.[7] In order to promote a more sustainable peace, clinics, schools, and other basic infrastructure should be constructed and provided for Hausa-Fulani herders during the seasons when they reside in these protected areas.

The development of solutions to the conflict in northern Nigeria and the Middle Belt has been hampered by incomplete information from the natural and social science spheres. Detailed state-specific maps that plot the overlapping factors involved, such as desertification patterns, land tenure holdings, grazing routes and reserves, and past locations of violence and conflict, are needed to inform policymaking. Assistance

Stemming the Tide of Water Weaponization 199

with map creation can come from international organizations such as multilateral development agencies and specialized agencies within the UN, United States, or European Union. These maps can help guide policies and interventions that build resilience and prevent or resolve farmer–pastoralist conflicts as they emerge.

Information gleaned from mapping should be coupled with downscaled data from regional climate models to assess the range of possibilities for the worsening impacts of climate change. In addition to their utility for national policymakers, maps can also be used as advocacy tools by local stakeholders to encourage sometimes reluctant state and federal organizations to take action to design the most effective water infrastructure and water management systems.

Countering the Water Weapon on a Broader Basis

The Water, Peace and Security Partnership (WPS) is a new organization that can provide information helpful to more effective water policymaking. The WPS is a collaboration of the German Agency for International Development, the Netherlands Ministry of Foreign Affairs, and a collection of international partner organizations, including the World Resources Institute. The WPS Global Early Warning Tool uses geographic information system (GIS) mapping to predict locations where the outbreak of water-related violence will most likely occur, even short-term conflicts. Although this project is still relatively new, there is hope that governments and NGOs operating in areas susceptible to water stress will adopt this tool in support of water policy decisions that can better avoid conflict.[8]

Many US government organizations have capabilities relevant to water that could also be brought to bear. The main mission of the US military is to fight and win America's wars. However, there are what can be referred to as "nonkinetic" roles for the US military too. For example, significant technical capacities reside in the US Army Corps of Engineers (USACE). Some of USACE's efforts in Africa include facilitating discussions among contentious Nile basin stakeholders, rebuilding hydrologic planning capacities in South Africa, and consulting over controversial water diversion projects in Kenya and Ghana.

On a technical level, the USACE cooperates with civilian agencies such as the US Geological Survey to build early-warning capabilities through application of remote sensing technologies that advance situational awareness for more effective policymaking and response to

200 *Weaponizing Water*

emerging water crises. The USACE has a long history of successful water projects in the United States, including on the Colorado River, for the Great Lakes, and in the Everglades. The USACE Institute for Water Resources helps with hydrological modeling, water resource planning, and conflict resolution regarding the use of water. USACE can provide a full range of services to international partners, including analysis of emerging water resources trends and issues, and state-of-the-art planning and hydrologic engineering methods, models, and training.[9]

USAID is responsible for the Famine Early Warning Systems Network (FEWS NET), which provides comprehensive coverage of Nigeria and up-to-date information on water availability in sub-Saharan Africa. This data enables USAID to make more accurate predictions of drought conditions that can impact food security.[10] FEWS NET also works with local governments to communicate potential migration patterns so that government agencies can pre-position water, food, and other relief supplies in the case of emergencies. In addition to climatic conditions, FEWS NET provides information about current livestock and cereals pricing.

USAID used climate change analysis based on FEWS NET data to modify irrigation techniques to help farmers in Niger, which neighbors Nigeria, modify crop growth. This best practice can be easily replicated.[11] Lessons learned from limited interventions by the US government could contribute to sustainable solutions to water stress in other areas prone to drought, such as Syria/Iraq and Somalia.

The timing to address these problems is auspicious because the United States is now developing a White House Action Plan on Global Water Security that could include approaches to counter water weaponization in these regions. Interventions should use all the tools of US foreign policy that provide the foundation for promoting and protecting US national interests. These are defense, development, and diplomacy—the 3 Ds—traditionally wielded by the Department of State, USAID, and the Department of Defense (DoD), respectively. A whole-of-society approach that includes contributions from academia and NGOs complements any USG interventions.

Countering water weaponization is an action that can easily fit into the larger framework of the US Global War on Terrorism. Despite the precipitous withdrawal from Afghanistan in August 2021, signs indicate the United States will likely remain engaged in the war against extremism in Iraq, Nigeria, and Somalia at some level. Therefore, the United States will and should continue to support military operations to counter VEOs.

One proposal is to repurpose US-supplied surveillance drones from the primary mission of targeted assassinations to supplying intelligence

Stemming the Tide of Water Weaponization 201

that can inform environmental missions, such as pinpointing the locations and effects of droughts.[12] Early military engagement in this case would be to support the framework of conflict prevention. The idea is to interrupt the momentum of the water and conflict cycle outlined in each chapter of this volume early enough to maintain peace and forestall situations of resource deprivation that create conflict and breed extremism. Extremism, in turn, enables the use of the water weapon. Unfortunately, in many locations around the globe the water and conflict cycle has already advanced beyond when early intervention is effective.

Proliferation of the Water Weapon

Under what conditions and in what geographies is water weaponization used in Iraq/Syria, Nigeria, and Somalia a harbinger? Sadly, ample evidence is emerging indicating that the practice of water weaponization is spreading in similar drought-affected countries in the wider Middle East and Africa regions.

On the African continent, developments in the small, tumultuous West African nation of Burkina Faso in 2020 are a prime cause for concern. By virtue of its geography, Burkina Faso is particularly vulnerable to extreme weather, including floods, dust storms, heat waves, and droughts. The adverse effects of drought have had outsized impacts on resource-based, extractive sectors of the country's economy, with more than one-third of arable land suffering degradation at a rate of 360,000 hectares per year. Rates of food insecurity have tripled. Agriculture contributes roughly 32 percent to the country's GDP, so the failings of the agricultural and other sectors impede planning for water resource management, maintenance of public health, and safeguarding the food supply.[13]

According to the World Food Program, in 2020, 2.1 million Burkinabes were food insecure under drought conditions, a number that had more than doubled from approximately 680,000 in 2019.[14] Cycles of drought are common throughout the Sahel, and Burkina Faso is no exception; but, though the country has suffered droughts before, notably from 1968 to 1973, currently a combination of high temperatures, lower-than-average rainfall, and water shortages has increased the severity of both contemporary and projected drought cycles.[15]

Consequently, food security, health, and water access have been threatened, with rural-to-urban migration rates accelerating, which places heavy pressures on infrastructure and state resources.[16] These issues exacerbate climatic and political struggles, with jihadi violence

202 *Weaponizing Water*

killing thousands of people and displacing almost a million. As violence rages in the countryside, protests of the government's inability to stop the violence have spread across Burkina Faso.

Unable to quell the civil unrest, President Roch Kaboré fired Prime Minister Christophe Joseph Marie Dabire from his post in December 2021. Kaboré was himself deposed in a military coup d'etat in January 2022. Paul-Henri Sandaogo, his replacement, has since been ousted by his colleague Ibrahim Traore.[17] Meanwhile Burkinabes continue to be caught in the crossfire between jihadi insurgents and a flailing central government.

These systemic vulnerabilities have been exploited by the Islamic State West Africa Province (ISWAP). Amid the central government's inability to guard against jihadi elements, water has played an indirect but vital role in the militants' subjugation of populations. As noted by UN Secretary-General Antonio Guterres, groups like Boko Haram in Nigeria have been able to gain new recruits "particularly from local communities disillusioned by a lack of economic opportunities and access to essential resources," with the same phenomenon occurring in central Mali on the border with Burkina Faso where "terrorist groups have exploited the growing tensions between herders and farmers to recruit new members from pastoralist communities who are cut off from water supplies and feel excluded and stigmatized."[18]

Extending its reach into Burkina Faso, ISWAP is leveraging access to water over subjected populations to build allegiance, much as did their brethren in Syria and Iraq. Many communities are caught between the encroaching Islamic State and the droughts that continue to negatively impact large swathes of the country. Since 2017, ISWAP has targeted civilian and military infrastructure alike, using it to coerce local populations into submission.

Although ISWAP lacks the institutional presence of a nation-state, it has been able to enforce the cooperation of local populations.[19] Through Islamic practices such as zakat, or almsgiving, jihadist groups have empowered themselves through the accumulation of capital and natural resources and dictated access to natural resources, including water. As a result, because of these consistent patterns of conflict, the Burkinabe government's inability to provide basic public services, and stressors on the environment, the state's ability to govern has eroded and radically buoyed jihadist influence and alternative governance structures.

This situation is analogous to ISWAP's actions in the Lake Chad region. Evidence suggests that, unlike Boko Haram in Nigeria, ISWAP in Burkina Faso is using the water weapon to win over the local peo-

Stemming the Tide of Water Weaponization   203

ple. Where Boko Haram earned a reputation for savagery, ISWAP is digging wells, giving out seeds and fertilizer, and providing safe pasture for herders.

The role of the water weapon in the ongoing crisis in Yemen is more established. Water continues to be weaponized by the various state and non-state actors embroiled in conflict. Here al-Qaeda in the Arabian Peninsula (AQAP) is garnering support and recruits through the provision of water services, such as well construction. Meanwhile, Iranian-backed Houthi rebels are blockading resources and preventing the population's access to water in some areas. Most significantly, the Saudi-led coalition opposing the rebels is continuing to commit war crimes as it targets civilian infrastructure, including desalination and water bottling plants.

The coalition's violations of international law should be especially troubling to the United States, which, in general, opposes water weaponization out of principle. Washington must reconcile its support for the international laws of war and for the Saudi-led coalition's air campaign of indiscriminate airstrikes. The United States has remained largely silent in the face of these violations of the laws of war.

However, since the murder of journalist Jamal Khashoggi in 2018, at the hands of Saudi agents, US congressional sentiment toward Saudi Arabia has hardened as the international community also pushed for an end to the conflict. Yet even those lawmakers who backed the Trump administration's support of Saudi Arabia generally began to yield to the increasing call to enact legislation that would punish Saudi human rights abuses, including the destruction of water infrastructure. The eventual consequence was to limit weapon sales to Saudis and their allies.

In March 2019, the US Senate narrowly voted 54–46 to end US support for the Saudi-led coalition fighting in Yemen in a resolution cosponsored by Senator Bernie Sanders (I-VT) and Senator Mike Lee (R-UT).[20] However, this progress was negated when in May 2019 the Trump administration sidestepped congressional review by declaring an emergency with respect to tensions with Iran as an excuse to proceed with $8 billion in military sales. The administration also vetoed a 2019 resolution that would have ended US military support for the Saudi-UAE air campaign, and the Republican-led Senate failed to override that veto.[21]

The warfighting tactics of the Saudi-led coalition and their effect on the supply of potable water were direct causes of what was then the worst cholera outbreak in the world. Areas under rebel Houthi control have become completely isolated from humanitarian supplies and potable water because of the continued airstrikes and blockades. Observers from the World Health Organization (WHO) assessing the ongoing situation noted that Saudi-led airstrikes have been perniciously destroying vital infrastructure, including hospitals and public water systems, and have displaced people into crowded areas with unsanitary conditions.[22]

Turning to southwest Asia, as of early 2022, the chaos in Afghanistan, precipitated by the withdrawal of US forces from the country in conjunction with drought conditions and depleted groundwater in many reservoirs, has brought misery to many communities. This dire situation raises the possibility that the Taliban could use the water weapon against citizens or the national branch of the Islamic State that has become the chief contender for power in Afghanistan. At this point, there are rumors but no solid evidence that this practice has already begun.

Beyond the drought, water stress in Afghanistan was driven by severe spring floods in 2021 that affected nearly half a million people. The degradation of arable land is leading to irregular livestock migration, which in turn stokes interethnic tensions and conflict between herders and farmers. Once again, as in other countries such as Somalia, citizens with diminished livelihoods are more prone to extremism.[23] On the international level, tensions are rising between Iran and the Taliban over the transboundary Harirund and Helmand Rivers, which are subject to diminishing flows. This problem is compounded by the fact that five major river basins in Afghanistan discharge water into neighboring states, Pakistan, Iran, Uzbekistan, Turkmenistan, and Tajikistan.

The impacts of water stress extend to Afghanistan's agricultural sector. Opium is a less water-intensive crop than many food crops. This is one factor, along with economic desperation, that has pushed Afghani farmers toward growing opium, a practice that brings more violence as gangs, warlords, and the Taliban itself fight for control over the opium trade.

Whether the Taliban choose to consciously weaponize water, the lack of water management capacity brought about by the flight and evacuation of technical professionals could still cause considerable damage to public health and welfare. One danger is that unsanitary conditions could cause a flare-up of Covid-19. Experts have voiced concerns that the Taliban's strict limitation of modern technology may limit options for building infrastructure needed for water control and climate change adaptation.

Conditions in geographies as distinct as Burkina Faso, Yemen, and Afghanistan, where use of the water weapon by both state and non-state actors is increasing, stand as a warning. It is imperative for the community of nations to prevent the practice of water weaponization from further metastasizing beyond a limited geography of countries that harbor

Stemming the Tide of Water Weaponization   205

extremists and becoming a norm in modern warfare. It is also important to forestall the possibility that use of the water weapon by terrorists causes upward proliferation to the national level. The international community must strongly discourage nation-states, including those engaged in combat with extremist groups, from considering water weaponization as an option to retaliate against extremists or against other states.

Although it has some inherent structural weaknesses, as described herein, an international legal framework exists for addressing water weaponization, at least at the nation-state level. This framework can be expanded to address all uses of the water weapon. Better coordination between the global community and national-level actors, including NGOs, is essential to prevent state-sponsored water weaponization in countries where deteriorating ecological and social conditions create growing instability.

However, the lingering, and wicked, problem is how to prevent proliferation of water weaponization by VEOs using the instrument of international law. It may be a fool's errand when it is applied to non-state actors. Extremists do not operate according to any ethical framework, let alone a legal one. Neither are they respectful of the rules of war.

The very assumptions of the neoliberal world order are under stress. Today, the prospect of global cooperation around the challenges posed by water weaponization is dim, as evidenced by the failure of consensus-based decisionmaking addressing the twin clear and present dangers of the climate crisis and the Covid-19 epidemic. The lack of enforcement mechanisms for global environmental agreements is a challenge that has only been overcome on rare occasions. Therefore, it is incumbent on individual nations and regional organizations to take matters into their own hands to stem the tide of water weaponization. In the case of the United States, this will take a whole-of-society effort that also includes government action.

To Stem the Tide

In the end, barring a binding, enforceable legal framework, the key to countering water weaponization may lie in conflict prevention through better international development that improve conditions in the water sector. Addressing water stress in Iraq and Syria, Nigeria, and Somalia is a test case for a US development strategy that foregrounds human security in fragile states important to US national security that have complex environmental problems.

Adapting US Foreign Policy

The Global Fragility Act is one US foreign policy vehicle for accomplishing this goal. The act was passed by the US Congress in December 2019 as part of a comprehensive government strategy to stabilize conflict-affected areas and strengthen US capacity to be an effective leader of international efforts preventing extremism and conflict. The Global Fragility Act is intended to establish a ten-year pilot strategy for USAID, the Department of State, and the Department of Defense to work together to prevent violence. The initial focus is on five of the countries deemed, under the act, to be the most fragile. The announcement of the selected countries is pending as of 2022, but there are indications that at least a few countries under active consideration are experiencing water stress.

The Department of State is the lead agency under the US Water Strategy, and USAID is at the forefront of efforts to improve social conditions. The Global Fragility Act could be a useful tool in Nigeria, for example, because it directs funding toward conflict prevention and peacebuilding activities that target water disputes and allocates resources that alleviate compound climate and water stressors.

It is also notable that at the time of this writing, USAID is leading a whole-of-government effort to develop the US Global Water Strategy. It has added Nigeria to its list of focal countries.[24] Focal countries were chosen because of a combination of national security considerations and development needs. Though the specific programs under these plans focus heavily on water, sanitation, and hygiene (WASH) and global health sectors, it might be possible to reprogram some of the funds to promote drought resilience in areas beset by extremist influence. Other funds could be made available by direct congressional appropriations.

Climate change and water weaponization are closely linked. International funding, known as climate finance, is mobilized for climate adaptation projects in lesser developed nations under the provisions of multilateral international climate change agreements such as the Paris Agreement. Some of the $200 billion pledged by developed nation-states at the 2021 United Nations Climate Change Conference (COP26) in Glasgow, should it be realized, could also be directed toward climate adaptation projects that target the water sector. Mobilizing climate finance necessitates coordination between national governments and multilateral development institutions such as the World Bank.

Investment in the prevention of water stress provides another set of strategic foreign policy goals in addition to hard security. Improving developing nations' water infrastructure can give the United States a

Stemming the Tide of Water Weaponization   207

comparative advantage in its rivalry with China, which is increasing foreign assistance investments with the Belt and Road Initiative as a vehicle to build goodwill across the developing world.

There are not many places where Chinese investment has been more influential than in Nigeria. According to a 2014 poll, 80 percent of Nigerians view China's influence positively, with only 10 percent expressing a negative view, making Nigeria the most pro-Chinese nation in the world.[25] The fact that Nigeria is an important source of petroleum for the Chinese economy has been a key factor leading to extensive economic, military, and political support. Accordingly, China signed a $1 billion memorandum of understanding with Nigeria about funding home construction and water supply improvement in Abuja in 2009.[26] Under such agreements, Chinese firms are systematically hired to oversee these projects, as is the case with the massive 3,050-megawatt Mambilla Hydroelectric Power Station under construction on the Benue River.[27]

Beyond international competition, US internal politics aligns with pursuit of a strategic advantage over China in the area of development assistance in the water sector. In the United States, foreign assistance for water projects in developing nations enjoys relatively high bipartisan support when compared to other foreign assistance projects. This trend has been discernible for decades.[28] Support among the conservative wing of the US Congress has been garnered especially when explanations of the global problem of water stress are not overtly conflated with climate change and thus imply that the blame can be placed on individual economic choices.

Pursuant to Senator Paul Simon's Water for the Poor Act of 2005, which was passed by Congress with broad bipartisan support, USAID annually allocated an average of $452 million to water activities between fiscal years 2003 and 2011. These funding levels have remained consistent. Historically, the USAID budget allocations for water programs have been made in four thematic areas: (1) water sanitation and hygiene, (2) water resources management, (3) water productivity, and (4) disaster risk reduction.[29]

USAID has made important progress in Nigeria under this act's umbrella. In 2017, USAID launched a successful two-year $2.5 million Water and Sanitation Coordination Project in Nigeria's Bauchi and Kaduna States to improve water governance. This project is an example of international cooperation because it also leveraged infrastructure investments from the World Bank and African Development Bank.[30]

More such projects are needed to improve human conditions in Nigeria and reverse the scarcity that legitimizes VEOs and allows them

208   *Weaponizing Water*

to weaponize water. Successful development projects are also a tool that builds national capacity and effectively counters the narratives of VEOs that claim national governments are unable to provide for their citizens.

These small examples of work in Nigeria could be scaled up in other regions. This provides the hope that it is still possible to invest wisely to stem the tide of water weaponization. From the perspective of the US government, systematic prioritization of global water challenges is an important and politically feasible basis for a renewed foreign policy that foregrounds human dignity while combating extremism and supporting the human security of future generations.

Developing a Research Agenda

Academia also has an important part to play. More research on water weaponization is needed as soon as possible. Such research should be based on interdisciplinary approaches. Scholars in the field of security studies should dedicate effort to new approaches examining the water and conflict cycle.

Scholars and scientists should devote special attention to the compound risks resulting from the physical impacts of climate change on human security. Interdisciplinary studies are crucial for determining where climate change and associated water scarcity increase the vulnerability of human systems and trigger responses that increase the risk of water conflict and water weaponization.

Designing and conducting meaningful studies on water and conflict can be challenging. These studies must draw on expertise from multiple academic departments even though there are often institutional barriers against collaboration. This problem is not exclusive to academia. Public and private research institutions rarely *maintain* capacity for interdisciplinary study on the scale necessary to address water and conflict.

The type of analysis called for must draw on expertise in the natural sciences, including earth science and ecology, as well as political science, economics, and social sciences, to better understand human behavior in the conflict cycle in drought-affected areas. Funding for this type of research should also be a priority for foundations and philanthropists interested in climate change and security issues.

Engaging the International Community

Some of these same challenges are echoed in the policy arena. Since at least the early 2000s, large swathes of the international community,

Experts have called for what they refer to as climatization of the UN Security Council (UNSC). Resolutions recognizing the connections between climate change and security issues have been proposed to the Security Council on about half a dozen occasions. The need to prepare for and prevent the worst impacts of climate change has also surfaced in Arria formula meetings, which are opportunities for experts outside the UN to testify in an informal consultative process.

including governance and security institutions, have developed a growing awareness of the connections between climate change and security. Climate security issues now shape the policy agenda at the highest levels globally, including at the United Nations and Group of Seven (G7) forums and at major annual international security conferences in Berlin and Halifax, Canada.

Experts have called for what they refer to as climatization of the UN Security Council (UNSC). Resolutions recognizing the connections between climate change and security issues have been proposed to the Security Council on about half a dozen occasions. The need to prepare for and prevent the worst impacts of climate change has also surfaced in Arria formula meetings, which are opportunities for experts outside the UN to testify in an informal consultative process.

The impetus for raising climate and security issues at the UNSC is usually recognition of the existential threat that sea level rise poses for small island nations, but other issues have been discussed. The debate that was most germane to water weaponization took place on March 31, 2017. On that day, the UN Security Council passed Resolution 2349 on peace and security in Africa in response to the upsurge in terrorism by Boko Haram and IS in the Lake Chad basin region.

In addition to offering policy prescriptions about more effective counterterrorism approaches, the resolution recognizes the adverse effects of climate change and ecological changes, among other factors, on the stability of the region. These effects include water scarcity, drought, desertification, land degradation, and food insecurity. Further, the resolution emphasizes the need for adequate regional climate change risk assessments, including drought prediction and risk management strategies, by national governments and United Nations members.[31]

Testifying before a subsequent Security Council meeting in March 2018, Mohammed Bila, a representative of the Lake Chad Basin Commission, underlined the continuing need for assessments recounting the experience of Kaukiri, a village near the tri-point marker between Niger, Nigeria, and Chad. In 2010, he observed, farming could not take place because the Komadugu Yobe River had run dry and failed to bring water to the areas around the village. Yet, there was no sign that local authorities or community organizations had noticed the three preceding years of similar agricultural losses, which could have signaled the impending drought, or that any action had been taken.[32]

In response to the recommendations for reform of climate risk assessment, the UN established the Climate Security Mechanism in 2018. This organization provides the United Nations with a small but

210   *Weaponizing Water*

dedicated capacity to connect and leverage existing resources and expertise across the system to address climate-related security risks more systematically. It is designed to inform the work of the United Nations specialized organizations operating in this space, such as the UN Development and Environmental Programmes. Although this is an important symbolic step, the main effect of the Climate Security Mechanism has been to raise awareness of climate risk assessments within the UN system rather than to implement tangible programs on the ground in impacted countries.[33]

Regional security organizations, most notably the North Atlantic Treaty Organization (NATO), have incorporated considerations of climate security into their engagement and operational plans. The NATO Climate and Security Plan of Action, released in 2021, recognizes the connection between water stress and conflict, describing the relationship as follows:

> The implications of climate change including drought, soil erosion . . . and degradation can lead to famine, floods, loss of land and livelihood, and have a disproportionate impact on women and girls as well as on poor, vulnerable or marginalized populations, as well as potentially exacerbate state fragility, fuel conflicts, and lead to displacement, migration, and human mobility, creating conditions that can be exploited by state and non-state actors that threaten or challenge the Alliance[34]

Intelligence and Defense

The mission of the US intelligence community is to provide timely and relevant information to policymakers, decisionmakers, and the military. Since the early 2000s, defense and intelligence agencies as well as many US and European think tanks have undertaken analyses of the security risks associated with climate change. In January 2021, as one of his first acts as president of the United States, Joe Biden issued an executive order calling for the preparation of a comprehensive national intelligence estimate on the national security implications of climate change.

An unclassified version released in late 2021 and widely distributed found that water stress associated with climate change was a significant driver of social and economic instability in countries that are important to US national security interests. Eleven countries, predominantly in the Middle East and North Africa (MENA) region, but some as close as Central American nations in the so-called dry corridor, were identified as being at the highest risk.

Stemming the Tide of Water Weaponization   211

This analysis underscores the importance of water in climate security. These assessments are good first steps. However, water stress as a factor leading to instability and enabling water weaponization should be considered more prominently in intelligence assessments.

The US Department of Defense is also an important actor in the climate and security space. The DoD has a history of building the practical realities of climate change, including water stress, into its operational plans, roles, and missions. The time is ripe for the DoD to consider the risks of global instability posed by water stress at a more strategic level. This warrants the inclusion of the issue in documents such as the National Defense Strategy but also in so-called theater engagement plans, which are used by regional combatant commands that contend with climate change–induced threats on the ground.

The defense sector also has the opportunity to engage military to military with partner nations in regions subject to water stress including droughts. Practitioners and scholars often see cooperation around the environmental challenges as a tool for peacebuilding, and this approach has been effective in the Middle East when it involved non-military actors such as the NGO Ecopeace. Renewed bilateral cooperation could include larger-scale projects such as the construction of resilient water infrastructure and smaller-scale projects such as pumping stations and boreholes.

Another impetus to address water stress is the United Nations Sustainable Development Goals (SDGs), seventeen interlinked global goals established by the UN General Assembly in 2015. They were designed to promote a better and more sustainable future by 2030. Promoting human security by maintaining access to natural resources is a central objective of the SDGs.

Sustainable Development Goal 6 was established to ensure availability and sustainable management of water and sanitation for all. Progress toward this goal is determined by eleven indicators. The one most relevant to water weaponization calls for the protection and restoration of water-related ecosystems in the face of climate change. This provision can serve as guidance for the international community in protecting drought-prone water ecosystems from being exploited on the national level for nefarious purposes.

In short, the issue of water weaponization should be incorporated into the growing climate and security agenda and should act as a factor in planning for organizations ranging from the US government to the United Nations and NGOs.

Conclusion

Water weaponization has begun to appear into the academic literature and discourse around climate and security. Some authors have examined actions by nation-states, but most of the prominent scholars quoted in this volume, such as Marwa Daoudy, Tobias von Lossow, and Jeannie Sowers, are focusing on weaponization in the Middle East perpetrated by non-state actors. Unfortunately, conditions in other regions are becoming ripe for water weaponization as climate change–induced water stress becomes more prevalent.

This volume documents both perpetrators and victims of water weaponization within the geography of the Middle East and Africa in the context of climate change and drought-induced scarcity. The prognosis for the Middle East and Africa is rather bleak. As internal conflicts continue and as scarcity increases due to climate change, water may become even more weaponized. It is my hope that this work opens the door to future inquiry about water's use as a weapon under various conditions and in regions across the globe as a step toward eradication of this ancient and odious approach to modern warfare.

Notes

1. "Nigeria: Migration Profiles," UNICEF, https://esa.un.org/miggmgprofiles /indicators/files/Nigeria.pdf.

2. Matthew Holdgate, "Why It Matters: Nigeria's Global Oil Impact," Nikko Asset Management, September 9, 2016, https://americas.nikkoam.com/files/pdf /insights/2016/20160909-Why-it-matters-Nigerias-Global-Oil-Impact.pdf.

3. "Primer: The Resource Curse," Natural Resource Governance Institute, April 27, 2015, https://resourcegovernance.org/analysis-tools/publications/primer-resource -curse.

4. Ojoma Akor, "How Drought-Tolerant Maize Variety Enhances Production," All Africa, February 13, 2014, https://allafrica.com/stories/201402130473.html.

5. Feed the Future, *Maximizing Agricultural Revenue and Key Enterprises in Targeted Sites: Markets II 2015 Mid-Term Update: April 2012–2015* (USAID, 2014), https://www.chemonics.com/wp-content/uploads/2017/10/MARKETS2_Mid TermUpdate_PrintVersion_Dollars.pdf.

6. Feed the Future, *Global Food Security Strategy: Nigeria Country Plan* (USAID, August 2018), https://cg-281711fb-71ea-422c-b02c-ef79f539e9d2.s3.us -gov-west-1.amazonaws.com/uploads/2018/11/Nigeria_GFSS_Country_Plan_-_Final _WS_Edits_2.pdf.

7. Al Chukwuma Okoli and Atelhe Georgee, "Nomads Against Natives: A Political Ecology of Herder/Farmer Conflicts in Nasarawa State, Nigeria," *American International Journal of Contemporary Research* 4, no. 2 (2014): 79, aijcrnet.com /journals/Vol_4_No_2_February_2014/11.pdf.

Stemming the Tide of Water Weaponization 213

8. "About the Water and Security Partnership," WPS, https://waterpeacesecurity.org/info/our-approach.

9. "Mission and Vision," Institute for Water Resources, US Army Corps of Engineers, http://www.iwr.usace.army.mil/About/Mission-and-Vision/.

10. "About Us," Famine Early Warning Systems Network (FEWS NET), https://fews.net/about-us.

11. "Environmental Security in Africa" (Proceedings of the 2012 Environmental Security Africa Dialogue, US Army War College, Carlisle, PA, July 11–12, 2012).

12. Sinead O'Sullivan, "Drones for Climate and Security," Center for Climate and Security, 2016, https://climateandsecurity.org/2016/08/10/drones-for-climate-and-security/.

13. John Pike, "Burkina Faso—Climate," Global Security, https://tinyurl.com/4k2nu5ef.

14. "Burkina Faso Crisis and Covid-19 Concerns Highlight Pressure on Sahel Food Security," UN News, April 2, 2020, https://news.un.org/en/story/2020/04/1060942.

15. "Climate Risks in Food for Peace Geographies: Burkina Faso," Climate Links, August 7, 2017, https://www.climatelinks.org/resources/climate-risks-food-peace-geographies-burkina-faso.

16. Ibid.

17. "Burkina Faso restores constitution, names coup leader president," Al Jazeera, January 31, 2022, https://www.aljazeera.com/news/2022/1/31/burkina-faso-restores-constitution-names-coup-leader-president.

18. Edith M. Lederer, "UN Chief: Climate Change Aggravates Conflict and Terrorism," AP News, December 9, 2021, https://apnews.com/article/climate-africa-poverty-united-nations-antonio-guterres-de6cf4b14d89537543cc4ac3a8288352.

19. Natasja Rupesinghe and Mikael Hiberg, "The Sahel's Jihadists Don't All Govern Alike: Context Matters," The Conversation, September 14, 2021, https://theconversation.com/the-sahels-jihadists-dont-all-govern-alike-context-matters-166998.

20. Joe Gould, "Senate Passes Resolution to End US Support of Saudi Arabia in Yemen, 54–46," DefenseNews, March 13, 2019, https://www.defensenews.com/congress/2019/03/13/us-senate-passes-yemen-resolution-54-46/.

21. Patricia Zengerle, "U.S. Lawmakers Still Plot to Push Saudi Arabia on Rights, Despite Trump," Reuters, August 1, 2019, https://www.reuters.com/article/us-usa-saudi-arms/u-s-lawmakers-still-plot-to-push-saudi-arabia-on-rights-despite-trump-idUSKCN1UR5T1.

22. Matthew Ponsford, "Saudi-Led Coalition Responsible for 'Worst Cholera Outbreak in the World' in Yemen: Researchers," Reuters, August 18, 2017, https://www.reuters.com/article/us-yemen-cholera-saudi/saudi-led-coalition-responsible-for-worst-cholera-outbreak-in-the-world-in-yemen-researchers-idUSKCN1AY2JH.

23. Harman Singh, "Can the Taliban Address Climate-Related Risks in Afghanistan?" Planetary Security Initiative, October 26, 2021, https://www.planetarysecurityinitiative.org/news/can-taliban-address-climate-related-risks-afghanistan.

24. These countries include Afghanistan, Democratic Republic of Congo, Ethiopia, Ghana, Haiti, India, Indonesia, Kenya, Lebanon, Liberia, Madagascar, Mali, Mozambique, Nigeria, Nepal, Senegal, South Sudan, Tanzania, and Uganda.

25. "Negative views of Russia on the Rise: Global Poll," BBC World Service poll, June 3, 2014, http://downloads.bbc.co.uk/mediacentre/country-rating-poll.pdf.

26. Michael J. Tierney et al., "More Dollars Than Sense: Refining Our Knowledge of Development Finance Using AidData," *World Development* 39, no. 11

(2011): 1891–1906, https://www.aiddata.org/publications/more-dollars-than-sense
-refining-our-knowledge-of-development-finance-using-aiddata.

27. "Nigeria Awards Dam Power Plant Contract to Chinese State Firm Again," Reuters, August 30, 2017, https://www.reuters.com/article/us-nigeria-hydro-china -idUSKCN1BA27P.

28. Marcus DuBois King, *Water, U.S. Foreign Policy and American Leadership* (Institute for International Economic Policy Working Paper Series IIEP-WP-2013-11, Elliott School of International Affairs, George Washington University, October 15, 2013), https://www2.gwu.edu/~iiep/assets/docs/papers/2014WP/KingIIEPWP 201311.pdf.

29. USAID, *Water and Development Strategy 2013–2018* (Washington, DC: USAID, n.d.), https://www.usaid.gov/sites/default/files/documents/1865/USAID _Water_Strategy_3.pdf.

30. "USAID Launches New Water and Sanitation Project in Nigeria," USAID, May 15, 2017, https://2017-2020.usaid.gov/nigeria/news-information/press-releases /usaid-launches-new-water-and-sanitation-project-nigeria.

31. UN Security Council, "Resolution 2349 (2017) / adopted by the Security Council at its 7911th Meeting, on 31 March 2017," United Nations Digital Library, https://digitallibrary.un.org/record/863830?ln=en.

32. "Better Governance of Underfunded, Poorly Managed Lake Chad Basin Key to Resolving Conflict, Suffering Across Region, Speakers Tell Security Council," UN Press Office, March 22, 2018, https://www.un.org/press/en/2018/sc13259 .doc.htm.

33. Marcus D. King, Caitlin Werrell, and Francesco Femia, "The Responsibility to Prepare and Prevent: Closing the Climate and Security Governance Gaps," in *Anthropocene (In)Securities: Reflections on Collective Survival After the Stockholm Conference* (Oxford: Oxford University Press, 2021).

34. "NATO Climate Change and Security Action Plan," North Atlantic Treaty Organization, June 14, 2021, https://www.nato.int/cps/en/natohq/official_texts _185174.htm.

Bibliography

"About Us." Famine Early Warning System Network. https://fews.net/about-us.

"About Us." International Law Association. https://www.ila-hq.org/index.php/about-us.

"About the Water, Peace and Security Partnership." Water Peace Security. https://waterpeacesecurity.org/info/our-approach.

Adnan, Tahir. "Shabaab Destroys Only Source of Water." *Somalia Report*, June 4, 2012. http://piracyreport.com/index.php/post/3418/Shabaab_Destroys_Only_Source_of_Water.

Agence France-Presse. "At Least 23 Killed in Somalia Clan Violence." *Daily Nation*, January 22, 2015. Updated July 3, 2020. http://www.nation.co.ke/news/africa/At-least-23-killed-in-Somalia-clan-violence/1066-2598404-wnk51rz/index.html.

———. "Isis Captured 2,300 Humvee Armoured Vehicles from Iraqi Forces in Mosul." *The Guardian*, May 31, 2015.

Aggestam, Karin. "Desecuritisation of Water and the Technocratic Turn in Peacebuilding." *International Environmental Agreements: Politics, Law and Economics* 15, no. 3 (2015): 327–340.

Akinrotoye, Kehinde Peter, and Uzal Umar. "Combating Diarrhoea in Nigeria: The Way Forward." *Journal of Microbiology and Experimentation* 6, no. 4 (2018): 191–197.

Akinwotu, E. "Drought Worsens Deadly Battle Between Fulani Herdsmen and Farmers in Nigeria." *The Guardian*, January 23, 2017.

Akor, Ojoma. "How Drought-Tolerant Maize Variety Enhances Production." *DailyTrust*, February 13, 2014. https://dailytrust.com/how-drought-tolerant-maize-variety-enhances-production.

Akpor, O. B., and M. Muchie. "Challenges in Meeting the MDGs: The Nigerian Drinking Water Supply and Distribution Sector." *Journal of Environmental Science and Technology* 4, no. 5 (2011): 480–489.

Al-Amin, Mohammed A. "Hydropower Resources as Target of Terrorism: Case Study of Selected Water Bodies in Northern Nigeria." *International Journal of Engineering and Science* 2, no. 11 (2013): 52–61.

Al-Ansari, Nadhir A. "Management of Water Resources in Iraq: Perspectives and Prognoses." *Engineering* 5 (2013): 677.

216 Bibliography

Alfifi, Majid, Parisa Kaghazgaran, James Caverlee, and Fred Morstatter. "Measuring the Impact of ISIS Social Media Strategy." Texas A&M University. 2018. https://snap.stanford.edu/mis2/files/MIS2_paper_23.pdf.

Al-Kinānī, Abū 'Amr. "It's Either Islamic State or the Flood." *Dabiq* 1435, Ramadan Issue no. 2.

Al-Marashi, Ibrahim. "The Dawning of Hydro-Terrorism." Al-Jazeera, June 19, 2015. https://www.aljazeera.com/opinions/2015/6/19/the-dawning-of-hydro-terrorism/.

America Abroad. "Al-Shabaab's 'Water Terrorism' Is Yielding Results and Tragedy in Somalia's Civil War." The World. August 12, 2014. https://www.pri.org/stories/2014-08-08/how-al-shabaab-using-water-tool-terrorism.

Amery, Hussein A. "Climate, Not Conflict, Drove Many Syrian Refugees to Lebanon." *The Conversation*, December 3, 2019.

"Annual Freshwater Withdrawals, Domestic (% of Total Freshwater Withdrawal)—Somalia." World Bank. 2014. https://data.worldbank.org/indicator/ER.H2O.FWDM.ZS?display=default%25%2525252020&locations=SO.

"Aqueduct Water Risk Atlas." Aqueduct, World Resources Institute. 2019. https://tinyurl.com/2p9hyj2f.

Arango, Tim, James Risen, Farnaz Fassihi, Ronen Bergman, and Murtaza Hussain. "The Iran Cables: Secret Documents Show How Tehran Wields Power in Iraq." *New York Times*, November 18, 2019.

"Are You Provided Electricity, Water or Basic Services Under the Oppression of the Daesh Caliphate?" (Arabic translation). YouTube video, Witness from Mosul, 2015. https://www.youtube.com/watch?v=2imQZdyI5Z8.

"The AS Finance System." Hiraal Institute. https://hiraalinstitute.org/the-as-finance-system/.

Associated Press. "A Look at the Nigerian Extremist Group Boko Haram." AP News, April 14, 2014. https://apnews.com/5a70eba16ff14934a16e4b63672cce59.

"At-a-Glance: Somalia Displacement Crisis." United Nations High Commission on Refugees Somalia (UNHCR Somalia), October 7, 2011. https://data.unhcr.org/en/news/9757.

"At Least a Million Sub-Saharan Africans Moved to Europe Since 2010." Pew Research Center, March 22, 2018. https://www.pewresearch.org/global/2018/03/22/at-least-a-million-sub-saharan-africans-moved-to-europe-since-2010/.

Azmeh, Shamel. "The Uprising of the Marginalised: A Socio-economic Perspective of the Syrian Uprising." London School of Economics Middle East Centre Paper Series, no. 6, November 2014. http://eprints.lse.ac.uk/60243/?from_serp=1.

"Bandit Attacks Displace Northern Nigeria Herders." IRIN, June 19, 2013. https://reliefweb.int/report/nigeria/bandit-attacks-displace-northern-nigeria-herders.

Barbooti, M. M., G. Bolzoni, I. A. Mirza, M. Pelosi, L. Barilli, R. Kadhum, and G. Peterlongo. "Evaluation of Quality of Drinking Water from Baghdad, Iraq." *Science World Journal* 5, no. 2 (2010).

Barrett, Richard. *Beyond the Caliphate: Foreign Fighters and the Threat of Returnees*. New York: Soufan Center and Global Strategy Network, October 2017. https://thesoufancenter.org/wp-content/uploads/2017/11/Beyond-the-Caliphate-Foreign-Fighters-and-the-Threat-of-Returnees-TSC-Report-October-2017-v3.pdf.

Bature, Yunana Magaji, Abubakar Aliyu Sanni, and Francis Ojo Adebayo. "Analysis of Impact of National Fadaa Development Projects on Beneficiaries Income and Wealth in FCT, Nigeria." *Journal of Economics and Sustainable Development 4*, no. 17 (2013): 11–23.

Bibliography   217

Baumgarten, Philip A. "Israel's Transboundary Water Disputes." Elisabeth Haub School of Law Student Publications, Pace Law School, May 14, 2009. https://digitalcommons.pace.edu/lawstudents/2.

Beehner, Lionel. "The Effects of 'Youth Bulge' on Civil Conflicts." Council on Foreign Relations, April 13, 2007. https://www.cfr.org/backgrounder/effects-youth-bulge-civil-conflicts.

Berger, Miriam. "Here's What We Know About the ISIS Prisons Controlled by the Syrian Kurds." *Washington Post*, October 12, 2019.

"Better Governance of Underfunded, Poorly Managed Lake Chad Basin Key to Resolving Conflict, Suffering Across Region, Speakers Tell Security Council." UN Press Office, March 22, 2018. https://www.un.org/press/en/2018/sc13259.doc.htm.

Bhojani, Fatima. "How ISIS Makes IEDs: The Supply Chain of Terrorism." *Foreign Affairs*, March 2, 2016.

Blair, Tony. "The Depth of the Challenge." Tony Blair Institute for Global Change, December 4, 2015. https://institute.global/policy/depth-challenge.

"Boko Haram Timeline: From Preachers to Slave Raider." BBC News, May 15, 2013. http://www.bbc.com/news/world-africa-22538888.

Botha, A., and M. Abdile. "Radicalization and Al-Shabaab Recruitment in Somalia." Institute for Security Studies, ISS Paper no. 266, September 2014. https://issafrica.s3.amazonaws.com/site/uploads/Paper266.pdf.

Bourne, Charles B. "The International Law Association's Contribution to International Water Resources Law." *Natural Resources Journal* 36, no. 2 (1996).

Buhaug, Halvard, J. Nordkvelle, T. Bernauer, T. Böhmelt, M. Brzoska, J. W. Busby, A. Ciccone et al. "One Effect to Rule Them All? A Comment on Climate and Conflict." *Climatic Change* 127 (December 2014): 391–397.

Burden, Jonathan. "Water Shortage and Unrest in Iraq." Global Risk Insights, November 24, 2019. https://globalriskinsights.com/2019/11/water-shortage-and-unrest-in-iraq/.

"Burkina Faso Crisis and Covid-19 Concerns Highlight Pressure on Sahel Food Security." UN News, April 2, 2020. https://news.un.org/en/story/2020/04/1060942.

Callimachi, Rukmini. "Described as Defeated, Islamic State Punches Back with Guerilla Tactics." *New York Times*, January 21, 2019.

Carlson, Andrew. "Pirates of Puntland, Somalia." Origins, June 2009. https://origins.osu.edu/article/pirates-puntland-somalia?language_content_entity=en.

Carsten, Paul, and Ahmed Kingimi. "Islamic State Ally Stakes Out Territory Around Lake Chad." Reuters, April 29, 2018. https://www.reuters.com/article/us-nigeria-security/islamic-state-ally-stakes-out-territory-around-lake-chad-idUSKBN1I0063.

Carty, Tracy. "A Climate in Crisis: How Climate Change Is Making Drought and Humanitarian Disaster Worse in East Africa" (Oxfam Media Briefing, Oxfam, London, April 27, 2017). https://www-cdn.oxfam.org/s3fs-public/mb-climate-crisis-east-africa-drought-270417-en.pdf.

Catovic, Saffet. "Islamic Sacred Texts Related to Water." GreenFaith Water Shield. faithinwater.org/uploads/4/4/3/0/44307383/islamic_sacred_texts-water-greenfaith.pdf.

Center for Preventive Action. "Al-Shabab in Somalia." Global Conflict Tracker. Published 2017. Updated May 12, 2022. https://www.cfr.org/global-conflict-tracker/conflict/al-shabab-somalia.

Cetorelli, Valeria, Isaac Sasson, Nazar Shabila, and Gilbert Burnham. "ISIS' Yazidi Genocide." *Foreign Affairs*, June 8, 2017. https://www.foreignaffairs.com/articles/syria/2017-06-08/isis-yazidi-genocide.

218   Bibliography

Chalecki, Elizabeth. "A New Vigilance: Identifying and Reducing the Risks of Environmental Terrorism." *Global Environmental Politics* 2, no. 1 (2002): 46–64. https://doi.org/10.1162/152638002317261463.

"Chapter 3: Somalia: Drought Conflict = Famine?" Brookings Institute, 2016. https://www.brookings.edu/wp-content/uploads/2016/06/03_nd_review_chapter3.pdf.

Chayes, Sarah. "Nigeria's Boko Haram Isn't Just About Western Education." *Washington Post*, May 16, 2014.

Chibueze, Nwokocha. "Historical Analysis of the Economic Effect of Drought on Tropical Forest Management in Northern Nigeria." *Journal of Political Sciences and Public Affairs* 4, no. 3 (2016).

Chonka, Peter. "What You Need to Know to Understand al-Shabaab." Tony Blair Institute for Global Change, September 21, 2016. https://institute.global/insight/co-existence/what-you-need-know-understand-al-shabaab.

Chulov, Martin. "How an Arrest in Iraq Revealed ISIS' $2bn Jihadist Network." *The Guardian*, June 15, 2014.

―――. "ISIS: The Inside Story." *The Guardian*, December 11, 2014.

"Climate Change, Charcoal Trade and Armed Conflict in Somalia." Climate Diplomacy. https://climate-diplomacy.org/case-studies/climate-change-charcoal-trade-and-armed-conflict-somalia.

Climate Projections and Extreme Climate Indices for the Arab Region. [Archived version.] United Nations Economic and Social Commission for Western Asia, 2016. https://archive.unescwa.org/publications/climate-projections-extreme-climate-indices-arab-region.

"Climate Risks in Food for Peace Geographies: Burkina Faso." Climate Links, August 7, 2017. https://www.climatelinks.org/resources/climate-risks-food-peace-geographies-burkina-faso.

CNA. *The Role of Water Stress in Instability and Conflict.* Report CRM-2017-U-016532. Arlington, VA: CNA, December 2017. https://www.cna.org/CNA_files/pdf/CRM-2017-U-016532-Final.pdf.

Cole, Juan. "Did ISIL Arise Partially Because of Climate Change?" Democratic Underground, July 26, 2015. https://www.democraticunderground.com/10027011582.

Coles, Isabel, and Ned Parker. "How Saddam's Men Help Islamic State Rule." Reuters, December 11, 2015. https://www.reuters.com/investigates/special-report/mideast-crisis-iraq-islamicstate/.

Collier, Paul, and Anke Hoeffler. "Greed and Grievance in Civil War." Policy Research Working Paper no. 2355, World Bank, Washington, DC, May 2000.

"Composite Drought Index." Food and Agriculture Organization of the United Nations (FAO). https://data.review.fao.org/map/catalog/srv/api/records/f186959b-c68b-42fb-be83-912cd72987b0.

Convention for the Pacific Settlement of International Disputes. [Archived version.] Netherlands Ministry of Foreign Affairs, no. 003316, October 18, 1907. https://archive.vn/20130616131806/http://www.minbuza.nl/en/key-topics/treaties/search-the-treaty-database/1907/10/003316.html#selection-47.0-47.63.

Convention on the Prohibition of Military or Any Hostile Use of Environmental Modification Techniques. United Nations, May 18, 1977. http://www.un-documents.net/enmod.htm.

Counter Extremism Project. *Al-Shabaab.* New York: Counter Extremism Project, 2019. https://www.counterextremism.com/threat/al-shabaab/report.

"Country Profile: Somalia." AQUASTAT—FAO's Information System on Water and Agriculture. 2005. http://www.fao.org/nr/water/aquastat/countries_regions/SOM/.

Bibliography   219

Crowcroft, Orlando. "Abu Bakr al-Baghdadi: How an Obscure Iraqi Academic Became the Leader of the Islamic State." Euronews, October 27, 2019. https://www.euronews.com/2019/10/27/how-abu-bakr-al-baghdadi-became-the-leader-of-isis.

Cunningham, Erin. "Islamic State Jihadists Are Using Water as a Weapon in Iraq." *Washington Post*, October 7, 2014.

"Daesh Wages Water War in Diyala in Northeastern Iraq (تنظيم داعش يشن حرب المياه في ديالى شمال شرق العراق)." YouTube video, 4:00. Al Aan TV, October 5, 2014. https://www.youtube.com/watch?v=6pGBtNbCkik.

Danilenko, Gennady M. "The Statute of the International Criminal Court and Third States." *Michigan Journal of International Law* 21, no. 3 (2000): 445.

Daoudy, Marwa. "Water Weaponization in the Syrian Conflict: Strategies of Domination and Cooperation." *International Affairs* 96, no. 5 (September 1, 2020): 1347–1366.

Debono, Gwendoline, and Simona Foltyn. "Iraq's Yazidis Still Haunted by Sinjar Massacres." France 24, June 28, 2019. https://www.france24.com/en/20190628-revisited-iraq-yazidis-still-haunted-sinjar-massacres-islamic-state-group-nadia-murad.

De Châtel, Francesca. "Drops of Faith: Water in Islam." *Water Resources IMPACT* 11, no. 6 (2009).

———. "The Role of Drought and Climate Change in the Syrian Uprising: Untangling the Triggers of Revolution." *Middle Eastern Studies* 50, no. 4 (2014): 521–535.

Dempsey, Michael P. "How ISIS' Strategy Is Evolving: What the U.S. Can Do to Counter the Group's Shifting Tactics." *Foreign Affairs*, January 18, 2018.

Dews, Fred. "Al Shabaab: Background on the Somalia-based Terrorist Group that Attacked a Nairobi Mall." Brookings Institute, September 23, 2013. https://www.brookings.edu/blog/brookings-now/2013/09/23/al-shabaab-background-on-the-somalia-based-terrorist-group-that-attacked-a-nairobi-mall/.

"Designation of Al-Shabaab." [Archived version.] US Department of State, March 18, 2008. https://2001-2009.state.gov/r/pa/prs/ps/2008/mar/102338.htm.

Dreazen, Yochi. "From Electricity to Sewage, U.S. Intelligence Says That Islamic State Is Fast Learning How to Run a Country." Foreign Policy, August 19, 2014. http://foreignpolicy.com/2014/08/19/from-electricity-to-sewage-u-s-intelligence-says-the-islamic-state-is-fast-learning-how-to-run-a-country/.

"Drought Conditions Exacerbated by Above-Average Surface Temperatures over Eastern Horn." FEWS NET, January 31, 2017. http://www.fews.net/east-africa/seasonal-monitor/january-2017.

"Drought Monitoring." Somalia Water and Land Information Management, Food and Agriculture Organization of the United Nations. http://www.faoswalim.org/water-resources/drought/drought-monitoring.

"Droughts, Livestock Prices and Armed Conflict in Somalia," Climate Diplomacy. https://climate-diplomacy.org/case-studies/droughts-livestock-prices-and-armed-conflict-somalia.

Dupuy, Beatrice. "President Obama Did Not Free Islamic State Leader Al-Baghdadi from Prison." AP News, October 30, 2019. https://apnews.com/afs:Content:8037620747.

"Dutch Flood Land to Repel French." Pacific Institute. https://www.worldwater.org/conflicts/dutch-flood-land-to-repel-french-2/.

Dwyer, Colin. "Drought Threatens to Drive Famine in Somalia As Hunger Kills More Than 100." NPR, March 5, 2017. http://www.npr.org/sections/thetwo

220 Bibliography

-way/2017/03/05/518624610/drought-threatens-to-drive-famine-in-somalia-as -hunger-kills-more-than-100.

"Ecoregions." World Wildlife Fund. www.worldwildlife.org/biomes.

Eisenstadt, Michael, Michael Knights, and Ahmed Ali. "Iran's Influence in Iraq." Washington Institute, April 26, 2011. https://www.washingtoninstitute.org/policy -analysis/view/irans-influence-in-iraq-countering-tehrans-whole-of-government -approach.

Eklund, Lina, and Darcy Thompson. "Differences in Resource Management Affects Drought Vulnerability Across the Borders Between Iraq, Syria, and Turkey," *Ecology and Society* 22, no. 4 (2017): 9.

"Environmental Security in Africa." Proceedings of the 2012 Environmental Security Africa Dialogue, US Army War College, Carlisle, PA, July 11–12, 2012.

Epatko, Larisa. "Al-Shabab Militants Try Food to Win Hearts and Minds in Somalia." PBS, April 20, 2017. https://www.pbs.org/newshour/world/al-shabab-militants -try-food-win-hearts-minds-somalia.

Erian, Wadid, Bassem Katlan, and Ouldbdey Babah. *Drought Vulnerability in the Arab Region: Special Case Study: Syria.* Global Assessment Report on Disaster Risk Reduction, United Nations Office for Disaster and Risk Reduction, 2010. http://www.preventionweb.net/english/hyogo/gar/2011/en/bgdocs/Erian _Katlan_&_Babah_2010.pdf.

Eze, Jude Nwafor. "Drought Occurrences and Its Implications on Households in Yobe State, Nigeria." *Geoenvironmental Disasters* 5, no. 18 (2018).

Faul, Michelle. "Violence Surges from Islamic Uprising in Nigeria." AP News, April 15, 2014. https://apnews.com/article/801dcb341f1e4e06b21ef9247af73d00.

"Fears That Syria's Tishrin Dam May Collapse Amid Rising Water Levels," Middle East Eye, December 31, 2015. https://www.middleeasteye.net/fr/news/fears -syrias-tishrin-dam-may-collapse-amid-rising-water-levels-705752950.

Federal Government of the Republic of Nigeria and the State Governments of Adamawa, Bauchi, Borno, Gombe, Taraba and Yobe. *North-East Nigeria: Recovery and Peace-Building Assessment, Volume II, Component Report.* Washington, DC: World Bank, 2016. https://openknowledge.worldbank.org /bitstream/handle/10986/25778/110424-v2-WP-NorthEastNigeriaRecovery andPeaceBuildingAssessmentVolumeIIweb-PUBLIC-Volume-2.pdf;sequence=1.

Feed the Future. *Global Food Security Strategy (GFSS): Nigeria Country Plan, August 2018.* Washington, DC: USAID, 2018. https://www.usaid.gov/sites/default /files/documents/1867/Nigeria_GFSS_Country_Plan_-_Final_WS_Edits_2.pdf.

———. *Maximizing Agricultural Revenue and Key Enterprises in Targeted Sites: Markets II 2015 Mid-Term Update.* Washington, DC: USAID, April 2012– 2015. https://www.chemonics.com/wp-content/uploads/2017/10/MARKETS2 _MidTermUpdate_PrintVersion_Dollars.pdf.

Fergusson, James. *The World's Most Dangerous Place: Inside the Outlaw State of Somalia.* New York: Da Capo Press, 2013.

Ferris, Elizabeth, and Daniel Petz. "A Year That Shook the Rich: A Review of Natural Disasters in 2011." Brookings Institute, March 1, 2012. https://www .brookings.edu/multi-chapter-report/the-year-that-shook-the-rich-a-review-of -natural-disasters-in-2011/.

"Finally Free of al-Shabaab, Daily Life Resumes in El Bur." Hiiraan Online, December 17, 2014. https://hiiraan.com/news4/2014/Dec/97372/finally_free _of_al_shabaab_daily_life_resumes_in_el_bur.aspx.

Flood, Derek Henry. "A Review of the French-Led Military Campaign in Northern Mali." *CTC Sentinel* 6, no. 5 (May 2013). https://ctc.westpoint.edu/a-review -of-the-french-led-military-campaign-in-northern-mali/.

Bibliography   221

FloodList News Desk. "Somalia—30,000 in Need of Food and Drinking Water After Flooding." FloodList, June 13, 2016. http://floodlist.com/africa/somalia-30000-need-food-drinking-water-flooding.

Food Security and Nutrition Analysis Unit—Somalia. "Special Brief—Focus on Post *Gu* 2017 Assessment Results." *Food Security & Nutrition*, September 28, 2017. https://reliefweb.int/sites/reliefweb.int/files/resources/FSNAU-Special-Brief-September-2017_0.pdf.

"Former National Leaders: Water a Global Security Issue, 3/20/2011." United Nations University, March 20, 2011. https://unu.edu/media-relations/releases/water-called-a-global-security-issue.html.

"Fragile States Index." US Fund for Peace. https://fragilestatesindex.org/.

"The Fragile States Index 2019." US Fund for Peace. https://fundforpeace.org/2019/04/10/fragile-states-index-2019/.

Funk, Chris, Sharon E. Nicholson, Martin Landsfeld, Douglas Klotter, Pete Peterson, and Laura Harrison. "The Centennial Trends Greater Horn of Africa Precipitation Dataset." *Nature*, art. no. 150050, September 29, 2015.

Gadain, Hussein, Z. Stevanovic, K. Upton. B. Ó Dochartaigh, and I. Bellwood-Howard. "Africa Groundwater Atlas: Hydrogeology of Somalia." British Geological Survey. 2016. http://earthwise.bgs.ac.uk/index.php/Hydrogeology_of_Somalia.

Gaulter, Steff. "Flooding Affects Tens of Thousands in Somalia." Al Jazeera, November 8, 2015.

Geneva Water Hub. *The Geneva List of Principles on the Protection of Water Infrastructure*. Geneva: Geneva Water Hub and Platform for International Water Law, 2019. https://www.genevawaterhub.org/resource/geneva-list-principles-protection-water-infrastructure.

———. *Geneva Water Hub: Hydropolitics Towards Peace and Security*. Geneva: World Meteorological Organization, n.d. https://www.genevawaterhub.org/sites/default/files/atoms/files/leaflet_gwh_eng_small.pdf.

Gettleman, Jeffrey, and Neil MacFarquhar. "Food Aid Bypasses Somalia's Needy, U.N. Study Finds." *New York Times*, March 10, 2010.

Gibbons-Neff, Thomas. "Piracy Back on the Rise Off Somalia, U.S. Military Says." *Washington Post*, April 23, 2017.

Gilsinan, Kathy, and Mike Giglio. "What ISIS Will Become." *The Atlantic*, November 22, 2019.

"GLAAS Nigeria 2018/2019 Country Highlights." World Health Organization. Accessed 2014. Updated September 12, 2018. https://www.who.int/publications/m/item/glaas-nga-2018-2019-country-highlights.

Gleick, Peter. "Water, Drought, Climate Change, and Conflict in Syria." *Weather, Climate, and Society* 6, no. 3 (February 2014): 331–340.

"Global High-Level Panel on Water and Peace—Secretariat." Geneva Water Hub. https://www.genevawaterhub.org/resource/global-high-level-panel-water-and-peace-secretariat-0.

Global Terrorism Database. National Consortium for the Study of Terrorism and Responses to Terrorism. https://www.start.umd.edu/gtd/.

Global Water Security. Intelligence Community Assessment, ICA 2012-08. Washington, DC: Office of the Director of National Intelligence, February 2, 2012. http://www.dni.gov/files/documents/Special%20Report_ICA%20Global%20Water%20Security.pdf.

Goldbaum, Christina. "To Ambush and Kill American Green Berets, Al Shabaab Diverted a River." Daily Beast, June 10, 2018. https://www.thedailybeast.com/to-ambush-and-kill-an-american-green-beret-al-shabaab-diverted-a-river.

222   Bibliography

Gould, Joe. "Senate Passes Resolution to End US Support of Saudi Arabia in Yemen, 54–46." *Defense News*, March 13, 2019. https://www.defensenews.com/congress/2019/03/13/us-senate-passes-yemen-resolution-54-46/.

Grech-Madin, Charlotte. "The Water Taboo: Restraining the Weaponisation of Water in International Conflict." PhD diss., Department of Peace and Conflict Research, Uppsala University, 2020. http://urn.kb.se/resolve?urn=urn:nbn:se:uu:diva–397700.

———. "Water and Warfare: The Evolution and Operation of the Water Taboo." *International Security* 45, no. 4 (April 20, 2021): 84–125.

Haken, Nate. Interview with Lourdes Eliacin Mars, Alyssa Gomes, and Maya Jacobs. In "Environmental Peacebuilding: Nigeria." Elliott School of International Affairs Report, Fund for Peace, March 13, 2015.

Halaby, Jamal. "Syria Rebels Recruit at Refugee Camp." AP News, November 11, 2013. https://apnews.com/3ac366b07f5b4ff3ae7be6b5873a968a.

Hashem, Ali. "The Many Names of Abu Bakr al-Baghdadi." Al-Monitor, March 20, 2015. https://www.al-monitor.com/pulse/originals/2015/03/isis-baghdadi-islamic-state-caliph-many-names-al-qaeda.html.

Hashim, Ahmed S. "The Islamic State: From Al-Qaeda to Caliphate." *Middle East Policy* 21, no. 4 (Winter 2014). http://www.mepc.org/journal/middle-east-policy-archives/islamic-state-al-qaeda-affiliate-caliphate.

Hatami, Haleh, and Peter H. Gleick. "Conflicts over Water in the Myths, Legends, and Ancient History of the Middle East." *Environment: Science and Policy for Sustainable Development* 36, no. 3 (1994): 10–11.

Haynes, Jeffrey. "Conflict, Conflict Resolution and Peace-Building: The Role of Religion in Mozambique, Nigeria and Cambodia." *Commonwealth & Comparative Politics* 47, no. 1 (2009): 52–75.

Heaton, Laura. "Somalia's Climate for Conflict: How Drought Brings War to Somalia." Ground Truth Project, April 19, 2017. https://thegroundtruthproject.org/somalia-conflict-climate-change/.

Hersh, Seymour M. "Rainmaking Is Used as a Weapon by U.S." *New York Times*, July 3, 1972.

High-Level Panel on Water and Peace. *A Matter of Survival: Report of the Global High-Level Panel on Water and Peace*. Geneva: Geneva Water Hub, September 14, 2017. https://www.genevawaterhub.org/resource/matter-survival.

Hoerling, Martin, Jon Eischeid, Judith Perlwitz, Xiaowei Quan, Tao Zhang, and Philip Pegion. "On the Increased Frequency of Mediterranean Drought." *Journal of Climate* 25, no. 6 (March 2012): 2146–2161.

Hohtadi, Shahrzad. "Climate Change and the Syrian Uprising." *Bulletin of the Atomic Scientist*, August 16, 2012. http://thebulletin.org/climate-change-and-syrian-uprising.

Holdgate, Matthew. *Why It Matters: Nigeria's Global Oil Impact*. Nikko Asset Management, September 2016. https://americas.nikkoam.com/files/pdf/insights/2016/20160909-Why-it-matters-Nigerias-Global-Oil-Impact.pdf.

Homer-Dixon, Thomas F. *Environmental Scarcity and Violence*. Princeton, NJ: Princeton University Press, 1999.

"How to Stop the Decline of Lake Chad?" United Nations Development Programme, November 21, 2017. https://stories.undp.org/how-to-stop-the-decline-of-lake-chad.

Hsiang, Solomon M., Marshall Burke, and Edward Miguel. "Quantifying the Influence of Climate on Human Conflict." *Science* 341 (September 2013).

"Inter-Agency Initial Investigation Report—Inter Clan Fighting in Deefow, Deefow, Hiraan Region." United Nations Office for the Coordination of Humanitarian

Affairs, June 25, 2015. https://www.humanitarianresponse.info/sites/www.humanitarianresponse.info/files/assessments/150625_deefow_initial_investigation_inter_clan_conflict.pdf.

International Committee of the Red Cross. "Protection of Objects Indispensable to the Survival of the Civilian Population." Protocol Additional to the Geneva Conventions of 12 August 1949, and Relating to the Protection of Victims of Non-International Armed Conflicts (Protocol II), 8 June 1977. International Committee of the Red Cross, 1977. https://www.icrc.org/applic/ihl/ihl.nsf/Article.xsp?action=openDocument&documentId=ACF5220D585326BCC12563CD00 51E8B6.

International Gas Union. *2019 World LNG Report*. Barcelona: International Gas Union, 2019. https://www.igu.org/wp-content/uploads/2019/06/IGU-Annual-Report-2019_23.pdf.

International Law Association. *Resolution on the Protection of Water Resources and Water Installations in Times of Armed Conflict, Madrid, 1976, from Report of the Fifty-Seventh Conference, Madrid 30 August–4 September 1976*. London: International Law Association, 1978. https://www.internationalwaterlaw.org/documents/intldocs/ILA/ILA-Resolution_on_Protection_of_Water_Resources_and_Water_Installations-Madrid1976.pdf.

Ireogbu, Senator. "Expert Proffers Solution to Fulani Herdsmen, Farmers Clashes." *This Day Live*, July 9, 2016. http://www.thisdaylive.com/index.php/2016/07/09/expert-proffers-solution-to-fulani-herdsmen-farmers-clashes-2/.

"ISIL Confirms Death of al-Baghdadi, Names New Chief." Al Jazeera, November 1, 2019. https://www.aljazeera.com/news/2019/10/isil-confirms-death-leader-al-baghdadi-names-chief-191031151709004.html.

"ISIS." Counterextremism Project. https://counterextremism.com/threat/isis.

"ISIS Cuts Off Water, Electricity, Destroys Churches." Assyrian International News Agency, June 18, 2014. http://www.aina.org/news/20140618172333.htm.

"Islamic State and the Crisis in Iraq and Syria in Maps." BBC, March 28, 2018. https://www.bbc.com/news/world-middle-east-27838034.

"Islamist Extremist Strategy: Executions." Tony Blair Institute for Global Change, September 13, 2018. https://institute.global/policy/islamist-extremist-strategy-executions.

Jayamaha, Buddhika, Jahara Matisek, William Reno, and Molly Jahn. "Changing Weather Patterns, Climate Change and Civil War Dynamics: Institutions and Conflicts in the Sahel." *Seton Hall Journal of Diplomacy and International Relations* 20, no. 1 (Fall/Winter 2018): 70–87.

"The Juba and Shabelle Rivers and Their Importance to Somalia." Food and Agriculture Organization of the United Nations. http://www.faoswalim.org/article/juba-and-shabelle-rivers-and-their-importance-somalia.

Kaplan, Michael. "Nigeria's Boko Haram to Poison Water? Army Urges Northeast to Stock Up Amid Fears of Terrorist Plot." IBTimes, October 26, 2015. https://www.ibtimes.com/nigerias-boko-haram-poison-water-army-urges-northeast-stock-amid-fears-terrorist-plot-2155999.

Katzenstein, Peter. "Introduction: Alternative Perspectives on National Security." In *The Culture of National Security*, edited by P. Katzenstein, 1–32. New York: Columbia University Press, 1996.

Kelley, Colin P., Shahrzad Mohtadi, Mark A. Cane, Richard Seager, and Yochanan Kushnir, "Climate Change in the Fertile Crescent and Implications of the Recent Syrian Drought." *Proceedings of the National Academy of Sciences* 112, no. 11 (March 7, 2015): 3241–3246.

224 Bibliography

King, Marcus. "Water Security." In *An Introduction to Non-traditional Security Studies*, edited by Mely Caballero-Anthony. Thousand Oaks, CA: Sage, 2016.

King, Marcus DuBois. "Water, U.S. Foreign Policy and American Leadership." Institute for International Economic Policy Working Paper Series IIEP-WP-2013-11, Elliott School of International Affairs, George Washington University, Washington, DC, October 2013. https://www2.gwu.edu/~iiep/assets/docs/papers/2014WP/KingIIEPWP201311.pdf.

King, Marcus D., and Rianna LeHane. "Drought Is Leading to Instability and Water Weaponization in the Middle East and North Africa." Center for Climate and Security, April 30, 2021. https://climateandsecurity.org/2021/04/drought-is-leading-to-instability-and-water-weaponization-in-the-middle-east-and-north-africa/.

King, Marcus D., Caitlin Werrell, and Francesco Femia. "The Responsibility to Prepare and Prevent: Closing the Climate and Security Governance Gaps." In *Anthropocene (In)Securities: Reflections on Collective Survival After the Stockholm Conference*. New York: Oxford University Press, 2021.

Klobucista, Claire, Jonathan Masters, and Mohammed Aly Sergie. "Al-Shabab." Council on Foreign Relations, 2015. Last updated May 19, 2021. https://www.cfr.org/backgrounder/al-shabab.

"Lake Chad: Can the Vanishing Lake Be Saved?" BBC News, March 31, 2018. https://www.bbc.com/news/world-africa-43500314.

"Lake Chad Basin: Crisis Overview—Nigeria." ReliefWeb, January 23, 2019. https://reliefweb.int/report/nigeria/lake-chad-basin-crisis-overview-23-january-2019.

"Lake Chad Basin Crisis—Response Strategy (2017–2019)—Short Version." Food and Agriculture Organization of the United Nations, March 2017. https://www.fao.org/resilience/resources/resources-detail/en/c/471497/.

Lederer, Edith M. "UN Alarm That Most of al-Shabab's Force in Somalia Are Kids." AP News, January 19, 2017. https://apnews.com/85093315baa644a6bee802b13fc343e5/un-alarm-most-al-shababs-force-somalia-are-kids.

Ligtvoet, Willem, A. Bouwman, J. M. Knoop, Sophie de Bruin, Kersten Nabielek, Hiddo Huitzing, Jan H. Janse et al. *The Geography of Future Water Challenges*. The Hague: PBL Netherlands Environmental Assessment Agency, 2018.

Lister, Charles. *Profiling Islamic State*. Brookings Doha Center Analysis Paper, no. 13. Doha, Qatar: Brookings Doha Center, November 2014. https://www.brookings.edu/wp-content/uploads/2014/12/en_web_lister.pdf.

"Livestock and Agriculture." Somali Development and Reconstruction Bank. https://sodevbank.so/livestock-and-agriculture/.

Macheve, Berta, Alexander Danilenko, Roohi Abdullah, Abel Bove, and L. Joe Moffitt. "Water Sector Institutions and Governance." In *State Water Agencies in Nigeria: A Performance Assessment*, Directions in Development—Infrastructure. Washington, DC: World Bank, 2015. https://doi.org/10.1596/978-1-4648-0657-5_ch2.

Marama, Ndahi. "JTF, Vigilante Arrest Female Boko Haram Suspects." Vanguard, August 17, 2013. https://www.vanguardngr.com/2013/08/jtf-vigilante-arrest-female-boko-haram-suspects/.

Maruf, Harun. "Somalia: Al-Shabaab Battles Islamic Militants in Northeastern Somalia." All Africa, February 1, 2019. https://allafrica.com/stories/201902010619.html.

Maruf, Harun, and Dan Joseph. *Inside Al-Shabaab: The Secret History of Al-Qaeda's Most Powerful Ally*. Bloomington: Indiana University Press, 2018.

Maystadt, Jean-Francois, and Olivier Ecker. "Extreme Weather and Civil War: Does Drought Fuel Conflict in Somalia Through Livestock Price Shocks?" *American Journal of Agricultural Economics* 96, no. 4 (2014): 1157–1182.

Mednick, Sam. "Burkina Faso's Prime Minister Is Fired amid Growing Violence." ABC News, December 9, 2021. https://abcnews.go.com/International/wireStory /burkina-fasos-prime-minister-fired-amid-growing-violence-81652462.

Mendis, Lucius O. "Ancient Water and Soil Conservation Ecosystems of Sri Lanka." Paper presented at International History Seminar on Irrigation and Drainage, Tehran, Iran, May 2–5, 2007.

"Migration and Displacement Country Profiles (MDCP): Nigeria." UNICEF, July 2021. https://data.unicef.org/resources/migration-and-displacement-country -profiles-mdcp/.

Mironova, Vira. "The Year the Islamic State Lost Its Last Strongholds." Foreign Policy, December 27, 2019. https://foreignpolicy.com/2019/12/27/the-year-the -islamic-state-lost-its-last-strongholds/.

"Mission and Vision." Institute for Water Resources, US Army Corps of Engineers. http://www.iwr.usace.army.mil/About/Mission-and-Vision/.

Mohamed, Hamza. "Somali Farmers Benefit from al-Shabab Reforms." Al Jazeera, March 11, 2014. https://www.aljazeera.com/indepth/features/2014/03/somali -farmers-benefit-from-al-shabab-reforms-201431053038814400.html.

Mohammed, Khalid. "Obama Applauds Recapture of Mosul Dam, Says Iraq Must Unite Because 'the Wolf's at the Door.'" *Globe and Mail*, August 18, 2018. http://www.theglobeandmail.com/news/world/latest-round-of-us-airstrikes -aimed-at-helping-iraqis-reclaim-mosul-dams/article20091967/.

Moran, Ashley, Clionadh Raleigh, Joshua W. Busby, Charles Wight, and Management Systems International. *Country Brief: Fragility and Climate Risks: Nigeria.* Washington, DC: USAID, 2019. https://pdf.usaid.gov/pdf_docs/PA00TKRT.pdf.

Morris, Loveday, and Louisa Loveluck. "Killing of ISIS Leader Has Not Hurt Groups' Operations, Says Iraqi Kurdish Leader." *Washington Post*, February 15, 2020. https://www.washingtonpost.com/world/killing-of-isis-leader-has-not -hurt-groups-operations-says-iraqi-kurdish-leader/2020/02/15/d3e7303a-4ff8 -11ea-a4ab-9f389ce8ad30_story.html.

Mubarak, Mohamed. "Al-Shabab's Military Machine." Hiraal Institute. 2018. https://hiraalinstitute.org/al-shababs-military-machine/.

"Mujahideen Shura Council (Islamic State of Iraq)." Terrorism Research and Analysis Consortium, 2020. https://www.trackingterrorism.org/group/mujahideen-shura -council-islamic-state-iraq.

Munoz, Michael. "Selling the Long War: Islamic State Propaganda After the Caliphate." *CTC Sentinel* 11, no. 10 (November 2018). https://ctc.usma.edu /selling-long-war-islamic-state-propaganda-caliphate/.

Mutambo, Aggrey. "Kismayu on the Spot Over Charcoal Trade." Business Daily, February 13, 2018. https://www.businessdailyafrica.com/economy/Kismayu -on-the-spot-over-charcoal-trade/3946234-4303554-b786icz/index.html.

Naharnet Newsdesk. "PM Says Iraq Lost 2,300 Humvee Armored Vehicles in Mosul." Naharnet, May 31, 2015. http://www.naharnet.com/stories/en/180602.

NAN. "Boko Haram Destroyed 75% Water, Sanitation Infrastructure in Northeast— UNICEF." *The Guardian*, August 30, 2017. https://guardian.ng/news/boko -haram-destroyed-75-water-sanitation-infrastructure-in-northeast-unicef/.

Nasser, Shanifa. "Somali Politician with Canadian Citizenship Killed in al-Shabaab Hotel Attack." CBS News, June 26, 2016. https://www.cbc.ca/news/canada

226 Bibliography

/toronto/somali-politician-with-canadian-citizenship-killed-in-al-shabaab-hotel
-attack-1.3653654.

National Intelligence Council. "Implications for US National Security of Anticipated
Climate Change." Office of the Director of national Intelligence, September 21,
2016. https://www.dni.gov/files/documents/Newsroom/Reports%20and%20Pubs
/Implications_for_US_National_Security_of_Anticipated_Climate_Change.pdf.

"NATO Climate Change and Security Action Plan." North Atlantic Treaty Organization,
June 14, 2021. https://www.nato.int/cps/en/natohq/official_texts_185174.htm.

Natural Resource Governance Institute. *Primer: The Resource Curse*. New York:
Natural Resource Governance Institute, April 27, 2015. https://resource
governance.org/analysis-tools/publications/primer-resource-curse.

"ND-GAIN Country Initiative." Notre Dame Global Adaptation Initiative, University
of Notre Dame. https://gain.nd.edu/our-work/country-index/.

Niang, I., O. C. Ruppel, M. A. Abdrabo, A. Essel, C. Lennard, J. Padgham, and P.
Urquhart. "Africa." In *AR5 Climate Change 2014: Impacts, Adaptation, and
Vulnerability. Part B: Regional Aspects*, contribution of Working Group II to the
Fifth Assessment Report of the Intergovernmental Panel on Climate Change. New
York: Cambridge University Press, 2014. http://www.ipcc.ch/report/ar5/wg2/.

———. "Executive Summary, Chapter 22 Africa." In *Intergovernmental Panel on
Climate Change 5th Assessment Report*, edited by Core Writing Team, R. K.
Pachauri, and L. A. Meyer. Geneva: Intergovernmental Panel on Climate Change,
2014. https://archive.ipcc.ch/pdf/assessment-report/ar5/wg2/WGIIAR5-Chap22
_FINAL.pdf.

"Nigeria." Notre Dame Global Adaptation Index, University of Notre Dame, July
18. 2022. https://knoema.com/NDGAIN2017/university-of-notre-dame-global
-adaptation-index?country=1001270-nigeria.

"Nigeria." Transparency International. https://www.transparency.org/country/NGA.

"Nigeria." WaterAid. https://www.wateraid.org/ng/.

"Nigeria: Investigate Massacre, Step Up Patrols: Hundreds Killed by Mobs in Villages
in Central Nigeria." Human Rights Watch, March 8, 2010. https://www.hrw
.org/news/2010/03/08/nigeria-investigate-massacre-step-patrols.

"Nigeria: Migration Profiles." UNICEF. https://esa.un.org/miggmgprofiles/indicators
/files/Nigeria.pdf.

"Nigeria: Scramble for Land, Water Deadlier Than Boko Haram." APA News, June
18, 2019. http://apanews.net/en/news/nigeria-scramble-for-land-water-deadlier
-than-boko-haram/.

"Nigeria Awards Dam Power Plant Contract to Chinese State Firm Again." Reuters,
August 30, 2017. https://www.reuters.com/article/us-nigeria-hydro-china-id
USKCN1BA27P.

"Nigeria Economic Outlook." African Development Bank Group. https://www.afdb
.org/en/countries/west-africa/nigeria/nigeria-economic-outlook.

"Nigeria Facts and Figures." Organization of the Petroleum Exporting Countries.
Accessed 2019. Updated 2022. https://www.opec.org/opec_web/en/about
_us/167.htm.

Nigerian Federal Ministry of Agriculture and Rural Development (FMARD). *Agri-
cultural Transformation Agenda Support Program—Phase One (Atasp–1).
Strategic Environmental and Social Assessment*. African Development Bank
Group, July 2013.

"Nigerians Got Poorer in Muhammadu Buhari's First Term." *The Economist*, May
30, 2019.

"Nigeria's Food Crisis: Hunger Games." *The Economist*, September 1, 2016.

Bibliography 227

Nor, Omar, and Greg Botelho. "At Least 50 Dead in Somalia After Drinking from Contaminated Well." CNN, December 11, 2014. https://www.cnn.com/2014/12/11/world/africa/somalia-drinking-water-deaths/index.html.

"Number of Somali Refugees Grows Sharply in 2011." United Nations High Commission on Refugees, April 29, 2011. https://www.unhcr.org/news/briefing/2011/4/4dba949d9/number-somali-refugees-grows-sharply-2011.html.

Nwajiuba, Chinedum. "Nigeria's Agriculture and Food Security Challenges." Green Deal Nigeria study paper, Heinrich-Böll-Stiftung, 2013. https://ng.boell.org/sites/default/files/uploads/2013/10/agriculture_-_green_deal_nigeria_study.pdf.

Nzwili, Fredrick. "Terrorist Group al-Shabab Delivers Food to Drought-Stricken Somalia." Catholic Register, March 31, 2017. https://www.catholicregister.org/home/international/item/24761-terrorist-group-al-shabab-delivers-food-relief-to-drought-stricken-somalia.

Obaji, Philip, Jr. "Recharging Lake Chad Key to Ending the Conflict Between Nigeria's Farmers and Herders." IPI Global Observatory, September 5, 2018. https://theglobalobservatory.org/2018/09/recharging-lake-chad-end-conflict-farmers-herders/.

"OCHA Somalia." Human Data Exchange. https://data.humdata.org/organization/ocha-somalia.

Ochonu, Moses. "The Roots of Nigeria's Religious and Ethnic Conflict." GlobalPost, The World, March 10, 2014. http://www.pri.org/stories/2014-03-10/root-nigerias-religious-and-ethnic-conflict.

Odjugo, Peter Akpodiogaga-a Ovuyovwiroye. "An Analysis of Rainfall Pattern in Nigeria." *Global Journal of Environmental Science* 4, no. 2 (2005): 139–145.

———. "General Overview of Climate Change Impacts in Nigeria." *Journal of Human Ecology* 29, no. 1 (January 2010): 47–55. https://doi.org/10.1080/09709274.2010.11906248.

Oduah, Chika. "Nigeria: Deadly Nomad-Versus-Farmer Conflict Escalates." Al Jazeera, July 6, 2016. http://www.aljazeera.com/news/2016/07/nigeria-deadly-nomad-farmer-conflict-escalates-160704043119561.html.

Ohanesian, Adriane. "In Photos: Tracking al Shabaab in Somalia." France 24, May 19, 2014. https://www.france24.com/en/20140516-operation-eagle-somalia-fight-against-al-shabaab.

Okoli, Al Chukwuma, and Atelhe George Atelhe. "Nomads Against Natives: A Political Ecology of Herder/Farmer Conflicts in Nasarawa State, Nigeria." *American International Journal of Contemporary Research* 4, no. 2, (2014): 76–88.

Ola, Timothy. "How Boko Haram Leader Beheaded 3 Pastors for Refusing to Accept Islam—Violent Crimes." Nairaland Forum, August 6, 2009. http://www.nairaland.com/307020/how-boko-haram-leader-beheaded.

Olanrewaju, John S. "Terrorism and Its Socio-Economic Impacts on Nigeria: A Study of Boko-Haram in the North East." PhD diss., Kwara State University, Malete, Nigeria, January 2019. https://search.proquest.com/docview/2217883483/?pq-origsite=primo.

Oldenborgh, Geert Jan Van, M. Collins, J. Arblaster, J. H. Christensen, J. Marotzke, S. B. Power, M. Rummukainen, and T. Zhou. "Annex I: Atlas of Global and Regional Climate Projections." In *Climate Change 2013: The Physical Science Basis*. New York: Cambridge University Press, January 2013.

Omo-Ikirodah, Osigwe. "B'Haram Poison Water Sources of Abandoned Villages—Army." IReporterOnline.com.ng, September 30, 2015. https://www.linkedin

228   *Bibliography*

.com/pulse/bharam-poison-water-sources-abandoned-villages-army-osigwe -ikirodah.

Ononihu, Simon Chukasi, and Mike Chidebe. "Nigeria's Quest for a Permanent Seat at the United Nations Security Council: An Appraisal." *IOSR Journal of Humanities and Social Science* 22, no. 4 (2017).

O'Sullivan, Sinead. "Drones for Climate and Security," Center for Climate and Security. https://climateandsecurity.org/2016/08/10/drones-for-climate-and -security/.

Oxfam. *Lake Chad's Unseen Crisis: Voices of Refugees and Internally Displaced People from Niger and Nigeria*. London: Oxfam, 2016. https://www.oxfam.org /sites/www.oxfam.org/files/file_attachments/bn-lake-chad-refugees-idps-190816 -en.pdf.

Oxford Dictionary, 7th ed. s.v. "weapon." Oxford: Oxford University Press, 2010.

Pagliery, Jose. "Inside the $2 Billion ISIS War Machine." CNN Money, December 11, 2015. http://money.cnn.com/2015/12/06/news/isis-funding/.

Paraszcuk, Joanna. "The ISIS Economy: Crushing Taxes and High Unemployment." *The Atlantic*, September 2, 2015.

Parrish, Karen. "Stopping Flow of Foreign Fighters to ISIS 'Will Take Years,' Army Official Says." US Army, April 6, 2017. https://www.army.mil/article/185550 /stopping_flow_of_foreign_fighters_to_isis_will_take_years_army_official_says.

Picker, Les. "Where Are ISIS's Foreign Fighters Coming From?" National Bureau of Economic Research, June 2016. https://www.nber.org/digest/jun16/w22190 .html.

Pike, John. "Burkina Faso—Climate." Global Security, 2022. https://www.global security.org/military/world/africa/bf-climate.htm.

Ponsford, Matthew. "Saudi-Led Coalition Responsible for 'Worst Cholera Outbreak in the World' in Yemen: Researchers." Reuters, August 18, 2017. https://www .reuters.com/article/us-yemen-cholera-saudi/saudi-led-coalition-responsible-for -worst-cholera-outbreak-in-the-world-in-yemen-researchers-idUSKCN1AY2JH.

Pope, Cody. "Vanishing Lake Chad—a Water Crisis in Central Africa." Circle of Blue, June 24, 2008. https://www.circleofblue.org/2008/world/vanishing-lake -chad-a-water-crisis-in-central-africa/.

"The Power of Sadaqah Jariyah." Islamic Relief USA. http://irusa.org/sadaqah -jariyah/.

"Profile of Nigeria's Boko Haram Leader Abubakar Shekau." BBC News, May 9, 2014. http://www.bbc.com/news/world-africa-18020349.

Raleigh, C., A. Linke, H. Hegre, and J. Karlsen. Armed Conflict Location and Event Data (ACLED) Project. 2018. https://www.acleddata.com/data/.

"Rebels Threaten Damascus Water over Zabadani Assault." Aamanalwsl, August 2015. https://en.zamanalwsl.net/news/article/10709.

"Recent Floods Damage Supply Routes, Vital Infrastructure in Somalia, UN Relief Wing Warns." UN News, November 23, 2015. https://news.un.org/en/story /2015/11/516312-recent-floods-damage-supply-routes-vital-infrastructure-somalia -un-relief-wing.

"Remembering the Sinjar Massacre." Voice of America, August 3, 2018. https:// editorials.voa.gov/a/remembering-the-sinjar-massacre/4512154.html.

Rhodes, Tom. "Saddam Drives 100,000 Marsh Arabs from Homes." *The Times*, 2014.

Rice, Doyle. "It Was 129 Degrees in Iran Thursday, Which Is One of the Earth's Hottest Temperatures Ever Recorded." *USA Today*, June 29, 2017.

Richard, Martin C, ed. *Encyclopedia of Islam & the Muslim World*. New York: Macmillan Reference USA, 2016.

Bibliography   229

Ringler, Claudia. "What's Really Causing Water Scarcity in Africa South of the Sahara?" International Food Policy Research Institute, August 29, 2013. http://www.ifpri.org/blog/what%e2%80%99s-really-causing-water-scarcity -africa-south-sahara.

Robbins, Nicholas S., and James Fergusson. "Groundwater Scarcity and Conflict— Managing Hotspots." *Earth Perspectives* 1, art. no. 6 (2014).

Rono, Moses. "Somalia Food Crisis: Has al-Shabab Adopted New Approach to Food Aid?" BBC News, March 22, 2017. http://www.bbc.com/news/world -africa-39296517.

Ross, Will. "Nigerians' Fear of Northern Atrocities." BBC News, November 1, 2012. http://www.bbc.com/news/world-africa-20166065.

Rupesinghe, Natasja, and Mikael Hiberg. "The Sahel's Jihadists Don't All Govern Alike: Context Matters." The Conversation, September 14, 2021. https://the conversation.com/the-sahels-jihadists-dont-all-govern-alike-context-matters -166998.

"Sahih Bukhari." Hadith. https://www.sahih-bukhari.com/Pages/Bukhari_3_40.php.

Salama, Vivian. "Obama: Iraq forces Retake Mosul Dam from Militants." AP News, August 18, 2014.

Salehyan, Idean. "From Climate Change to Conflict? No Consensus Yet." *Journal of Peace Research* 45, no. 3 (2008): 315–326.

Salehyan, Idean, Cullen S. Hendrix, Jesse Hamner, Christina Case, Christopher Linebarger, Emily Stull, and Jennifer Williams. "Social Conflict in Africa: A New Database." *International Interactions* 38, no. 4 (2012): 503–511.

Sattar, Sardar. "KRG Announces Public Holiday Due to Heat Wave." BasNews, 2015. http://www.basnews.com/index.php/en/lifestyle/health/288389.

Sauer, Natalie. "Lake Chad Not Shrinking, but Climate Is Fuelling Terror Groups: Report." Climate Home News, May 16, 2019. https://www.climatechangenews .com/2019/05/16/lake-chad-not-shrinking-climate-fuelling-terror-groups -report/.

Sayne, Aaron. "Climate Change, Adaptation and Conflict in Nigeria." Special report 274. United States Institute of Peace, Washington, DC, June 7, 2011. http:// www.usip.org/publications/climate-change-adaptation-and-conflict-in-nigeria.

———. "Rethinking Nigeria's Indigene-Settler Conflicts." Special report 311. United States Institute of Peace, July 24, 2012. http://www.usip.org/publications /rethinking-nigeria-s-indigene-settler-conflicts.

Schleussner, Carl-Friedrich, Johnathan F. Donges, Reik V. Donner, and Hans Joachim Schellnhuber. "Armed-Conflict Risks Enhanced by Climate-Related Disasters in Ethnically Fractionalized Countries." *Proceedings of the National Academy of Sciences* 113, no. 33 (2016): 9216–9221. https://doi.org/10.1073 /pnas.1601611113.

Schwartzstein, Peter. "The History of Poisoning the Well." *Smithsonian Magazine*, February 13, 2019, https://www.smithsonianmag.com/history/history-well -poisoning-180971471/.

———. "Why Water Conflict Is Rising Especially on the Local Level." Center for Climate and Security, February 26, 2021. https://climateandsecurity.org/2021 /02/why-localized-water-violence-is-flourishing-even-as-transboundary-water -wars-are-not/.

"The 'Secretive Sect' in Charge of Syria." BBC News, May 17, 2012. http://www .bbc.com/news/world-middle-east-18084964.

Semple, Kirk. "Missiles of ISIS May Pose Peril for Aircrews." *New York Times*, October 27, 2015.

230 *Bibliography*

Shinkman, Paul D. "ISIS Remains Potent, Deadly Despite Baghdadi's Death, Top Spy Says." *US News & World Report*, October 30, 2019. https://www.usnews.com/news/world-report/articles/2019-10-30/isis-remains-potent-deadly-despite-baghdadis-death-top-spy-says.

Shiru, Mohammed Sanusi, Shamsuddin Shahid, Noraliani Alias, and Eun-Sung Chung. "Trend Analysis of Droughts During Crop Growing Seasons of Nigeria." *Sustainability* 10 (2018): 871. https://www.mdpi.com/2071-1050/10/3/871/pdf.

Singh, Harman. "Can the Taliban Address Climate-Related Risks in Afghanistan?" Planetary Security Initiative, October 26, 2021. https://www.planetarysecurityinitiative.org/news/can-taliban-address-climate-related-risks-afghanistan.

Smith, Alexander. "ISIS Owns Headlines, but Nigeria's Boko Haram Kills More Than Ever." NBC News, 2016. http://www.nbcnews.com/storyline/2015-year-in-review/isis-owns-headlines-nigeria-s-boko-haram-kills-more-ever-n480986.

Snow, Shawn. "DIA Says ISIS Took Advantage of Turkish Invasion of Northern Syria, Baghdadi Death Did Not Degrade Jihadi Group." Military Times, February 4, 2020. https://www.militarytimes.com/flashpoints/2020/02/04/dia-says-isis-took-advantage-of-turkish-invasion-of-northern-syria-baghdadi-death-did-not-degrade-jihadi-group/.

"Social Conflict Analysis Database." University of Texas at Austin. https://www.strausscenter.org/scad.html.

"Somalia." One World Nations Online. http://www.nationsonline.org/oneworld/somalia.htm#Search2.

"Somalia." World Bank. https://data.worldbank.org/country/somalia.

"Somalia: Events of 2016." Human Rights Watch. https://www.hrw.org/world-report/2017/country-chapters/somalia.

"Somalia: Forest Change." Global Forest Watch. https://www.globalforestwatch.org/dashboards/country/SOM?category=forest-change.

"Somalia: Humanitarian Access Map—as of August 2012." UN Office for the Coordination of Humanitarian Affairs. https://reliefweb.int/map/somalia/somalia-humanitarian-access-map-august-2012.

"Somalia: Improved Water Source, Rural (% of Rural Population with Access): 2011." World Development Indicators. Last updated April 23, 2017. https://time.graphics/statistic/wb244672.

"Somalia: Local Admin Forces, Militia Clash in Deadly Battle in Galgaduud." Garowe Online, November 29, 2014. https://www.garoweonline.com/index.php/en/news/somalia/somalia-local-admin-forces-militia-clash-in-deadly-battle-in-galgaduud.

"Somalia: Overview." World Bank. Accessed 2017. Updated April 14. 2022. https://www.worldbank.org/en/country/somalia/overview.

"Somalia: World Bank Approves US$50 Million in Support of Emergency Drought Response and Recovery." World Bank, May 30, 2017. http://www.worldbank.org/en/news/press-release/2017/05/30/somalia-world-bank-approves-us50-million-in-support-of-emergency-drought-response-and-recovery.

"Somalia Famine Killed Nearly 260,000 People, Half of Them Children—Reports UN." UN News, May 2, 2013. https://news.un.org/en/story/2013/05/438682-somalia-famine-killed-nearly-260000-people-half-them-children-reports-un.

"Somalia Livestock Price Bulletin, June 2016." FEWS NET, June 2016. https://fews.net/east-africa/somalia/price-bulletin/june-2016-0.

"Somalia Profile—Timeline." BBC News, January 4, 2018. http://www.bbc.com/news/world-africa-14094632.

Bibliography 231

Stocker, T. F., D. Qin, G.-K. Plattner, M. Tignor, S. K. Allen, J. Boschung, A. Nauels, Y. Xia, V. Bex, and P. M. Midgley. "Summary for Policymakers." In *Climate Change 2013: The Physical Science Basis*. New York: Cambridge University Press, January 2013.

"Stopping Nigeria's Spiraling Farmer-Herder Violence." International Crisis Group, July 26, 2018. https://www.crisisgroup.org/africa/west-africa/nigeria/262-stopping-nigerias-spiralling-farmer-herder-violence.

"Stress Tolerant Maize for Africa (STMA)." International Maize and Wheat Improvement Center, 2020. https://www.cimmyt.org/projects/stress-tolerant-maize-for-africa-stma/.

Swain, Ashok. "Water and Post-Conflict Peacebuilding." *Hydrological Sciences Journal* 61, no. 7 (2016): 1313–1322.

"Syria: Drought Driving Farmers to the Cities." New Humanitarian, September 2, 2009. http://www.irinnews.org/report/85963/syria-drought-driving-farmers-to-the-cities.

"Syria in Crisis." Oxfam Hong Kong, December 5, 2014. https://www.oxfam.org.hk/en/news-and-publication/syria-in-crisis.

"32 People Die in Somalia After Drinking from Well." *Gulf Times*, January 30, 2017.

Thomas, Tres. "3 Notes on the Al-Shabaab Attack on U.S. Allied Forces in Somalia." Somalia Newsroom, June 12, 2018. https://somalianewsroom.com/2018/06/12/3-notes-on-the-al-shabaab-attack-on-u-s-allied-forces-in-somalia/.

Tierney, Jessica E., Caroline C. Ummenhofer, and Peter B. deMenocal. "Past and Future Rainfall in the Horn of Africa." *Science Advances* 1, no. 9 (2015): e1500682.

Tierney, Michael J., Daniel L. Nielson, Darren G. Hawkins, J. Timmons Roberts, Michael G. Findley, Ryan M. Powers, Bradley Parks, Sven E. Wilson, and Robert L. Hicks. "More Dollars Than Sense: Refining Our Knowledge of Development Finance Using AidData." *World Development* 39, no. 11 (2011): 1891–1906.

Tony Blair Institute for Global Change. https://institute.global/.

"UN Warns Millions of Somalis Are at Risk of Famine." *Financial Times*, January 17, 2017.

UNICEF. *Progress for Children: A Report Card on Water and Sanitation*. Washington, DC: UNICEF, 2006. https://www.unicef.org/reports/progress-children-no-5.

"UNICEF Somalia Annual Report 2015." UNICEF, December 31, 2015. https://somalia.un.org/en/19192-unicef-somalia-annual-report-2015.

UNICEF. "Somalia Water, Sanitation and Hygiene." https://www.unicef.org/somalia/water-sanitation-and-hygiene#:~:text=Only%2052%20percent%20of%20the,and%20from%20unsafe%20open%20wells. Accessed June 20, 2020.

United Nations. *Report of the United Nations Conference on Human Development, 5–16 June 1972*. New York: United Nations, 1973. https://digitallibrary.un.org/record/523249?ln=en.

United Nations. "Right to water and sanitation is legally binding, affirms key UN body." UN News, October 1, 2010. https://www.un.org/en/?_gl=1*4cbv8y*_ga*ODMyMTc3Njc0LjE2NjUxNTUwNTY.*_ga_TK9BQL5X7Z*MTY2NTE1NTA1Ni4xLjEuMTY2NTE1NTA5My4wLjAuMA.

———. "Resolution 64/292: The Human Right to Water and Sanitation." United Nations Department of Economic and Social Affairs, July 28, 2010. https://www.un.org/waterforlifedecade/human_right_to_water.shtml.

232 Bibliography

United Nations Department of Economic and Social Affairs. *World Population Prospects 2019*. New York: United Nations, 2019. https://population.un.org/wpp/Publications/Files/WPP2019_Highlights.pdf.

United Nations Office for the Coordination of Humanitarian Affairs. *Somalia Humanitarian Bulletin*. United Nations Office for the Coordination of Humanitarian Affairs, June 2016. https://reliefweb.int/sites/reliefweb.int/files/resources/Somalia%20Humanitarian%20Bulletin%20for%20June.pdf.

United Nations Office of the High Commissioner Human Rights. "International Covenant on Economic, Social and Cultural Rights." General Assembly resolution 2200A (XXI). United Nations Office of the High Commissioner Human Rights, December 16, 1966. https://www.ohchr.org/en/instruments-mechanisms/instruments/international-covenant-economic-social-and-cultural-rights?ref=hackernoon.com.

United Nations Security Council. *Resolution 2349 (2017) / Adopted by the Security Council at Its 7911th Meeting, on 31 March 2017*. New York: UN Security Council, 2017. https://digitallibrary.un.org/record/863830?ln=en.

United States Army Corps of Engineers. "Mission and Vision." Institute for Water Resources, Army Corps of Engineers. http://www.iwr.usace.army.mil/About/Mission-and-Vision.

United States Central Intelligence Agency. "Nigeria." In *World Factbook*. https://www.cia.gov/the-world-factbook/countries/nigeria/.

———. "Somalia." In *World Factbook*. https://www.cia.gov/the-world-factbook/countries/somalia.

USAID. "USAID Launches New Water and Sanitation Project in Nigeria." [Press release, archived version.] USAID, May 15, 2017. https://2017-2020.usaid.gov/nigeria/news-information/press-releases/usaid-launches-new-water-and-sanitation-project-nigeria.

USAID Water and Development Strategy 2013–2018. Washington, DC: USAID, n.d. https://www.usaid.gov/sites/default/files/documents/1865/USAID_Water_Strategy_3.pdf.

Veilleux, Jennifer, and Shlomi Dinar. "A Global Analysis of Water-Related Terrorism, 1970–2016." *Terrorism and Political Violence* 33, no. 6 (2019): 1191–1216.

"A Very Black Market." *The Economist* 426, no. 9085 (2018): 52.

Vidal, John. "Water Supply Key to Outcome of Conflicts in Iraq and Syria, Experts Warn." *The Guardian*, July 2, 2014.

Von Lossow, Tobias. "Water as Weapon: IS on the Euphrates and Tigris." German Institute for International and Security Affairs, January 2016. https://www.swp-berlin.org/en/publication/water-as-weapon-is-euphrates-tigris/.

———. "Weaponizing of Water in the Middle East: 'Lessons Learned' from IS." In *Water and Conflict in the Middle East*, ed. Marcus DuBois King, chap. 7. London: Hurst, 2020.

Wabala, Dominic. "Kenya: KDF Airlifts Water to Troops as Wells Poisoned." AllAfrica, September 24, 2012. https://allafrica.com/stories/201209250173.html.

Wada, Yoshihide, L. P. H. van Beek, and Marc Bierkens. "Nonsuitable Groundwater Sustaining Irrigation: A Global Assessment." *Water Resources Research* 48 (January 2012).

Walker, Andrew. *What Is Boko Haram?* Special report no. 308. United States Institute for Peace, 2012. http://www.usip.org/publications/what-boko-haram.

The War of the Rebellion: A Compilation of the Official Records of the Union and Confederate Armies. Series III, vol. 3. Washington, DC: Government Printing Office, 1899. https://archive.org/details/warrebellionaco17offigoog.

Bibliography 233

Ward, Alex. "Guess Who Has Drones Now? ISIS." Vox, May 30, 2017. https://www.vox.com/world/2017/5/30/15686240/drones-isis-iraq-syria.

"Water Conflict Chronology." Pacific Institute. http://www.worldwater.org/conflict/map/.

"Water and Sanitation Program." Islamic Relief USA. http://irusa.org/water-and-sanitation/.

Waters, Nick. "Types of Islamic State Drone Bombs and Where to Find Them." Bellingcat, May 24, 2017. https://www.bellingcat.com/news/mena/2017/05/24/types-islamic-state-drone-bombs-find/.

"Weapons of the Islamic State." Conflict Armament Research. https://www.conflictarm.com/reports/weapons-of-the-islamic-state/.

Werrell, Caitlin E., and Francesco Femia, eds. *The Arab Spring and Climate Change*. Climate and Security Correlation Series. Washington, DC: Center for American Progress, February 2013. https://cdn.americanprogress.org/wp-content/uploads/2013/02/ClimateChangeArabSpring.pdf.

Werrell, Caitlin E., Francesco Femia, and Troy Sternberg. "Did We See It Coming? State Fragility, Climate Vulnerability, and the Uprisings in Syria and Egypt." *SIAS Review* 25, no. 1 (Winter–Spring 2015): 29–46. https://doi.org/10.1353/sais.2015.0002.

Werz, Michael, and Laura Conley. "Climate Change, Migration and Conflict in Northwest Africa: Rising Dangers and Policy Options Across the Arc of Tension." Center for American Progress, April 18, 2012. https://www.americanprogress.org/article/climate-change-migration-and-conflict-in-northwest-africa/.

West, Sunguta. "Al-Shabaab Plays on Aid Distribution Role to Win Over Desperate Somalis." *Terrorism Monitor* 15, no. 7 (April 7, 2017). https://jamestown.org/program/al-shabaab-plays-aid-distribution-role-win-desperate-somalis/.

———. "Resurgence of Al-Shabaab." *Terrorism Monitor* 16, no. 3 (February 8, 2018).

Westing, Arthur. *Warfare in a Fragile World: The Military Impact on the Human Environment*. Oxfordshire, UK: Taylor & Francis, 1980.

"Who Are Somalia's al-Shabab?" BBC News, December 22, 2017. https://www.bbc.com/news/world-africa-15336689.

"WHO Calls for Immediate Action to Save Lives in Somalia." World Health Organization. 2017. http://www.who.int/mediacentre/news/releases/2017/save-lives-somalia/en/.

Wilkinson, John C. "Muslim Land and Water Law." *Journal of Islamic Studies* 1 (1990): 60.

Wolf, Aaron T., Annika Kramer, Alexander Carius, and Geoffrey D. Dabelko. "Water Can Be a Pathway to Peace, Not War." *Navigating Peace*, no. 1 (July 2006).

Worth, Robert F. "Earth Is Parched Where Syrian Farms Thrived." *New York Times*, October 14, 2010.

"Zakat." BBC, September 8, 2009. https://www.bbc.co.uk/religion/religions/islam/practices/zakat.shtml.

Zeitoun, Mark, and Jeroen Warner. "Hydro-Hegemony: A Framework for Analysis of Trans-Boundary Water Conflicts." *Water Policy* 8, no. 5 (September 2006): 443.

Zelin, Aaron Y. "The War Between ISIS and al-Qaeda for Supremacy of the Global Jihadist Movement." *Research Notes: Washington Institute for Near East Policy*, no. 20, June 2014. https://www.washingtoninstitute.org/media/2714.

234 Bibliography

Zengerle, Patricia. "U.S. Lawmakers Still Plot to Push Saudi Arabia on Rights, Despite Trump." Reuters, August 1, 2019. https://www.reuters.com/article/us -usa-saudi-arms/u-s-lawmakers-still-plot-to-push-saudi-arabia-on-rights-despite -trump-idUSKCN1UR5T1.

Zittis, George, Panos Hadjinicolaou, Mansour Almazroui, Edoardo Bucchignani, Fatima Driouech, Khalid El Rhaz, Levent Kurnaz et al. "Business-as-Usual Will Lead to Super and Ultra-Extreme Heatwaves in the Middle East and North Africa," *Climate and Atmospheric Science* 4, no. 20 (2021): 1–9.

Index

Abacha, Sani, 111
al-Abadi, Haider, 80
Abdul Hamid, Mustafa, 35
Abdul-Mahdi, Adil, 48, 87
Abdulwahed, Hezha, 51
ablution, 28
absolute water scarcity, 1
Abu Ghraib prison, 46, 76
Abu Ubaidah, Ahmed Umar, 155
al-Adnani, Abu Muhammad, 63
Afghanistan, 62, 204
Africa: precipitation in, 2; VEOs in, 4,
   19; water availability in sub-Saharan,
   200; water stress in, 2–3, 6, 24, 195.
   See also Middle East and North
   Africa; Nigeria; Somalia
African Development Bank, 207
African Union Mission to Somalia
   (AMISOM), 154, 176–178, 181, 183–
   185
Agricultural Transformation Agenda
   (ATA), Nigeria, 113
Ajuran Empire, 159
Alawites, 38–39, 56
Allers, Sire, 81–82
Alwash, Azzam, 75–76
AMISOM. *See* African Union Mission to
   Somalia
Annan, Kofi, 5
AQAP. *See* al-Qaeda in the Arabian
   Peninsula
AQI. *See* al-Qaeda in Iraq

AQIM. *See* al-Qaeda in the Islamic
   Maghreb
Aqueduct Water Risk Atlas, 159–160
Arab League, 45
Arab Spring, 40, 54–55
al-Assad, Bashar, 38–39, 43, 55–58, 74,
   78, 81, 83, 86
al-Assad, Hafez, 38
ATA. *See* Agricultural Transformation
   Agenda
Ayn al Fijah spring, 78
Ayro, Aden Hashi, 155

Baath Dam, 73–74
Baath Party: in Iraq, 45–47, 64; in Syria,
   36, 38
Babangida, Ibrahim, 112
Bab-el-Mandeb Straits, 184, 196
al-Baghdadi, Abu Omar, 62–65, 69–71
Ban Ki-moon, 5
Barre, Mohamed Siad, 151, 153, 158
Barzani, 71
Basra Water Supply Improvement
   Project, 88–89
Belt and Road Initiative, China, 206–207
Biafra, 113
Bila, Mohammed, 209
Blackwater, 46–47
Boko Haram, 9, 28; in Borno State, 125,
   127, 131–135; emergence of, 123–
   127; Hausa-Fulani militants and,
   138–139; IDP camps infiltrated by,

235

132; on Islamic caliphate, 114, 123–124; ISWAP and, 120, 125, 133, 202–203; kidnappings and trafficking by, 125–126, 134; Lake Chad basin and, 126–127, 129–130, 132, 140, 209; MNJTF and, 112; in Nigeria, 4, 19, 109, 112, 114, 120–121, 123–135, 136*tab*, 138–141, 181, 183, 202–203; al-Shabaab and, 154–155, 181; on Sharia law, 123–124, 126; Shekau in, 124–125; on social media, 125–126; tactics of, 125–126; terrorist attacks by, 124–125, 128; water insecurity and, 126–127; on Western education, 124; Yusuf in, 123–124

Boko Haram, water weaponization by: conflict cycle and water stress in, 135–136, 137*fig*; dam infrastructure in, 130–131; incentivization and coercive, 132–134; IS and, 127–128; psychological terrorism in, 134; strategic, 129–131, 140; summary of incidents in Nigeria, 136*tab*; tactical, 131–132; unintentional, 134–135; as water terrorism, 128–129

Borno State, 125, 127, 131–135, 198
Boutros-Ghali, Boutros, 5
Bremer, Paul, 46, 63
Buhari, Muhammadu, 111
Burkina Faso, 201–204

Campbell, John, 126
CARE, 167
Chalecki, Elizabeth, 14–15, 78
Châtel, Francesca de, 43
China, 206–207
cholera, 165
Christian extremists, in Nigeria, 140
Civil War, US, 21
climate, water stress and, 10–11
Climate and Security Plan of Action, NATO, 210
climate change: in drought, 55–56; environment-conflict thesis on, 9–10; intelligence and defense agencies on, 210–211; migration induced by, 58; in Nigeria, 116–117, 132–133, 199; in precipitation decline, 2–3; in Somalia, 162–163, 169; in Syrian uprising, 43; in temperature increases, 2–3; terrorism and, 209; UNSC on, 209; in

water stress, 2, 85, 171, 210–211; water weaponization and, 206, 211
climate finance, 206
climate security, 208–211
Climate Security Mechanism, UN, 209–210
Clinton, Bill, 173
cloud seeding, 20–21
Code of Hammurabi, 26
Cold War, 36
Collier, Paul, 11–12
conflict cycle: ecological changes and, 59; water stress and, 12–14, 59–60, 59*fig*, 135–136, 137*fig*, 140, 141*fig*, 182, 182*fig*
COP26. *See* United Nations Climate Change Conference
Covid-19, 204–205
cowpea, 198
crimes against humanity, 25

Dabiq, 28, 99*n*3
Dabire, Christophe Joseph Marie, 202
Daoudy, Marwa, 8–9
de-Baathification, 46
deforestation, 159, 173
Department of Defense, US, 20, 200, 206, 211
Department of State, US, 206
desalinization, 88–89
desertification, 118, 173
diarrhea, 84, 115, 165–166
Dinar, Shlomi, 128, 140
Druze people, 39

Ecopeace, 211
eco-violence theory, 11–12
Egypt, 12, 37
Environmental Modification Techniques (ENMOD) treaty, 23, 90
environmental peacebuilding, 7–8, 88
Environmental Scarcity and Violence (Homer-Dixon), 10
environmental terrorism, water weaponization and, 14
environment-conflict thesis, water stress and, 9–12
Ethiopia, 159, 167, 177–178, 184
Euphrates River, 4, 9, 15, 36, 41; IS control of upper, 61; in Syria, 50–51, 72, 74; Tabqa Dam, 72–73; Tigris–

Euphrates river system, 44, 48, 50–52, 71, 82, 85–86, 89, 130; valley, 38
extreme heat, 3

Fallujah, 46–47
Fallujah Dam, 76–77
Famine Early Warning Systems Network (FEWS NET), USAID, 200
FAO. *See* Food and Agriculture Organization
Feed the Future Program, 198
FEWS NET. *See* Famine Early Warning Systems Network
FFS. *See* Funding Facility for Stabilization
First Battle of Fallujah, 46–47
Foley, James, 66
Food and Agriculture Organization (FAO), UN, 158, 161
food insecurity, 3; in Burkina Faso, 201; migration and, 53–55
food security, in Nigeria, 119–120, 137–138, 197–198
food weaponization, 35
foreign policy, US, 206
Fragile State Index, 151
Franco-Dutch War, 19
Frederick Barbarossa (emperor), 77
Free Syrian Army, 58
freshwater ecosystem, 1–2
Funding Facility for Stabilization (FFS), 88

G7. *See* Group of Seven
GAP. *See* Güneydoğu Anadolu Projesi
General Orders No. 100 (Lieber Code), 21
Geneva Conventions, 22
Geneva List of Principles on the Protection of Water Infrastructure, 24, 90
Geneva Water Hub, 24
genocide, 25
GHG. *See* greenhouse gas
Global Coalition to Defeat Daesh/ISIS, 88
Global Early Warning Tool, WPS, 199
Global Fragility Act of 2019, 206
Global High-Level Panel on Water and Peace, 24
Global Terror Database (GTD), 128

Global War on Terror, 46, 200
Global Water Strategy, US, 206
Godane, Ahmed Abdi, 153, 155, 174, 183
Grand Ethiopian Renaissance Dam, 12
Grech-Madin, Charlotte, 21
greed and grievance theory, 11
greenhouse gas (GHG) emissions, 2–3
Group of Seven (G7), 209
GTD. *See* Global Terror Database
Güneydoğu Anadolu Projesi (GAP), 51
Guterres, Antonio, 157, 202

Hague Conventions of 1899 and 1907, 22
Hamza, Buri, 179
Harakat al-Shabaab al-Mujahideen. *See* al-Shabaab
Hausa-Fulani militants, 138–141
Henning, Alan, 66
Hezbollah, 78–79
high temperatures, 2–3
Hoeffler, Anke, 11
Homer-Dixon, Thomas, 10–12
Houthi rebels, 203
HRWS. *See* human right to water and sanitation
Huayuankow Dike, 19
human right to water and sanitation (HRWS), 25
Human Rights Council, UN, 26
human rights law, 25–26, 203
Human Rights Watch, 52
Hussein, Saddam, 45–47, 53, 60–61, 63–64
hydro-diplomacy, 8, 89–90
hydroelectric dams and power, 12, 20, 71–77, 86, 88, 130; in Iraq, 51, 53; in Nigeria, 114–115
hydrohegemony, 15
hydro-terrorism, 78

ICC. *See* International Criminal Court
ICESCR. *See* International Covenant on Economic, Social and Cultural Rights
ICU. *See* Islamic Courts Union
IDPs. *See* internally displaced people
IEDs. *See* improvised explosive devices
Igbo people, 113
IITA. *See* International Institute of Tropical Agriculture

238   Index

ILA. *See* International Law Association
Ilısu Dam, 51
improvised explosive devices (IEDs), 67, 78
Indus Water Treaty, 90
InterAction Council, 5
Intergovernmental Panel on Climate Change (IPCC), 116, 158
internally displaced people (IDPs), 54, 132, 165, 196
International Covenant on Economic, Social and Cultural Rights (ICESCR), 25
International Criminal Court (ICC), 24–25
International Institute of Tropical Agriculture (IITA), 198
international law: human rights, 25–26; on water weaponization, 21–26
International Law Association (ILA), 23–24
International Organization for Migration (IOM), 84
IPCC. *See* Intergovernmental Panel on Climate Change
Iran, 3, 203–204
Iran-Iraq War, 46, 56
Iraq: agriculture in, 44, 52; Arabization of, 44; Baath party in, 45–47, 64; demographics and economy of, 48–50; drought in, 43–44; ethnic Arabs in, 48; Fallujah Dam in, 76–77; geography of, 44; hydro-diplomacy with, 90; hydroelectric dams in, 51, 53; IS in, 47–48, 58, 67–71, 75–80, 82, 85–86, 131, 181, 183, 195–196, 202; Islamic radicalization in, 56–57; Kurds in, 46, 48–51, 85; map of, 45*fig*; Mosul Dam in, 75–76, 83, 131; political history of, 44–48; reconstruction of, 86–89; Shiites in, 46, 48–49, 60–61, 63–64; Sunnis in, 46, 48–49, 63–64; Tigris–Euphrates river system in, 44, 48, 50–52, 71; water pollution in, 86–87; water resources of, 50–53; water weaponization incidents in, summary of, 81*tab*; al-Zarqawi in, 62
Iraq, Syria and, 4, 8–9, 12, 15, 18, 89; conflict cycle and water stress in, 59–60, 59*fig*; drought in, 43–44;

Euphrates River in, 50–51; IS in, 35–36, 58, 67–83, 85–86, 130–131, 181, 183, 195–196, 202; systemic responses to water stress in, 53–58; water weaponization in, 60–61, 71–85, 91*tab*–98*tab*
Iraq War (US invasion of Iraq), 46–47, 56–57, 63–64, 67–68, 83, 87
Iraqi Kurdistan, 9, 44, 50, 66, 71, 85, 89–90
Iraqi refugees, 53
IS. *See* Islamic State
Islamic caliphate, 57, 63, 114, 123–124
Islamic Courts Union (ICU), 153
Islamic extremism and extremists, 14, 21, 57, 123
Islamic Institutes system, 155–156
Islamic radicalization, 56–57
Islamic State (IS), 4, 8–9, 18–19, 28; administrative organization of, 69–70; in Afghanistan, 204; Baath Dam and, 73–74; al-Baghdadi in, 62–65, 69–71; battlefield tactics and weapons, 66–68; combatants, 68–69, 69*tab*; dams seized and destroyed by, 71–77, 77*tab*, 83, 130–131; Fallujah Dam and, 76–77; financing, 70; hydro-terrorism of, 78; ideology of, 63–64; in Iraq, 47–48, 58, 67–71, 75–80, 82, 85–86, 131, 181, 183, 195–196, 202; on Islamic caliphate, 63; ISWAP and, 125; in Lake Chad basin region, 209; leadership of, 62–65; media manipulation by, 65–66; methods of, 65–70; Mosul Dam and, 75–76, 83, 131; names for, 61–62, 62*tab*; oil revenue, 70; al-Shabaab and, 153–155, 178, 181, 183; on social media, 65–66; in Syria, 57–58, 67–70, 72–75, 78–80, 85, 130, 175, 181, 183, 195–196, 202; in Syrian Civil War, 35–36, 40, 71–72, 78–79; Tabqa Dam and, 72–73; terrorist tactics of, 66, 78, 195; Tishrin Dam and, 74–75; at upper Euphrates River, 61
Islamic State (IS), water weaponization by, 35–36, 60–61; Boko Haram and, 127–128; patterns of, 80–82, 81*tab*; strategic, 71–77, 82–85; tactical, 77–80; as terrorism tactic, 195; US military perspective on, 86

Index 239

Islamic State in West African Province (ISWAP), 120, 125, 133, 139–141, 197, 202–203
Islamic theology, 26–27
Islamic water law, 27–29
Israel, 6
ISWAP. *See* Islamic State in West African Province
al-Itihad al-Islami, 153

al-Jaafari, Ibrahim, 46
Jabahaat, 156
Jabhat al-Nusra, 82
Jama'at al-Tawhid wal-Jihad (JTWJ), 62
Jamaat Jaysh Ahl al-Sunnah wa'l Jamaah, 64
Japan International Cooperation Agency (JICA), 88
Jihad al-Asghar (the lesser jihad), 63
Johnson, Lyndon, 20
Jonathan, Goodluck, 112
Jordan, 62
Jordan River, 6, 8
JTWJ. *See* Jama'at al-Tawhid wal-Jihad
Jubba River, 159, 171, 176, 178
al-Julani, Abu Muhammad, 65
July 17 Revolution, 45
jus in bello, 5

Kaboré, Roch, 202
Al-Kadhimi, Mustafa, 48
Katzenstein, Peter, 21
Kelley, Colin, 3
Kenya, 167, 170–171, 176–177, 179, 184
Khashoggi, Jamal, 203
Komadugu Yobe River, 209
Korean Conflict, 19, 21
Kosovo conflict, 88
Kurdistan Regional Government (KRG), 85
Kurds and Kurdistan, 8–9, 15, 46, 48–51, 73, 85; Iraqi Kurdistan, 9, 44, 50, 66, 71, 85, 89–90; Syria and, 39, 70–71

Lake Chad, 4, 118–120, 197, 202; Boko Haram and, 126–127, 129–130, 132, 140, 209
Lebanon, 55, 79
Lee, Mike, 203
the lesser jihad *(Jihad al-Asghar),* 63
Lieber Code, 21

Lincoln, Abraham, 21
Lossow, Tobias von, 81
Louis XIV, 19

Madrid Conference, ILA, 23
al-Maliki, Nuri, 46–47, 58, 63–64
Mambilla Hydroelectric Power Station, 207
Mao Zedong, 129
Marsh Arabs, 60–61
al-Masri, Abu Ayyub, 62
Mekong Committee, 8
Mekong River Commission, 8
MENA. *See* Middle East and North Africa
Mesopotamia, 6, 36, 44, 52, 60, 82
meteorological warfare, 20, 23
Middle East: environmental challenges and peacebuilding in, 211; IS recruits from, 68; precipitation in, 2–3; VEOs in, 4, 19; water stress in, 2–3, 6, 24, 195
Middle East and North Africa (MENA), 3–4, 6, 9, 85; Arab Spring in, 40; climate change and water stress in, 210; drought and famine in, 172, 195
migration: climate change induced, 58; conflict cycle and water stress in, 60; food insecurity and, 53–55; to Nigeria, 120–121; Somalia and, 169–170; to US and UK, 196
migratory patterns, in Nigeria, 137–138
MNJTF. *See* Multinational Joint Task Force
Mosul Dam, 75–76, 83, 131
Muhammad (prophet), 26, 44, 149
Muhasasa Ta'ifia, 49
Multinational Joint Task Force (MNJTF), 112
Mumin, Abdulqadir, 154
Muslim Brotherhood, 64

Nasser, Gamal Abdel, 37
National Geospatial-Intelligence Agency (NGA), 89
National Range Agency, 158
NATO. *See* North Atlantic Treaty Organization
natural resource scarcity or abundance, 11–12
ND-GAIN. *See* Notre Dame Global Adaptation Index

240 *Index*

NGA. *See* National Geospatial-
Intelligence Agency
Niger Delta Avengers, 196–197
Niger River, 109, 113, 117, 130, 137
Nigeria, 7, 12, 18; AQIM in, 197; ATA,
113; Biafran separatists against, 113;
Boko Haram in, 4, 19, 109, 112, 114,
120–121, 123–135, 136*tab*, 138–141,
181, 183, 202–203; characteristics of
society, 110–114; Chinese investment
in, 207; Christian extremists in, 140;
climate change in, 116–117, 132–133,
199; demographic challenges of, 120–
121; development projects in,
207–208; droughts in, 118–120, 122–
123, 137–138; drought-tolerant seeds
for food crops in, 197–198; flooding
in, 118–119; food security in, 119–
120, 137–138, 197–198; gender-based
violence in, 132; Hausa-Fulani
militants in, 138–141; hydroelectric
power in, 114–115; IDPs in, 196; Igbo
people in, 113; ISWAP in, 197, 202–
203; Lake Chad in, 4, 118–120,
126–127, 129–130, 132, 140, 197;
land governance policies of, 198; map
of, 110*fig*; Middle Belt, 137–140,
141*fig*; migration to, 120–121;
migratory patterns in, 137–138; as
model for countering water weapon,
196–199; natural resources of, 109–
110, 112–113; northeastern, 122–136,
136*tab*, 137*fig*, 197; oil production
and oil sector in, 112–113, 196–197;
Sahelian region of, 116, 118, 163,
170; Syria and, 109, 162; US policy
and, 142, 206–207; USAID in, 207;
water governance in, 117, 121–122,
141; water resources of, 114–117,
122; water scarcity in, 115, 121–122,
132; water stress in, 114–120, 197.
See also Boko Haram
Nile River, 12
Nixon, Richard, 20
North Atlantic Treaty Organization
(NATO), 210
North Korea, 20
Notre Dame Global Adaptation Index
(ND-GAIN), 117, 163
al-Nusra Front, 65
Nzeogwu, Chukwuma Kaduna, 111

Obama, Barack, 47
Obama, Michelle, 125
Okoroigwe, Pamela, 132
Omar, Ahmed, 174
Operation Anfal, 49
Operation Phantom Fury, 47
Operation Popeye, 20–21, 23
Operation Restore Hope, 173
Operation Rolling Thunder, 20
Ottoman Empire, 36, 44

Pacific Institute, 6, 82
Persian Gulf, 86–87
Persian Gulf War, 46, 56
Port of Kismayo, 157
precipitation, 2–3
PSAWEN. *See* Puntland State Agency
for Water, Energy and Natural
Resources
psychological terrorism, 134
Puntland, 151, 154, 160, 178, 185
Puntland State Agency for Water, Energy
and Natural Resources (PSAWEN),
160

al-Qaeda, 46, 130, 153
al-Qaeda in Iraq (AQI), 58, 65
al-Qaeda in the Arabian Peninsula
(AQAP), 203
al-Qaeda in the Islamic Maghreb
(AQIM), 139–141, 154, 197
al-Quraishi, Abu Ibrahim al-Hashimi, 70
Quran, 26–27, 69

Renaud, Fabrice, 5
resource curse theory, 112–113
Robow, Mukhtar, 174

sadaqah, 26
Sadaqah Jariyah, 26–27
al-Sadr, Muqtada, 48
Safavid Empire, 44
the Sahel, 2, 116, 118, 163, 170, 201
Salafism and Salafists, 28–29, 63, 155,
195
salinization, 52, 87
Sandaogo, Paul-Henri, 202
Sanders, Bernie, 203
Saudi Arabia, 203–204
SCAD. *See* Social Conflict Analysis
Database

Index 241

Schwartzstein, Peter, 7
Scientific American, 35
SDF. *See* Syrian Democratic Forces
SDGs. *See* Sustainable Development Goals
Second Battle of Fallujah, 47
Second Sino-Japanese War, 19
al-Shabaab, 9, 19, 28; advent of, 152–
158; AMISOM and, 154, 177–178,
181, 183–185; Boko Haram and,
154–155, 181; doctrine and
organizational structure, 155–156;
financing, 156–157, 175; food aid
obstructed and stolen by, 167, 172–
175; IS and, 153–155, 178, 181, 183;
Islamic Institutes system and, 155–
156; Jabahaat and, 156; mass casualty
attacks by, 154, 154*tab*; recruitment,
157–158; in Somalia, 153–159, 167,
170–181, 183–186
al-Shabaab, water weaponization by,
170; desertification from, 173; at
Jubba and Shabelle Riers, 176–177;
radicalization and, 179–181; strategic,
171–175; summary of incidents in
Somalia, 180*tab*; tactical, 175–178,
183; water terrorism and, 178–179
Shabelle River, 159, 166, 171, 176–177
shafa, 27
Shagari, Shehu Usman Aliyu, 111
Sharia Council, of IS, 69
Sharia law, 26–27, 29, 63, 123–124, 126
Sharmarke, Abdirashid Ali, 151
Shatt al-Arab, 86–87
Shekau, Abubakar, 124–125
Shia Islam, 38–39
Shia Muslims, 46, 48–49, 60–61, 63–64
shirb, 27
Shura Council, of IS, 69–70
Simon, Paul, 207
Six-Day War, 6
Social Conflict Analysis Database
(SCAD), 122–123
social media: Boko Haram on, 125–126;
IS on, 65–66
Soleimani, Qasem, 48
Somali immigrants, to Minneapolis, 156
Somali refugees, 169–170, 196
Somalia, 2, 12, 18; agriculture and rural
livelihoods in, 159, 164–165; aid
workers attacked in, 173; central
government and economy, 151–152;

charcoal trade in, 168–169, 173; clan
structure in, 149–151, 155, 170;
climate change in, 162–163, 169;
deforestation in, 159, 173;
demographics, 152; development
projects in, 186; drought in, 161–165,
168, 172–174, 177–180, 184;
ecological context of, 158–163;
environmental degradation in, 168–
169; famine in, 166–168, 172,
174–175, 183; flooding in, 166; GDP,
152, 164; groundwater in, 160–161;
ICU in, 153; irrigation infrastructure,
159; Islamic Institutes system on,
155–156; Jubba and Shabelle Rivers
in, 159, 166, 171, 176–178; map of,
150*fig*; migration and displacement,
169–170; National Range Agency,
158; piracy and, 169; al-Shabaab in,
153–159, 167, 170–181, 183–186;
Sunnis in, 149; TFG, 153–154, 176–
177; TNG, 151; UN on, 167, 173,
175; water governance in, 160–161;
water resources and management,
159–161, 168; water stress and
conflict cycle in, 182, 182*fig*; water
stress in, 164–168; water-related
illness in, 165–166; Zakat and
taxation in, 156–157
Somalia Water and Land Information
Management Project (SWALIM),
158–160, 185
Somaliland and Somaliland Republic,
151, 160, 185
Sotloft, Steven, 66
Soviet-Afghan War, 62
spectrum of conflict, water stress and, 4–
9
Stockholm Declaration of 1972, 22
Suez Crisis, 1956, 36–37
Sui-ho Dam, 20
Sunni Islam, 63
Sunni Muslims, 46, 48–49, 57–58, 63–
64, 83, 149
Sustainable Development Goals (SDGs),
UN, 211
SWALIM. *See* Somalia Water and Land
Information Management Project
Sykes-Picot Agreement, 36
Syria, 3, 6, 12–15; agriculture in, 39–42,
54; Alawites in, 38–39, 56; Arab

242 *Index*

Spring uprising in, 40, 54–55; Arabic language in, 39; Baath Dam in, 73–74; Baath Party in, 36, 38; Daraa City, 54–55; demographics and economy of, 38–40; drought in, 43–44, 54–55, 57–60; Druze people in, 39; economic liberalization by, 55–56; Egypt and, 37; ENMOD treaty and, 23; Euphrates River in, 50–51, 72, 74; food weaponization in, 35; geography of, 36; groundwater of, 42; hydro-diplomacy with, 89–90; IDPs in, 54; Iraqi refugees in, 53; IS in, 57–58, 67–70, 72–75, 78–80, 85, 130, 175, 181, 183, 195–196, 202; Islamic radicalization in, 56–57; Kurds in, 39, 70–71; map of, 37*fig*; national policy failures, 55–56; Nigeria and, 109, 162; political history of, 36–38; sectarian issues in, 56; Sunnis in, 57; Tabqa Dam in, 72–73; Tishrin Dam in, 74–75; Turkic people in, 39; water resources and management, 41–44, 60; water stress in, 41–42, 53–60, 59*fig*; water weaponization incidents in, summary of, 81*tab*. *See also* Iraq, Syria and
Syrian Arabs, 38
Syrian Civil War, 4, 13–14, 40–42, 56; IS in, 35–36, 40, 71–72, 78–79
Syrian Democratic Forces (SDF), 40, 73–75
Syrian refugees, 35, 40–41, 58

Tabqa Dam, 72–73
Talabani, Jalal, 46–47
Taliban, 204
terrorism: by Boko Haram, 124–125, 128; climate change and, 209; environmental, 14; hydro-terrorism, 78; IS tactics, 66, 78, 195; psychological, 134; water, 128–129, 139–140, 178–179; water weaponization and, 17–18, 24–25, 205
TFG. *See* Transitional Federal Government
Tigris River, 4, 9, 15, 44, 48, 50–52, 75
Tigris–Euphrates river system, 44, 48, 50–52, 71, 82, 85–86, 89. 130
Tishreen (October) movement, 87

Tishrin Dam, 74–75
TNG. *See* Transitional National Government
Transitional Federal Government (TFG), Somalia, 153–154, 176–177
Transitional National Government (TNG), Somalia, 151
Traore, Ibrahim, 202
Treaty of Sèvres, 44
Trump, Donald, 70, 203
Turkey, 15, 41, 50–52, 70–71, 85
Turkic people, 39

UAR. *See* United Arab Republic
UN. *See* United Nations
UNESCO, 53, 61
UNICEF, 24, 50, 84, 158
United Arab Republic (UAR), 37–38
United Iraqi Alliance Party, 63–64
United Nations (UN): on climate security, 209–210; on crimes against humanity, 25; FAO, 158, 161; Global Conference on the Human Environment, 22; Human Rights Council, 26; IPCC, 116, 158; Iraq in, 45; Nigeria in, 112; Oil-for-Food Programme, 49; SDGs, 211; on Somalia, 167, 173, 175; Syria in, 36; on Syrian water contamination, 78; on water stress, 1, 85; on water wars, 5; World Food Programme, 167, 201
United Nations Climate Change Conference 2021 (COP26), 206
United Nations Security Council (UNSC), 25, 209
United Nations University, 5
UNSC. *See* United Nations Security Council
Urlama (king), 60
US Agency for International Development (USAID), 87–88, 117, 158, 172, 198, 200, 206–207
US Army Corps of Engineers (USACE), 199–200
USAID. *See* US Agency for International Development

Veilleux, Jennifer, 128, 140
VEOs. *See* violent extremist organizations
Vietnam War, 8, 20–23, 47

Index   243

violent extremist organizations (VEOs): environmental peacebuilding and, 8; US-supported military operations against, 200–201; water stress and, 3–5, 86, 195; water weaponization by, 15, 17–19, 61, 205, 207–208. *See also* Boko Haram; Islamic State; al-Shabaab

Vivekananda, Janani, 119

volumetric availability, 1

Wadi Barada water supply, 78

Wahhabism, 155

Waldhauser, Thomas, 169

war crimes, 24–25, 66

Water, Peace and Security Partnership (WPS), 199

Water and Sanitation Coordination Project, USAID, 207

Water Conflict Chronology database, of Pacific Institute, 82

Water for the Poor Act of 2005, 207

water infrastructure, of developing nations, 206–207

water poisoning, 134, 177

water pollution, 41, 52, 86–87, 132

water stress: in Africa, 2–3, 6, 24, 195; climate and, 10–11; climate change in, 2, 85, 171, 210–211; conflict cycle and, 12–14, 59–60, 59*fig*, 135–136, 137*fig*, 140, 141*fig*, 182, 182*fig*; environment-conflict thesis and, 9–12; in Iraq and Syria, conflict cycle and, 59–60, 59*fig*; in Iraq and Syria, systemic responses to, 53–58; in Middle East, 2–3, 6, 24, 195; in Nigeria, 114–120, 197; in Somalia, 164–168; spectrum of conflict and, 4–9; in Syria, 41–42, 53–60, 59*fig*; UN on, 1, 85; US development strategy for, 205; VEOs and, 3–5, 86, 195

water terrorism, 128–129, 139–140, 178–179

water wars, 5–6, 9

water weaponization: categories, 15, 16*tab*, 17–18; climate change and, 206, 211; coercive, 17–18, 132–134; countering, 196–201; development of research agenda on, 208; environmental terrorism and, 14; farmer-herder violence and, 139–140; health crises and, 84; by Hussein, 60–

61; international law on, 21–26; in Iraq and Syria, 60–61, 71–85, 91*tab*–98*tab*; Islamic theology on, 26–27; Islamic water law and, 27–29; by ISWAP, 202–203; by nation-states, 19–22, 177–178; in poverty and gender inequality, 85; proliferation of, 201–205; by al-Shabaab, 170; strategic, 15, 17, 19, 71–77, 129–131, 140, 171–175; tactical, 17, 77–80, 83, 131–132, 175–178, 183; terrorism and, 17–18, 24–25, 205; unintentional, 18, 134–135; US military perspective on, 86; by VEOs, 15, 17–19, 61, 205, 207–208; water terrorism and, 128–129, 139–140, 178–179; in Yemen, 203. *See also* Boko Haram, water weaponization by; Islamic State (IS), water weaponization by; al-Shabaab, water weaponization by

waterborne diseases, 83–84, 165–166

Watson, Murray, 158

Wendle, John, 35

White House Action Plan on Global Water Security, 200

WHO. *See* World Health Organization

World Bank, 207

World Food Program, 167, 201

World Health Organization (WHO), 203–204

World Resources Institute (WRI), 159–160

World War I, 36, 44

World War II, 19, 21–22, 110–111

World Water Conflict Chronology, 6

WPS. *See* Water, Peace and Security Partnership

WRI. *See* World Resources Institute

Yalu River, 20

Yarmuk River, 8

Yazidis, 66

Yellow River, 19

Yemen, 170, 203–204

Yusuf, Mohammed, 123–124

Zakat, 156, 175, 202

zamzam, 28

al-Zarqawi, Abu Musab, 62, 65

Zawahiri, Ayman, 65

About the Book

DROUGHT, LACK OF ACCESS, POOR QUALITY . . . WATER SUP-
plies are in jeopardy across Africa and the Middle East. These same
areas are rife with conflicts involving Islamic extremist groups. Marcus
King explores linkages between water stress and violent conflict by
looking closely at how ISIS in Syria and Iraq, Boko Haram in Nigeria,
and al-Shabaab in Somalia have weaponized water in the pursuit of
political ends.

Marcus D. King is professor of practice in environmental and international affairs at Georgetown University.